RICHARD OLNEY
AND HIS PUBLIC SERVICE

A Da Capo Press Reprint Series

THE AMERICAN SCENE
Comments and Commentators

GENERAL EDITOR: WALLACE D. FARNHAM
University of Illinois

RICHARD OLNEY

AND HIS PUBLIC SERVICE

BY

HENRY JAMES

With Documents, including Unpublished
Diplomatic Correspondence

DA CAPO PRESS • NEW YORK • 1971

A Da Capo Press Reprint Edition

This Da Capo Press edition of
Richard Olney and His Public Service
is an unabridged republication of the
first edition published in Boston and
New York in 1923.

Library of Congress Catalog Card Number 70-87445

SBN 306-71516-3

Copyright, 1923, by Houghton Mifflin Company

Published by Da Capo Press
A Division of Plenum Publishing Corporation
227 West 17th Street, New York, N. Y. 10011

RICHARD OLNEY
AND HIS PUBLIC SERVICE

RICHARD OLNEY

AND HIS PUBLIC SERVICE

BY

HENRY JAMES

With Documents including Unpublished
Diplomatic Correspondence

AND WITH ILLUSTRATIONS

BOSTON AND NEW YORK
HOUGHTON MIFFLIN COMPANY
The Riverside Press Cambridge
1923

The Riverside Press
CAMBRIDGE · MASSACHUSETTS
PRINTED IN THE U.S.A.

ACKNOWLEDGMENTS

BEFORE all I wish to thank Mr. Olney's daughters, Mrs. George R. Minot and Mrs. Charles H. Abbot, who have placed every facility at my disposal, have given me much information, and have allowed me the most complete liberty in using it. Miss A. M. Straw, one of Mr. Olney's executors, who was his confidential clerk for thirty-one years, has furnished invaluable assistance by searching out and arranging papers that were preserved in his voluminous private files, by providing transcripts, and by supplying data which I should never have found by myself. I have also been helped by conversations and correspondence with a number of Mr. Olney's associates and acquaintances. Among these, it is a pleasure to name particularly Mr. Ira C. Hersey, Mr. Charles H. Tyler, Mr. William C. Endicott, Mr. Nathan Matthews, Mr. Edgar J. Rich, Mr. Richard Olney, 2d, Mr. Robert Lincoln O'Brien, and Mr. James Ford Rhodes, of Boston; Professor F. W. Taussig, of Cambridge; Dr. Gaillard Hunt, Mr. A. A. Adee, and Miss Mary W. Goss, of the State Department; Dr. James Brown Scott and Mr. Charles S. Hamlin, of Washington; Mr. Judson Harmon, of Ohio, who succeeded Mr. Olney as Attorney-General; Mr. Henry White, Mr. Elihu Root, Mr. J. Roosevelt Roosevelt, and Mr. Sigourney Olney, of New York; and the Honorable John Bassett Moore, now of The Hague. Professor Robert McNutt McElroy has kindly allowed me to examine documents in his collection of Cleveland papers, and has recently sent me some of the proof-sheets of his forthcoming *Life of Cleveland*.

Mr. White, Dr. Hunt, Professor R. B. Merriman, of Harvard, Miss Straw, and Mrs. Minot have kindly read parts or all of my manuscript and have made suggestions which have aided me in completing it.

Although I have tried to cite every published work on which I have relied for a particular statement, I should like to mention here that the following books have been of more help to me than footnotes can indicate: J. F. Rhodes, *History of the United States* and *The McKinley and Roosevelt Administrations;* H. T. Peck, *Twenty Years of the Republic;* F. E. Chadwick, *The Relations of the United States and Spain, Diplomacy;* A. C. Coolidge, *The United States as a World Power;* R. B. Merriman, "The Monroe Doctrine" (in the *Political Quarterly*, No. 7, Oxford, 1915).

Mr. Olney's family proposes to deposit in the Congressional Library in Washington such of his correspondence and papers as deal with his public service, and it is my understanding that this will be accomplished shortly. Documents referred to as "Olney Collection" (or "Olney Coll.") will be understood to be among them.

I am indebted for permission to reprint the map of the Venezuelan boundary, several cartoons, and several quotations and whole articles which appear in the text and appendices, to the courtesy of the publishers and journals which are identified in each instance. Mrs. T. J. Preston has contributed the snap-shot of Cleveland and Olney on the veranda at Falmouth. To Mrs. William S. Hilles, to

Mrs. Payne Whitney, to Mr. Rodman Gilder, to Mr. Henry White, and to Mr. R. H. Dana I owe thanks for permission to print semi-official or private correspondence with the late Thomas F. Bayard, the late John Hay, the late R. W. Gilder, and with Mr. White and Mr. Dana themselves.

Also I wish to express here my thanks to Mr. George B. Ives, who has prepared the topical index.

Finally I should add that, while making these acknowledgments most gratefully, I assume full responsibility for all statements which may appear to be my own.

H. J.

New York, *July*, 1923

CONTENTS

ILLUSTRATIONS

RICHARD OLNEY

I

OLNEY'S APPOINTMENT TO THE CABINET

IN 1893, Richard Olney, fifty-seven years of age, was absorbed in an excellent but quiet law practice which he had been pursuing in Boston for thirty-five years, when all of a sudden Cleveland, anxious to include a New-Englander in his list of Cabinet appointments, pounced upon him and bore him off to Washington to duties which were new and honors which he had never sought.

It is quite usual for the "cabinet" of an American President to include one or more secretaries whose names are unfamiliar to the public when their appointments are announced; and almost as often they retire from the national stage and disappear from public memory completely when their periods of office expire. Meanwhile they grapple for a term with such business as the course of events pushes across their desks, and their achievements and failures go to make up a curious chapter of our history.

Olney was one of the unknown, but also one of the few whose achievements are memorable. From the outset it fell to the lot of the Administration into which he was drawn to deal with unusual difficulties. As its Attorney-General, and then as Secretary of State, he displayed that kind of discretion which prefers imposing the conditions of an encounter to waiting in the hope of somehow avoiding it. He went out boldly, and sometimes rather brusquely, to meet the oncoming emergencies. Lacking political experience, and temperamentally indifferent to opinion, it was his way to act without offering any explanations. So what he did seemed to have a dramatic quality, and twice he threw the country into such a clangor of popular applause and abuse as only a surprising and exciting *fait accompli* can arouse. The Chicago strike, the Venezuela dispute, the General Arbitration Treaties were primarily his affairs. Several of the characters in which Cleveland's second term inscribed itself upon the pages of history were indelible because of Olney, although he took no particular pains to make them appear like his own handwriting. Then, when the four years were over and he had proved his fitness for public service and was better qualified than ever to go on, the fortunes of politics retired him to private life for the rest of his days.

To say what Richard Olney contributed to the Administration is not to detract from what is due to the President under whom he served. Both men understood the give-and-take that must go on between a responsible chief and a trusted aide. Cleveland knew how to rely upon a man of ability and rugged honesty without surrendering his own judgment. His Secretary's policies, when adopted, became his policies. He faced such risks and criticism as they entailed, threw his rough energy into their enforcement, and accepted full responsibility. The President, who is reported to have said about his Secretary of the Treasury (Carlisle), "We are just right for each other; he knows all

I ought to know, and I can bear all we have to bear," was a chief who encouraged initiative — and always won devotion.

Olney on his side played the part which our system of government prescribes for a Cabinet officer with a fidelity which it is appropriate to call lawyer-like. Unknown to the voters and untested in the public service, his contribution to the Administration was neither political influence nor popular prestige, but just his native ability and unqualified loyalty. He regarded himself as the President's personal adviser — as a zealous member of what the newspapers quite appropriately call the "official family." In whatever he initiated and whatever was entrusted to him for execution, he acted without reference to his own political fortune. Even after the Administration had gone out of office, he seems to have considered that explanations, reminiscences, and critical comments were not his to publish. It is true that nature disinclined him to gossip and discourse. But considering how often he was tempted and invited, in the twenty years during which he survived Cleveland's last term, to rehearse its history, it is remarkable that he seems never to have added anything to the public's knowledge of what happened in Washington while he was there.

But now material which has hitherto been scattered or locked up has become available, and it is possible to trace the simple outline of his career and to examine his part in certain important episodes which occurred between 1893 and 1897. What Olney did in Washington during those years is what is worth considering. Nothing else in his life

will matter much to posterity. The many services that he
rendered to his clients and his local community during his
long and honorable professional career, were not such as to
excite general interest. Like most similar services rendered by other members of the great profession he adorned,
their destiny always was — to be forgotten; and Olney
himself would have called it vanity to pretend otherwise.
Nothing in his public life requires to be explained by
reference to their detail. To attempt to review them in
this brief memoir would be to delay the reader's approach
to incidents that are equally revealing and much more
important.

The story of Olney's appointment can be given in his
own words:

I never saw Mr. Cleveland but once prior to February,
1893 [said he in a memorandum which he dictated in 1901],
when at his request I went to Lakewood. (In the summer
of 1890 or 1891, his former Secretary of War, Judge Endicott, and his wife, wishing to call upon the Clevelands who
were then living at Gray Gables, spent the night with me,
and on the following day I accompanied them in their call
on the Clevelands.)

So far as I know, I was requested to go to Lakewood
with the view to a Cabinet position in consequence of an
interview between Mr. Cleveland and my cousin, Sigourney Butler, who had been Second Comptroller of the
Treasury during Mr. Cleveland's first administration. Mr.
Cleveland offered Sigourney the position of Private Secretary, which office his duty to his own family compelled him
to decline. As I remember Sigourney's account to me, the
composition of the Cabinet was the subject of some talk

between himself and Mr. Cleveland, and Mr. Cleveland told him that he had filled all the positions except those of Secretary of the Navy and Attorney-General. A discussion of names for each position followed and mine was brought up — with the suggestion on Sigourney's part that it was possible I might be induced to accept the office of Attorney-General. Mr. Cleveland thereupon asked him to request me to come to Lakewood on the day which he named.

On Sigourney's mentioning the matter to me I at first declined to consider it or to go to Lakewood on what seemed to me a perfectly useless errand. But on reflection, it seemed discourteous not to do so and I went. Mr. Cleveland first offered me the office of Secretary of the Navy, which I positively refused. He then offered me the office of Attorney-General, which I did not peremptorily decline, though I expressed my aversion to leave the practice of my profession and enter into public life. Mr. Cleveland urged it, with the result that, after a good deal of discussion, I left the matter with him in this way: I told him there was much better Cabinet material in New England than myself — men much more familiar with politics and much more ambitious in that direction — and that I could name one who, I thought, would undoubtedly accept the position. He thereupon called for the name and I mentioned John Quincy Adams of Boston. Mr. Cleveland said if I could get Mr. Adams to serve he should be delighted to have him in the Cabinet as Secretary of the Navy. He, however, insisted that, if Mr. Adams for any reason would not serve, I should consider myself as booked for the position of Attorney-General. I assented to the condition, not feeling in my own mind at the time the slightest doubt that Mr. Adams would readily accede to Mr. Cleveland's wishes. It was arranged, therefore, that I should see Mr. Adams and offer him the naval portfolio, and that, upon obtaining his answer I should telegraph a message in a form which Mr. Cleveland wrote out and is as follows:

"A — (Yes) He will go with you" — (which meant that Adams would accept.)

"O — (Yes) I will go with you" — (which meant that Adams declined and I would be Attorney-General.)

"A — (To consult) He will meet you at ——" (which meant that Adams would go to see Cleveland.)

My recollection is that I arrived in Boston about six in the afternoon and immediately went to Mr. Adams's house, saw him personally, and on behalf of Mr. Cleveland tendered him the office of Secretary of the Navy. To my astonishment as well as dismay, he absolutely declined. . . .[1]

I had counted on Mr. Adams's willingness to go into the Cabinet with so much certainty that his refusal to do so entirely upset my calculations. Instead of sending the agreed-upon message to Mr. Cleveland, therefore, in the afternoon of the next day I telegraphed him as follows: [Telegram not preserved.] In the course of the next forenoon I received the following telegram in reply — "Nothing will now excuse you but the act of God or the public enemy."

Upon receipt of this telegram — no new circumstances having intervened upon which I could fairly ground my declination of the office — I considered myself fairly com-

---

[1] Olney here ventured upon a supposition which appears not to have been wholly correct and which, being unnecessary to his own story, is therefore omitted.

mitted to Mr. Cleveland and arranged to be in Washington by the 4th of March.[1]

When the news of this selection got about, most of the country asked, Who is Olney? The newspapers began to be humorous about the impossibility of obtaining a photograph. They sought interviews in vain, and published biographies which were meager and uninforming. It is possible to do a little better now.

[1] Mr. George F. Parker, who was much with Cleveland at the time here referred to, has given an account of this appointment which differs from the foregoing with respect to minor points. (*Saturday Evening Post*, June 9, 1923.) Among Olney's contemporary papers there are some which confirm Mr. Parker's idea that Peter B. Olney, Richard's younger brother, had as much or more to do with the preliminary stages of the appointment than did Sigourney Butler. Olney's abilities had been drawn to Cleveland's attention as early as 1888. Patrick Collins then urged the President to appoint him to the Supreme Court. It doesn't appear whether Olney had any knowledge of the matter.

II
HIS EARLIER YEARS

OLNEY was born in Oxford, Worcester Country, Massachusetts, September 15, 1835. A grandfather after whom he was named had moved from Rhode Island in 1811. This first Richard came of the large Olney family which had descended from the original Thomas, a Salem settler of 1635, who followed Roger Williams to Rhode Island, and became a proprietor and founder of the Providence Plantations. Richard, who settled in Massachusetts, is reputed to have been a large person physically and a man of great energy, who possessed even more than his fair allowance of the individualism and strongheadedness for which the citizens of Rhode Island were famous — or notorious, according to the point of view — from Roger Williams's time until days within living memory. He turned his back on his native State and his relatives there so completely that his descendants have never known more than that he was one of the Rhode Island Olneys and had been born in Smithfield. In Massachusetts he became a pioneer in the textile industry and established mills at East Douglas and later in Oxford. In that sturdy little community he became a "prominent citizen, merchant and manufacturer, who held many town offices and showed marked ability as a man of affairs." He had a number of children whom he ruled with an iron hand as long as he could and with some of whom he then quarreled and parted. His eldest son Wilson, a man of more kindly

WILSON OLNEY

ELIZA BUTLER OLNEY

THE PARENTS OF RICHARD OLNEY

and complying temper, made an unsuccessful trip down the Ohio into Kentucky while still young, but returned to accept Oxford as his fate. He married Eliza L. Butler, a descendant through one of her maternal ancestors of André Séjourné, who had fled from France after the revocation of the Edict of Nantes, and who became known as Andrew Sigourney in the country of his adoption. She thus brought into the family some of the warm blood of the little colony of French Huguenots who settled Oxford in 1687. She was a more energetic and positive person than her husband—a woman of "commanding and abrupt manner." Her eldest son, Richard, the hero of this sketch, appears to have derived his temper and the cast of his mind from her and from the grandfather after whom he was named, rather than from his gentle and rather unenterprising father. He was brought up and given his early schooling in his native village, graduated from Léicester Academy at the head of his class, then went through Brown University with honors, and through the Harvard Law School in a way that led Theophilus Parsons to commend him as "among the best men we ever had here." [1] In 1859 he began practice in Boston as a law clerk in the office of Benjamin F. Thomas, who was an ex-Justice of

[1] In sending a check for $1000 to the Oxford town library in 1904, to establish a "Wilson Olney Fund," Richard Olney wrote: "For whatever advantages I have derived from a liberal education I am specially indebted to my father, whose early opportunities had been small and whose resources were always slender. But he cheerfully economized and saved that his children might enjoy privileges denied to himself, and would have deemed a library like that now accessible to the people of Oxford of inestimable value to his family and himself." Wilson Olney had three other sons, Peter Butler, George W., and Frederick A. He had one daughter, Gertrude, who married Eben S. Stevens.

the State Supreme Court, an ex-Congressman, and a man
of very unusual parts. He married Thomas's daughter
Agnes, became his junior associate, and continued to
practice with him until Thomas died.

Wilson Olney had been a Whig in politics and in later
life became a Democrat. Richard seems to have been a
Democrat from the beginning although little is known
about his early political beliefs. Having a wife to support
and his way to make in the world, he stuck to his practice
during the Civil War. In 1874 he served one term in the
Massachusetts Legislature, and in 1876 — a year in which
there was no possibility of a Democratic victory — he let
himself be nominated as a candidate for the State attorney-
generalship. But these incidents had little significance. The
modest incursion into public affairs which they signalized
ended in 1876, and by the time Cleveland appointed him to
the attorney-generalship of the United States most people
had probably forgotten them.[1] An appointment to the
highest court in Massachusetts had been offered him and
he had refused it, but very few people knew about that.
By the nineties it seemed that he regarded himself as entirely out of politics. The fact that, although his summer
place at Falmouth was within a few miles of Cleveland's
"Gray Gables," he had never tried to take advantage of

[1] Mr. Ira C. Hersey has kindly supplied the following figures: 1873,
Richard Olney elected representative from 2d Norfolk District (West
Roxbury); 1874, candidate for representative, Ward 17, Boston (West
Roxbury District): vote was, Olney 578, Joseph S. Ropes, 582, scattering
3; 1875, candidate for State Senator (Norfolk County, 1st District): vote
was, Olney 2108, Palmer 2878; 1876, candidate for Attorney-General: vote
was, Olney 107,185, Charles R. Train 141,260, scattering 8904. The part
of West Roxbury in which Olney lived was known as "Forest Hills" and
was annexed to Boston in 1874.

his opportunities to establish a personal acquaintance with the leader of the Democratic Party, showed this clearly. Naturally, therefore, it was difficult to report much about him except that he was a lawyer of high standing who never sought the public eye, and that the Boston Bar and State Street knew him as an able counselor who "appeared" not infrequently before the courts of appeal and such special tribunals as the Railway Commission, though almost never in the trial courts, and who was to be reckoned with as an aggressive force in any affair into which he was drawn.

But upon those who had come into contact with him, even casually, the impression the man made was anything but dim and uncertain. A stranger, observing a gathering in which Olney was present, would have found himself looking curiously at that almost motionless figure and remarkable physiognomy. "Imagine," said a slangy reporter who 'did' the new Cabinet for the New York "World," "a square block of wood with a slightly retroussé nose and two lumps of coal for eyes and a Dan Lamont moustache, and you've got him — the worst-looking feller of the gang." His "retroussé" nose was straight enough, but seemed to be tipped up because his open and mobile nostrils were so apparent. "They were his most expressive feature." "His nose always told me what his mood was, and sometimes the look of it made me quake," said a member of his family. "Il a une figure à faire aller promener les Anglais," remarked M. Tardieu on a later occasion. All his portraits do him the justice of making him look more like the directing head of some long-prosperous New England industry than like a supple-minded advocate. His stature was nearly six feet when he stood up, but his legs were so long and his body so compact that, sitting behind a desk, he appeared to be a short man. His dark brown hair was just beginning to turn gray. There was an amount of vigor as well as pugnacity in the forward carriage of his head which made him look younger than his years, and his whole person was hale and tough. Somehow his aspect suggested strong feelings disciplined by a lifelong practice of decision and emotional economy; suggested a man whom it would be hard to overthrow; who would have convictions to act upon, who would take measures accordingly before there was any reason to get excited, who would never bother himself to think of receding, who would be obstinate; — a hard-thinking, accomplishing, ruthless being like one of those modern war-tanks which proceeds across the roughest ground, heedless of opposition, deaf alike to messages from friends and cries from the foe, able to crush every person and every obstacle that gets between it and its chosen objective.

It would have been astonishing if some one had come up and clapped him on the shoulder. His well-bred deportment — the memory of him calls up the old phrase — his reserve, his dignity — these as much as his stern physiognomy forbade impertinence or intrusion. His secretary was always surprised when anybody called him by his first name. "There was one old gentleman who sometimes wrote to the office and began his letters *Dear Dick*, and Colonel Henry Lee used to walk in and call him Richard."

MR. AND MRS. RICHARD OLNEY IN 1861

But no one knew what the "old gentleman" looked like, and Colonel Lee was a being whose geniality none might resist! Others were less familiar, for, though Olney was called "urbane" and "charming" by people whom he respected and who did not waste his time, his manners were tinged with the kind of courtesy which maintains a certain distance.

Both accident and temperament had doomed him to be somewhat a man apart in Boston. He had never been thrown, in school, in college, or in the army, with the little groups of Boston and Harvard men who were the inner circle of the New England business world in which he practiced law. Between them and him there were no close personal ties, none of the free-masonries of boyhood. And he never made up for the deficiency; he established many professional associations and congenial acquaintances as time went on, but attached no intimates. His cousin Sigourney Butler seems to have been the only person with whom he carried on the free and equal give-and-take of a real friendship. One could not imagine him as "sauntering the street and covering with his arm the shoulder of his friend." On the contrary, the pace at which he walked from his house on Commonwealth Avenue to his office in Court Street was remarkable and the uncompromising determination with which he pressed it discouraged companionship. It is related that one morning when an elderly gentleman tried to keep up with him and talk politics, he marched him along Commonwealth Avenue so much more than briskly that the unfortunate man collapsed on the sidewalk and had to be helped into the nearest doorway to be resuscitated. Although he belonged to one or two good clubs, he never frequented them, nor joined dining associations, nor traveled abroad alone or with friends,[1] nor "went about" near home. His office and some hard exercise by day, and in the evening his family and a very few relatives or neighbors, books and magazines, or a rubber of whist — these, with a summer vacation at Falmouth on Martha's Vineyard Sound, were the elements that made up the almost changeless routine of his existence between the seventies and eighteen-ninety-three.

According to the ideas of these days, the office which he maintained on the top floor of the old Adams Building, in Court Street, was a curious place. "Organization," stir, and bustle were alien to it. Its old-fashioned simplicity made younger men wonder if it had changed at all since Judge Thomas's time. There were no younger partners, law-clerks, or students. After Thomas's death, Olney had in fact divided the old suite of rooms with Francis I. Amory and Sigourney Butler — at first employing one clerk for the three and occasionally availing himself of the services of the younger men. When business grew upon him, his own force became and remained just his own "clerk" plus an office boy. The clerk, Miss A. M. Straw, during the last thirty-one years of his life, was stenographer, bookkeeper, and secretary in one, and Olney

[1] Except that in the seventies Olney and his brother Peter took a walking trip in the British Isles one summer, and extended it to Paris, and that later he made a business trip to London and Paris once, and once a similar trip to Cuba. Practicing without partners he could not get away easily; but he preferred to practice that way.

gratefully named her in his will to be one of his executors and trustees. There were only three rooms. In a large one at the end Olney worked in a seclusion which was somehow honored without being elaborately protected; from the adjoining room Miss Straw could see persons who entered the outer office and could communicate with Olney's room in the other direction. There were no adornments, not even a rug in the outer office. There was no telephone until the Boston and Maine Railroad slyly installed an instrument there one dark night in order that its president might telephone to its counsel. If he wanted to dictate, Miss Straw sat at a little table which was completely hidden from his desk chair by his high roll-top desk, and Olney sometimes addressed her invisible person from behind this fortress. Sometimes he paced the room or stood before the open fire with his hands behind his back; more often he stationed himself before a stand-up desk. But generally he worked his thoughts out on paper, marshaling his premises and penciling his way to his conclusions in a hand that no one else but his clerk found it easy to read. Practicing in this wise, he limited his responsibilities to cases in which he could give his personal attention to all questions of any consequence, and what he did not want to do himself he farmed out or refused to be concerned with at all.

Out of business hours Olney's relaxations seem to have assumed a strenuous, or at any rate an active expression. In his early years he was fond of riding; later he and the three neighboring families of George R. Minot, William Minot, and Charles E. Guild had one of the first tennis-courts in Forest Hills, and Olney developed an excellent game for a man who had not played in his youth. His style on the court was "exasperating," for, though he looked awkward, he got about to return the ball somehow, usually cut it, and "always returned it where you weren't." He played aggressively rather than defensively. One winter he contrived a sort of indoor rackets-court in his attic and used to make his little girls play against him. After he began spending his summers at Falmouth he often went out in a sailboat. He never hunted, but was fond of fishing — and when fishing "could be extraordinarily patient." That was remarked as if it were contradictory of what might have been expected; for on the whole it was competition and exercise which he most enjoyed in his sports. When nothing better offered he walked, hard and fast. In the days when he lived in Forest Hills he used to get off the morning train at the Roxbury station, and could then have been seen streaking more than three miles to his office, always with his overcoat over his arm and often with two leggy schoolgirls, his daughters, whom he had pulled off the train and was leading to school by his way and at his pace, running along to keep up. Some of his pleasures would have led other men much into society, but Olney managed to gratify them at home. Indoors he enjoyed cards and almost any game, was a good loser, and wanted nothing from his opponent so much as a real contest. He managed to read a good deal in a miscellaneous way which included history, fiction, and the more serious magazines. Frequently he read aloud to his family, "pleasantly and with a beautiful enunciation." He had an excellent ear and taste in music too, read music well, and was especially fond of singing. For this he had a sweet though not strong voice and Mrs. Olney had a beautiful voice of which he was very proud. He collected a good deal of interesting church music, and preferred music at home to going out to concerts.

But this mention of his relaxations and exhilarations is not to be taken as meaning that his working days were short or easy during his younger years. When success began to flirt with him in the early seventies, he courted her with the diligence which must usually be paid for her favors. Great as was his admiration for Judge Thomas and cordial as were all his personal relations with his senior associate, Olney soon decided to build up a line of practice of his own. His appetite for work and learning amounted to a "rapacity." Such elasticity and geniality as had been the portion of his youth dried out of him in those years. His children remember the house in Forest Hills as a place where they often saw a light shining from his study door when they awoke in the small hours of the night. He settled into the groove of daily forward-and-back between office and home, and those who were near him were made to conform their ways to his needs and desires. His daughters had to learn the games which refreshed him; Mrs. Olney and they sang part songs with him. If he was preoccupied, the family table deferred to his mood in silence; if not, everybody was expected to sit up and apply her best wits to conversation.

Living and working in the manner that has been described, Olney's professional prosperity was, clearly, not an expression of the size of his practice, but a result of the ever-growing importance of the affairs that were confided to his care. Manifestly, too, he had won his position by ability and force of character, not by "pull" or any petty arts of self-advancement. It should be recalled that his years of active practice coincided with a period of truly immense prosperity during which modern business came into its own — indeed, into somewhat more than its own, as events were to demonstrate; during which much of the country was industrialized, capital was piled up, railroads were built and reorganized, trusts were developed, and the modern law of corporations was evolved from simplicity to technical complexity. New England money, New England brains, Massachusetts courts and railway commissions, and Boston business men played an important part in guiding and organizing that complex and gigantic expansion. Some of the strongest business men about him had drawn upon Olney for assistance as counselor and fellow director — as a partial list of his directorships showed: the Eastern Railroad until it was leased to the Boston and Maine (he was a director as early as '79); the Boston and Maine Railroad (he was director from 1884); lesser New England roads like the Worcester, Nashua and Rochester and the Boston, Revere Beach and Lynn; (for certain New England interests in) the Kansas City and Fort Scott system; the Atchison, and the Chicago, Burlington and Quincy (he was a director in that company after Mr. Sidney Bartlett's death in 1889); the Old Colony Trust Company (he was a director from its incorporation in 1890).

And as a result of it all and at fifty-seven — what was the bias of his mind?

Woven by such experience its tissue had become a serviceable stuff of simple pattern. Its warp and woof were legal and economic. Concerned mainly with corporation law and the law of wills and estates — in other words, with the conduct of the community's immensely expanding business — his thought was usually searching for the palpable structure of some matter in hand. Being thus strenuously concerned with the osteology of practical questions, he showed little discernment for the complexion and graces of a situation. But yet his processes were neither obvious nor commonplace. He was compounded of extremes and superlatives. His intellect was no gentle pendulum swinging — tick-tock — in one appointed arc. It sometimes moved erratically; it always moved boldly and without returning upon itself.

Something has been said of the way in which he depended on his family for games, for music, for society. After the wedding of his younger daughter (which took place in Olney's house, for she had chosen a man whom he had liked and had encouraged to come to the house), he was overcome by such a fit of jealous resentment as other fathers have felt and as any man of less domineering temper would have controlled. Olney sent word to his girl that she need never return to the home she had chosen to leave. His family accepted it that such a decree, once issued, could not be reversed; and Olney — one pities him as the years go on — was apparently as incapable of modifying the cruel fiat, no matter what suffering resulted to

those who were nearest to him and to his own spirit, as if
he had been the victim of a sort of lockjaw of the will.
"It would have happened to whichever daughter married
first," said an intimate of the house; but of course a
family breach for no real reason was quite unexplainable.
Olney's daughter and her husband, Dr. Charles H. Abbot,
were placed in a painful position, and in the Boston world
in which he and his daughter were both known, reproach,
silent in his presence, but as unforgiving as he was unbend-
ing, attended him for the remainder of his days. If he
divined that fact — and surely he must have — it would
have been for him an almost insurmountable obstacle in
the path of retreat.

He could commit himself to an unamiable hammer-and-
tongs manner of going through life and yet it was among
the many contradictions of his nature that there could
still well up in one corner of his inner being genuine
springs of responsiveness to the beauty and variety
of the world. It was as if he closed a hatch over the
springs and never opened it save in idle hours. He would
not lift it upon the business of the day for a moment.
The springs never flooded his nature; were never allowed
to soften his passions, his resentments, his ambitions. It
seemed that, even when he must have wanted to, *he could
not* let them do that. His active principle was at war with
everything soft and affectionate. And yet, though he
indulged his minor side solely for purposes of recreation —
and the word purposes might fairly be underlined — he
really loved a noble song, a sunset seen from a hill, a fine
stanza of verse, a good picture, a clean wit; and any one

who was often in his company could not fail to discern the fact.

In this connection the few brief memorial addresses which he delivered in honor of deceased members of the Bench or Bar are revealing. They are the only surviving proofs of what he could do when he was not just arguing, and they are not ordinary or dry. They are brief, appropriate to the occasion which called them forth, discriminating and sympathetic. They refrain from unmeasured expressions and venture upon strictures, but do so helpfully. They get at other qualities in the men of whom they treat besides the professional virtues of "rectitude," "learning," "fidelity to the client's interest," which are too often the stupidly iterated total of what is attributed to a dead lawyer. Take, for a single example, the following passage from remarks which he made at the meeting of the Bar of the Supreme Court after Justice Jackson's death:

Tennessee boasts a long line of illustrious public men, but cannot point to any one among them that does her greater honor. She has, indeed, had sons whose lives were fuller of incident and motion and dramatic surprises. There was the Jackson of "The Hermitage," the Jackson who triumphed at New Orleans, who hanged Arbuthnot, who made Peggy O'Neil a character of national consequence, who removed the deposits, who fought with equal energy Nullification and a United States Bank, and whose erect commanding person crowned with its wealth of whitened hair, "By the Eternal" on his lips, and in his grasp both the baton of the political leader and the sword of the soldier, forms one of the most picturesque figures on the whole canvas of modern history. If such a life be phenomenal in its power to fix the public gaze and fascinate the popular imagination, that of Judge Jackson cannot be too much extolled as a potent center of beneficent influence none the less valuable and far-reaching in its effects because neither glittering nor noisy. If any criticism could be made upon Judge Jackson's youth, it would seem to be that it was beyond criticism, that he was uniformly good, that he was not young enough, that he was always free from those follies and foibles which, as the bubbling over of the irrepressible spirits natural to that period of life, make the young dear to us almost in the proportion that we have to forbear and forgive and forget. That the freedom from such frailties indicates a certain lack of imagination and of humor is unquestionable, and justifies a deduction borne out by all we know of the man. He never at any time of life, in any marked degree certainly, exhibited qualities of that sort. On the contrary, the child was emphatically father to the man, and from his youth up he was hard-working, exact, logical, loyal to his convictions and his affections, self-contained and self-poised, conscientious and God-fearing. It was these traits which surely, if not very swiftly, placed him in the front rank of an exceptionally able and learned local bar.

Olney seems to have become a Democrat, not in the least from doctrinaire sympathy with Jeffersonian principles, but because he somehow got started that way and was a born individualist to whom it was natural to incline toward the teachings of the *laissez-faire* school, and consequently also natural to incline away from protection; and perhaps, too, because he was blessed with a certain temperamental contrary-mindedness toward some of the theories that went along with the Republicanism of his day. On that head it may be that his native bias was corroborated by the spectacle of Judge Thomas's independence. Thomas, though a Whig, lost his seat in Congress and was retired from public life because he maintained that it was wrong not to compensate the slave-owners when the slaves were emancipated. Olney seems to have been skeptical about the negro's fitness for citizenship even while the popular faith in racial equality was most bright and triumphant around him. Thus it is to be noted that he joined what seemed then to be a hopeless minority at a time of life when political associations might have been attractive to him for their own sake and would certainly have helped him in his profession. If the Republican Party failed to attach him while its war-time prestige was fresh and imposing, and its claim to be the ordained instrument of national salvation was advanced with an assurance that amounted almost to social compulsion in the North, it could hardly have won him over later. In politics men are moved by their antipathies as much as by their sympathies, and Olney was perhaps endowed with more than the ordinary man's capacity for obstinacy and resentment. The bullying follies of the reconstruction period, the scandals of Grant's Administration, Blaine's essential vulgarity, the cant of which the high-tariff Republicans were often guilty — these, he being what he was, necessarily confirmed his dislike of the party in power.

After Cleveland took the national stage in 1884, the Democratic Party may well have appeared to a Bay State free-trader to be looking up. Such a personality counted immensely. In a rally over which Olney was induced to preside during the campaign of 1892 (before there had been any suggestion of his entering the Cabinet) he said with characteristic candor:

In [the Democratic Party's] success we see, or think we see, our best chance of obtaining some measure of that good government which is the sole end and aim of all our political desires. Why do we see it in that way? Upon what foundation do we build our faith? Discarding all other and doubtless sufficient considerations, I answer it is because the name of Grover Cleveland is at the head of the Democratic ticket.

It will be said that the Democratic Party has a platform, as well as a candidate, and that in the coming presidential contest the one is to be considered as well as the other. I entirely agree, and I know of nothing in the Democratic declaration of principles which any patriotic American citizen may not honestly subscribe to and heartily support. Nevertheless, the true function and place and value of a party platform, adopted by that non-deliberative body known as a national convention, are not to be lost sight of. No intelligent man supports a party because he thinks it is perfect, or because he approves of everything it does, or everything it says. He supports it because of its general trend and tendency, of which a particular platform is only a single and partial indication. ... Mr. Cleveland has not been at the head of the National Government for four years for nothing. ... Mr. Cleveland is his own best platform; and, in my judgment, the most effective criticism possible upon the Chicago platform is this, that with Mr. Cleveland as a candidate, it is practically superfluous.

But now Olney has been kept standing on the threshold long enough. The reader will be ready to follow him into the office of the Attorney-General.

III

THE ATTORNEY-GENERALSHIP

WHEN Cleveland's Administration entered office, "the burning question," said Olney in the Memorandum, "was of the immediate convocation of Congress. The campaign had been fought and won by the Democrats on the question of tariff reform. The elections had been overwhelmingly in favor of the new administration on that issue and the immediate enactment of a new tariff bill was expected by the country and would have been simply carrying out the pledges given by the Democratic Party. Nevertheless, the conclusion of the President and those whom he consulted was against a special session of Congress. It was said in support of the conclusion, among other things, that the preparation of a new tariff law would necessarily be a work of immense labor and of a long time, and that Mr. Carlisle, the new Secretary of the Treasury, who was expected to prepare it, would, with his other duties, have no more time than he needed for the work between the 4th of March and the regular session of Congress in the following December. That any special session of Congress would be required on account of the currency or because purchases of silver under the Sherman Law threatened to bring the country to a silver basis was not thought of or anticipated. Consequently, Congress was not convened and the President and all the members of the Cabinet soon found themselves completely engrossed in the organization of the various Departments and in considering the claims of office-seekers."

In Olney's case "considering" such claims would often have sounded to the claimant like euphemism for denying and dismissing them. He would not discuss appointments unless the good of the service required changes.

I have never said a word [so runs a letter to one of the United States District Attorneys[1]] or had a thought, which authorized Mr.—— to telegraph you that I was anxious for the removal of Marshal Hunt, or that you were timid in the matter of his removal. . . . Your letter to me on the subject seemed to me non-committal and to indicate, at most, only a personal preference for a marshal in political accord with yourself. If that is all that is to be said in favor of a change of marshal, my inference is that he is a valuable officer and should be allowed to serve out his time.

And to Senator Hoar,[2]

The rule of the Department, since my connection with it, has been not to ask for removals on political grounds.

His manners to callers were frequently brusque and peremptory, and the first name he got for himself in Washington was that of being "difficult to approach," "formidable," and "icy." Exaggerated stories went abroad, for iciness is sure to annoy the political hangers-on who expect to find that every door in every department is standing hospitably open to them after their party has got into office. Among the news-correspondents, too, he soon made and always maintained a reputation for keeping his own counsel and being hard to interview. But before long

[1] To W. O. Hamilton, Texas, August 9, 1894.　　[2] December 12, 1894.

all this served him as a protection rather than a handicap. ˴
In fact, whoever understood the political situation at all
realized that the new Attorney-General was not qualified
by experience to be one of the Administration's dispensers
of patronage. Any thought that he might be ambitious to
assume such a rôle being soon disposed of, and the flood-
tide of office-seekers having ebbed away, he enjoyed an
immunity from political callers which amounted to the
most that any Cabinet officer can ever expect.

The duties of the Attorney-General are many and various. He directs and controls the Federal Government's
immense law business, not only in the Department in
Washington, but also in all the Judicial Districts into
which the United States and its Territories are divided.
He also exercises certain quasi-judicial functions, inter-
prets the law for the other executive departments and
for the President, and considers applications for pardons
before they go to the President.

The details of all this were more than enough to absorb
a new department head for many months. Olney immediately fell into the sound practice of letting the
Solicitor-General and Assistant Attorney-Generals represent him in court, and devoted himself to overseeing, and
to keeping himself prepared to advise the President on
questions which came before the Cabinet.[1] Knowledge of

[1] To a correspondent who was considering an invitation to become
Attorney-General in President McKinley's Cabinet, Olney wrote:
"So far as strictly legal work is concerned, the duties of the Attorney-
General are not more exacting than those of any lawyer having a large
general practice. But the truth is that the Attorney-Generalship cor-
responds to what is known in European countries as the 'Ministry of
Justice' — that is, the duties are very largely administrative. For the

the law, a habit of dispatch, decision of character — these amply assured his success in dealing with routine, and during his first year only one matter emerged to provoke discussion.

This concerned the Sherman Anti-Trust Law, which was still new and almost untested. Olney's estimate of the meaning of the Act corresponded with the better opinion of the Bar; but not with popular demand. He explained what he thought might and what might not be looked for

first year or two, while you were seeing to the appointments of proper persons as United States District Attorneys and Marshals and getting accustomed to the general duties of a Cabinet officer, you would probably have little or no time to prepare and argue cases in the Supreme Court of the United States. There is a vast deal of work to do in the way of giving opinions upon legal questions to other heads of Departments and to the President of the United States. It is probable, too, that President McKinley's Attorney-General will find a great deal of time occupied in the consideration of applications for pardon — a function of which, under President Cleveland's régime, Attorney-Generals have been almost entirely relieved. If I have made myself understood, you will perceive the great importance to the Attorney-General of having a first-rate Solicitor-General upon whom he can devolve the conduct of cases in the Supreme Court with entire confidence. In the same view, it is of great importance that the three Assistant Attorney-Generals should be carefully selected. They ought to render valuable assistance, not only to the Solicitor-General in connection with cases in the Supreme Court, but to the Attorney-General in all cases in which legal opinions are called for. . . . What you want particularly to bear in mind is the administrative character of the position. It took me two years to get the Department — in which term I include district attorneyships and marshalships all over the country — thoroughly organized. I then began to argue cases, but had an opportunity to argue only two — the Income Tax cases and the Debs case — before Judge Gresham died and I became Secretary of State."

During Olney's time his principal assistants were: Edward B. Whitney, later a judge of the New York Supreme Court; Lawrence Maxwell, Jr., of Cincinnati, who was Solicitor-General for a while; J. M. Dickinson, afterward Secretary of War under President Taft; Charles B. Howry, subsequently a judge of the United States Court of Claims; J. E. Dodge, later a judge of the Supreme Court of Wisconsin; and Holmes Conrad, Solicitor-General after January 30, 1895.

from the Act in two pages of his Annual Report, warning the public that it must not assume a broad interpretation, and consequently must not expect his Department to begin a multitude of prosecutions. It must be admitted that he thus interpreted the law more narrowly than the Supreme Court has since, but the law, it should be remembered, had not yet been passed upon by the highest court, and the lower courts which had been called upon to construe its difficult and uncertain provisions had found them unenforceable in almost every case. The most important and most thoroughly considered of these early decisions had been rendered by Mr. Justice Jackson, and he had been elevated to the Supreme Court by President Harrison shortly after rendering it and just before Olney took office. With the conservative reasoning of Judge Jackson's opinion Olney himself inclined to agree. Clearly he would have been guilty of demagogic and irresponsible extravagance had he launched the Government on a wide campaign of prosecution despite these early decisions, in disregard of his own well-grounded misgivings about the law, and in face of the business panic of '93. Although this appears obvious, it was quite natural too that his course should provoke a constant small-fire of criticism at the time. But it should not be judged by that nor by later events alone. It is hard to justify the extravagance with which Roosevelt and the Republican Party accused the Cleveland Administration, ten years later, of having favored the "trusts."

As a matter of fact, the Attorney-General did not merely pronounce an opinion on the law, but put it to the

test. He selected an important case and had it brought
before the Supreme Court as rapidly as possible. This was
the so-called Sugar Trust Case (U.S. *v.* Knight *et al.*, 156
U.S. 1), which was argued before the Supreme Court in
October, 1894.[1] The Court followed the earlier decisions
and decided against the Government, thus confirming
Olney's estimate of the then state of the law.

Meanwhile, his eye was also on the wider horizon outside his own Department. During that summer of 1893,
the country was rapidly slipping into a slough of financial
despond. In April the money market touched fifteen per
cent and during the next three months the business panic
developed in its full intensity and swept banks, railroads,
and commercial houses into bankruptcy all over the
country.[2] Olney's letter-books show that from April on he
was encouraging New England bankers and business men
like John M. Forbes, Henry L. Higginson, N. P. Hallowell,
Charles C. Jackson, and other men outside New England,
such as the veteran banker Samuel G. Ward, and Charles
E. Perkins of the Chicago Burlington & Quincy Railroad
to send him their observations and recommendations concerning the situation. What use he made of the comments
and hints which came to him no record discloses, but
Secretary Carlisle was being criticized for not communicating with "Wall Street" as freely and openly as the crisis

[1] See also, as to the Sherman Anti-Trust Law, Appendix II.

[2] Among the railroads that were hard hit was the Union Pacific. Fore-
seeing that the Government would be involved in the reorganization proceedings, Olney divested himself of his own interest in the company by
selling his stock at the price of $19 a share. (R. O. Memo.)

required, and the fact that Olney took pains to encourage these correspondents is worth noting with reference to his own conception of a Cabinet officer's rôle and with reference to the extent to which President Cleveland began very early to rely on his counsel and aid.

On June 30th an element of suspense was removed by Cleveland's proclamation calling Congress in special session. The President's departure from Washington followed immediately upon the signing of the proclamation. Other members of the Government went away too, and Olney betook himself to his summer house at Falmouth. But there disquieting rumors began to reach him. Cleveland had escaped from public observation on board Commodore Benedict's yacht, but it lingered inexplicably in New York Harbor. The fact was that Cleveland had hidden in its cabin in order to have a hurried operation for cancer of the jaw. No statement of any kind was given to the public for fear that the truth might aggravate the business panic, and even the Cabinet was left without information of the President's condition.[1] When at last the yacht moved up to Buzzard's Bay and put the President off at Gray Gables, Olney made several attempts to see him. After a fortnight, says his Memorandum, he succeeded in having an interview. Cleveland

had changed a good deal in appearance, had lost a good deal of flesh, and his mouth was so stuffed with antiseptic wads that he could hardly articulate. The first utterance that I understood was something like this — "My God,

[1] The facts were revealed by Dr. W. W. Keen in the *Saturday Evening Post* for September 22, 1917. See also Rhodes, VIII, 397–400.

Olney, they nearly killed me." He did not talk much, was very much depressed, and at the time acted, and I believe felt, as if he did not expect to recover. . . . The matter of repealing the "silver purchase" bill naturally came up. He had been thinking of it and had tried to do something towards his special message to Congress. He showed me what he had done. There were perhaps twenty or thirty lines, forming the first two paragraphs of the message as eventually sent to Congress. He was very depressed about the progress he was making and complained that his mind would not work, and, upon my suggesting that I might perhaps be of assistance, was evidently very much relieved. In the course of two or three days I went to Gray Gables with a draft of a message, which was approved by Mr. Cleveland practically as drawn.

Olney evidently dictated the last words without reëxamining the message,[1] for between it and his draft there are distinct differences. The two documents are interesting to compare, for they show how the minds of the two men, one a veteran, the other a beginner at such work, approached one and the same task at this time.

That task was, manifestly, to frame an appeal to the whole nation in the form of an address to Congress; to review briefly an economic question with which the business world was painfully familiar, and to define a "sound-money" policy with such tact and authority as to win or compel the support of Congress. Olney turned out a forensic argument, which certainly showed a grasp of the fiscal question; but he couched it in such needlessly challenging terms that, in reading it after reading the message, one realizes his political inexpertness. Some sentences

[1] Richardson, IX, 401. For the draft, see Olney Coll.

would have refreshed the spirits of the sound-money advocates, but would have given needless offense to the silver men. For instance:

It is indeed charged in some quarters that existing financial embarrassments ... have been purposely brought about by what are called the enemies of silver ... which is spoken of less as a material commodity than as a sort of benignant genius endowed with infinite potential faculties for good and now assailed by a foul conspiracy on the part of all the leading governments, banking institutions, and financiers of the world.

The President would not — no President could ever, without risk to his influence — refer thus mockingly to any party when speaking in a message to Congress about a matter which "rises above the plane of party politics." Indeed, the message of August 8th is, by comparison with Olney's draft, a lesson in message-writing. It shows that Cleveland either composed himself, or accepted from some one else, an introductory statement of fact so simple and clear that it gave to the whole document a tone of impartial authority. Then, following this introduction, Cleveland used a number of Olney's more argumentative paragraphs, so that, without any great alteration of phraseology, they fell into place like statements of necessary conclusions, and supplied most of the last half of the message.

Furthermore, the President confined himself, after asking definitely for the repeal of the silver purchase clauses of the Act of 1890, to a recommendation both broad and vague:

that other legislative action may put beyond all doubt or mistake, the intention and ability of the Government to fulfill its pecuniary obligations in money universally recognized by all civilized countries.

This named neither gold nor silver — the avoidance of both words is remarkable — and was not a categorical demand upon Congress. But at the same time it left no room to doubt the intention of the Executive. Olney's draft, on the other hand, looked beyond the repeal of the Sherman Law and explicitly urged Congress not only to repeal the silver purchase clauses, just as Cleveland's message did, but also to provide that all outstanding obligations of the Government (which would have included both bonds and paper money) should be payable in "gold coin," and to give the Secretary of the Treasury authority to issue bonds payable "in gold." The difference was only a question of how much to insist upon. Both men wanted everything that Olney named. Cleveland, who had the reputation of giving little thought to ways and means of avoiding collisions with Congress, seems to have had the better vision of the obstacles that lay ahead; and the pains he took to let no word or request add to the difficulty his opponents might find in meeting his chief request was justified by the outcome. A third of the Democrats in the House broke away and voted against the bill to repeal the silver purchase clauses. The Senate delayed over it until October 30th, and Republican votes were required to pass it. The Democratic Party began to disintegrate during the struggle, and Cleveland's message, moderate though it was, made him a host of enemies. When, later in 1895, he forwarded a definite request to Congress for authority to sell gold bonds to the Morgan-Belmont syndicate, and so to do in a single instance what Olney's draft would have demanded authority to do in all cases, Congress immediately refused and thus threw away a possible saving of $16,000,000 on the price of the issue.[1] Olney was right, though tactless in speaking as if it was a "state of mind" that confronted the Administration. "The silver craze" deserved to be so called; but Cleveland stands in American history as the great political champion of sound money, and he spoke more softly on this occasion.

During this first year in Washington, Olney was also drawn into the Hawaiian imbroglio. But it will be better to consider that strange episode at the point where this record brings him to the State Department.

[1] Noyes, *Forty Years of American Finance*, 197–99, 235. Cleveland, *Presidential Problems*, 156.

IV

LABOR TROUBLES AND THE COXEYITES

IT was not until the summer of 1894 that occurred the event which made Olney's attorney-generalship memorable. The disturbances which broke out in many parts of the country during the depressing winter and spring which followed the business panic were, in so far as they involved the Department of Justice, a prelude to the contest with Debs — they prepared the Department, and, as it were, led it to rehearse for the Chicago drama of July. Olney's Memorandum may be quoted again:

The times were so hard and work so scarce that, between the Pacific Coast and the Eastern States, especially in the more sparsely populated regions, there were large numbers of unemployed persons who were at a loss to know how to procure even the necessaries of life. [Jobless men and all the habitual tramps and vagabonds in the West began heading eastward, and "the notion of a general crusade of squalor spread all through the country,"[1] as if by some curious psychological impulse among them, although no leader and no objective for their crusade could at first be named.] In this state of things, an Ohio man by the name of Coxey... [proposed to lead] a vast army of the unemployed... to Washington for the purpose of stating their grievances.... The movement acquired considerable impetus in the West, contributions to a considerable amount were received, and a large number of persons actually started on the march for Washington.... They sympathized with the Coxey movement, not from conviction, it

[1] Peck, 373.

is believed, but because they were poor and suffering and without occupation, and any change seemed an improvement. By reason of the distance, despairing of getting to Washington on foot and lacking means to pay for their transportation, they organized and undertook to seize and operate railroad trains. [Some of them were men who had gone West to work at railroad construction before the panic, and who, now that they were left stranded by hard times, regarded themselves as having a sort of moral claim to a free ride home over any railroad.] It so happened that most, if not all, of the railroads running between Oregon and the East were then in the hands of receivers of the United States Courts. Accordingly, as soon as the train seizures began, the facts were brought to the attention of the United States Courts which, through their officers, were practically operating the railroads. The courts could not look on without an effort to save the situation, and at once issued injunctions against the persons seizing the trains, which injunctions the marshals were instructed to enforce by such number of deputy marshals as should be necessary.[1] Their orders were, however, practically ineffective for the reason that the very parties available as deputy marshals had either themselves taken part in the forcible capture of trains or sympathized with the actual captors. In these circumstances, the situation was capable of being relieved only through the action of the United States. On account of expense, perhaps for other reasons, the States

[1] What were the terms of these "injunctions"? In the Annual Report of the Attorney-General for 1894 Olney said, "The courts at once issued decrees for the protection of the receivers and their property." On May 2d, Beatty, J., in the Circuit Court for the District of Idaho issued an order to the United States Marshal to protect railroad property in the hands of receivers. A search which the Department of Justice has made in its existing files (1922) has turned up references which indicate that similar orders were issued to marshals and railroad receivers by other courts, but has disclosed no restraining order to unnamed persons such as the famous injunction issued later in the Chicago strike.

between Oregon and Minnesota, in which the lawless element was most rampant, were without any militia — so that the Government of the State, even if so disposed, was practically powerless either to prevent or to punish the disturbances connected with the seizure of trains, the interference with interstate commerce, and the carrying of the mails. The judges and the marshals thereupon joined in applications to the Department of Justice for such assistance as could be rendered by the army of the United States, and wherever the facts were clearly proven, the commanding officers of such troops of the United States as were in the vicinity of any disturbance were ordered to put in force the order of the United States Court wherever the United States Marshals and his deputies were unable to do so.

This — to interrupt the Memorandum — may be illustrated by the instructions which were telegraphed to the United States Marshal at Grafton, North Dakota, on April 25th:

Execute any injunction or other process placed in your hands by the United States Court for the protection of persons and property against lawless violence by employing such number of deputies as may be necessary. If execution resisted by force which cannot thus be overcome, let the facts be telegraphed by yourself and, if practicable, by the judge issuing the process, to the President with request for military assistance.[1]

Similarly, the following answer to a dispatch from the United States District Judge at Seattle was telegraphed on May 14th:

Yours of yesterday received. General Otis, Vancouver, will dispose troops so as to avert threatened danger, and in

[1] Files of the Department of Justice.

case of lawless resistance to the orders of the United States Court, too powerful to be overcome by the marshal and his deputies, will use the troops to enforce such orders. Communicate with him by wire. I rely upon you to see to it that troops are employed only in case of exigency making such employment necessary and legally justifiable.[1]

The result [letting the Memorandum resume the story] was that the capture of trains was stopped and that very large numbers of almost desperate men who would otherwise have found their way to Washington were compelled to remain at home. It was estimated at the time that if the Commonwealers could have used the railroads, at least sixty or seventy thousand of them would have rendezvoused in Washington. Such of them as did arrive there [about four hundred of them on April 28th] encamped in the vicinity and remained a week or more. They made a feeble demonstration upon Congress by attempting to attend a session at the Capitol *en masse* — the only visible result of which was that some of their leaders were arrested for trespassing on the lawns about the Capitol. Great vigilance was exercised by the Washington authorities to prevent house-breaking, robbery and pilfering of all sorts, and gradually they were edged out of the District into adjoining States and melted away and disappeared. As an organized movement, it was remarkable principally for its entire collapse without any serious consequences either to the Commonwealers themselves or to the communities visited by them.

For days, Coxey with his motley "Army of the Commonweal of Christ" had advanced slowly toward Washington — marching very conspicuously across the pages of the newspapers — and had distracted the public's

[1] Files of the Department of Justice.

attention from other disorders. Thanks to weather and distance he had lost marchers about as fast as he had enrolled them, and was never accompanied by a large contingent. But circumstances might have been more favorable to him. In a vague way he had threatened Washington with something it had never experienced, and the prospect had excited alarmists into talking about the march of the Paris mob to Versailles. What kept Coxey's movement from growing into an immense demonstration that would have disturbed Washington seriously and might have been imitated in a violent way in other centers too, what reduced it to the proportions which made possible its ludicrous anticlimax on the lawn of the Capitol, was not only the harsh spring weather and the skill of the District police, but in great measure the quiet and effective manner in which the disturbances on the Western railroads were snuffed out as fast as they occurred. That is the point which should at last be noted.

The procedure which the Department of Justice adopted was interesting because of its adequacy to these disorders; also because it was admirably adapted to the greater disorders which were about to break out in Chicago. Sporadic disturbances on the Western roads continued into May. The Chicago strike was called to enforce a strike at Pullman before the end of June. As Olney said, in writing to Cleveland in 1902, the Commonwealers and the Chicago strike "were dealt with in practically the same way." [1]

.[1] In 1877 there were railroad riots which were much more serious than anything that had occurred up to this moment in 1894, and which were marked by alarming violence in many places. The conduct of President

But the Chicago troubles were far more grave than anything that had preceded them.

Hayes's Administration was admirable in a different way from that of
President Cleveland's, and it would be interesting to look back and compare the two occasions fully. But it must suffice here to mention certain
important respects in which they differed. In 1894 the great extent of
railroad mileage in the hands of receivers appointed by the Federal
Courts, the fact that the disturbances of the spring months generally
began with attempts to seize the trains of the receivers instead of with
riot and destruction, and, last, the tacitly recognized feebleness of the local
authorities in the regions first affected, all made it appropriate for Olney
and Cleveland to interfere in the manner above described instead of leaving
matters to the local police and militia. In 1877 by contrast, the courts were
not much involved (although Mr. Rhodes says that the United States
Marshals called for troops in three States where there were Federal
receiverships). Generally the militia was first called out to quell the disorders. Where it proved, after trial, to be quite inadequate, as it did in
several States, the Governors themselves called upon President Hayes for
regular troops. (See Rhodes, VIII, 47; 13–51 *passim*.) In 1877 the Hayes
Administration based its important military dispositions on these requisi-
tions from the State authorities. But in 1894 the Cleveland Administration acted without waiting for appeals from the State authorities.

V
THE CHICAGO STRIKE

"THE Pullman strike," says the Memorandum, "originated in the fact that the entire business of the country, including that of railroad transportation, was greatly depressed, that the demand for cars from the Pullman Company had fallen off so that a large surplus of manufactured cars was on hand for which there was no demand, and that the alternative was either to stop the Pullman works altogether or to keep them running on short hours and at reduced rates of wages. The Company's attempt to resort to the latter mode of meeting the situation enraged its employees. . . ." They considered that they were being made to shoulder an unfair proportion of the Company's losses. Furthermore, their plight as strikers was peculiar, for the Company owned the town of Pullman and was in a position to impose living conditions as well as conditions of work and wages.

Their case might have excited the interest of union men elsewhere at any time. In 1894 it was certain to appeal forcibly to the railroad employees with whom they were affiliated. Recent wage-cuts on many different railway lines, blacklistings, and the activities of the so-called General Managers' Association — which was determining for twenty-four railroads centering on Chicago what their treatment of the employees should be — these had lately spread uneasiness and apprehension among railroad workmen generally, and so they "were ripe to espouse the cause of the Pullman strikers." [1] They were soon led to do it.

The American Railway Union, then recently organized by Eugene V. Debs as a protest against what he considered the feeble methods of the railroad "Brotherhoods," had just carried out a partially successful strike on the Great Northern Railway, and it met in Chicago for a stated convention in June. It had allowed a number of the men at Pullman to join its ranks, although they were not, strictly speaking, railroad men; and at the convention, Debs had their grievance brought up. After a fruitless attempt to arrange a settlement by negotiation and arbitration, the American Railway Union voted on June 21st that after the 26th its members should refuse to handle trains to which Pullman cars were attached. The avowed intention of this was to compel the railroads to *boycott* the Pullman Company. But no grievance against the roads was stated by the Union and no direct communication was sent to them by its convention.

To-day, as we look back, the action of the American Railway Union seems even more astonishing and even less possible to justify than it appeared at the moment. The gist of it was that, in order to help a strike by shop-workers in the town of Pullman, the Union planned to do nothing less than seize the country's transportation system by the

[1] See the Report on the Chicago Strike by the United States Strike Commission, Sen. Ex. Doc. 7 (53d Cong., 3d Sess.), Introd. p. xl. Carroll D. Wright, the Chairman of the Commission, said of the strike: "A share of the responsibility for bringing it on belongs in some degree to each and every party involved." (Wright, *Industrial Evolution of the United States* [New York, 1901], 316.)

throat and inflict more intolerable discomfort on the country than the country could bear. So inherently and essentially violent was this programme that Debs's orders to the members of the Union to refrain from individual acts of violence were reasonably regarded as formalism and mockery. Of course, too, the strike leaders knew that disorders and hoodlumism would attend such a strike as surely as camp-followers attend the march of the best disciplined army. Debs's plan, putting it baldly, was to hit the public rather than the Company, although his purpose was doubtless to draw the public's attention to the injustices of the Pullman situation and thus induce their removal. His error lay in not seeing that such methods were certain to focus criticism and bitter hostility against his own union. One of the "foolishest" as well as one of the "kindest" of men is what a sympathetic writer once called him.[1] Surely one of the foolishest! "When you say *strike* you mean *boycott* in this case," said Carroll D. Wright, and Debs replied with the candor which partly accounts for his personal magnetism, "Well, I do not exactly like the term *boycott*. It is a term I do not often use. There is a deep-seated hostility in this country to the term *boycott*."[2] Yet knowing that, he plunged ahead. There have been strikes and threats of strikes on a greater scale since then, but no strike of comparable magnitude has seemed so brutally oblivious of the interests of the nation, so careless of public opinion, so unmeasured, so surprising and consequently so menacing.

[1] Lincoln Steffens, *Everybody's Magazine*, October, 1908.
[2] Sen. Ex. Doc. 7 (53d Cong., 3d Sess.), 144.

This very quality of the Chicago strike relieved Cleveland and Olney of the need of elucidating the issues or 'making' public opinion in any way. It forced them to act without any reference to the merits of the dispute at the town of Pullman, and made it obvious that they were not attempting to pass upon such questions. "It is not germane," said Olney, "to consider the origin or the merits of the labor disturbance";[1] and neither at the moment nor later did he ever express his own opinion about them. He and the President had merely to protect the United States mails promptly, vigorously, and without preliminary proclamations or self-justifying explanations of any kind, and could dispense with all discussion of the strikers' claims. Debs had done for them the work of putting the country in the mood for just that. The boycott which he attempted to establish was so impudent a challenge to government that four people out of five realized, as soon as an injunction was published and the first troops began to move, that the Administration was doing what had got to be done. Debs himself admitted it all later. "Have you any doubt," he was asked, "that, if public opinion had been directly informed as to the entire situation, the strike would probably have been averted and that you would have succeeded in your just demands?" "I believe that is true," was his reply.[2]

President Cleveland described the magnitude of the disturbance fairly:

[It] is often called the "Chicago Strike." It is true that its

[1] Annual Report of the Attorney-General for 1894, xxxi.
[2] Sen. Ex. Doc. 7 (53d Cong., 3d Sess.), 167.

beginning was in that city; and the headquarters of those who inaugurated it and directed its operations were located there; but the name thus given to it is an entire misnomer so far as it applies to the scope and reach of the trouble. Railroad operations were more or less affected in twenty-seven States and Territories; and in all these the interposition of the general Government was to a greater or less extent invoked.

. . . [Complaints of obstruction of the mails,] sometimes accompanied by charges of forcible seizure of trains and other violent disorders, poured in upon the Attorney-General from all parts of the West and Southwest. These complaints came from post-office officials, from United States Marshals and District Attorneys, from railroad managers, and from other officials and private citizens.[1]

On the 28th of June, two days after the boycott started, the Postmaster-General's Department advised the Department of Justice that the mails were being detained at Chicago, San Francisco, St. Paul, Salt Lake City, Portland, Oregon, and Los Angeles, and asked that steps should be taken to protect them. The following telegram was thereupon dispatched to the United States Attorneys at the places named:

See that the passage of regular trains carrying United States mails in the usual and ordinary way, as contemplated by act of Congress and directed by the Postmaster-General, is not obstructed. Procure warrants or other available process from the United States Courts against any and all persons engaged in such obstruction, and direct marshal to execute the same by such number of deputies or such posse as may be necessary.[2]

[1] *Presidential Problems*, 80, 81, 87.
[2] Annual Report of the Attorney-General for 1894, xxxi.

Thus, as Olney explained in the Memorandum, the Department "took measures to put itself in the position which had induced the President to authorize the use of troops as against the Coxey movement." [1] It enlisted the services of Edwin Walker, an able local lawyer, as special counsel for the Government to aid United States District Attorney Milchrist in Chicago, and on June 30th Olney wrote to Walker:

It has seemed to me that if the rights of the United States were vigorously asserted in Chicago, the origin and center of the demonstration, the result would be to make it a failure everywhere else and to prevent its spread over the entire country. With yourself directing matters for the Government, I am sure all legal remedies will be resorted to that the facts will warrant.

In this connection it has seemed to me advisable not merely to rely on warrants against persons actually guilty of the offense of obstructing United States mails, but to go into a court of equity and secure restraining orders which shall have the effect of preventing any attempt to commit the offense. With that view I sent a telegram to Mr. Milchrist this morning citing some decisions, which I think may probably be availed of in the present exigency.

The Marshal and the District Attorney have wired me about the employment of fifty deputies. I authorized it, of course. But I feel that the true way of dealing with the matter is by a force which is overwhelming and prevents any attempt at resistance. In that particular, however, I must defer to the better judgment of one who is on the spot and familiar with all the facts of the situation. . . .

And the next day he telegraphed to Walker:

[1] R. O. Memo. 14.

Advantages of bill in equity restraining unlawful combinations against operation Federal laws, whether under Interstate-Commerce Law, Act of July 2, 1890, or on general grounds, are obvious and will doubtless be availed of by you, if practicable. Immediate, vigorous measures at center of disturbance immensely important.[1]

Olney also had other reasons for wanting an injunction — the only legal process by which a *prima facie* case against Debs could be judicially set up without delay. "The President might," he said later, "have used the United States troops to prevent interference with the mails and with interstate commerce on his own initiative — without waiting for action by the courts and without justifying the proceeding as taken to enforce judicial decrees. But . . . it is doubtful — at least seemed doubtful to me at the time — whether the President could be induced to move except in support of the judicial tribunals . . . it was unquestionably better to await its [the judiciary's] movements and make them the basis of executive action." [2]

Milchrist and Walker forthwith acted on their instructions and filed a bill in equity in the Attorney-General's name in which they asked for an injunction both on general grounds and to enforce the provisions of the Sherman Anti-Trust Law, and on July 2d Judges Woods and Grosscup issued a sweeping injunction against Debs and other officers of the Railway Union by name, and against "all other persons combining and conspiring with them, and to all other persons whomsoever."

[1] Appendix to Annual Report of the Attorney-General, 1896, pp. 60, 61.
[2] See Appendix I.

July 3d Olney telegraphed to Milchrist:

Congratulate you upon the legal situation, which is all that could be desired. Trust use of United States troops will not be necessary. If it becomes necessary, they will be used promptly and decisively upon the justifying facts being certified to me. In such case, if practicable, let Walker and Marshal and United States Judge join in statement as to the exigency.[1]

The following dispatch came from Chicago dated the same day:

When the injunction was granted yesterday a mob of from two to three thousand held possession of a point in the city near the crossing of the Rock Island by other roads, where they had already ditched a mail train, and prevented the passing of any trains, whether mail or otherwise. I read the injunction writ to this mob and commanded them to disperse. The reading of the writ met with no response except jeers and hoots. Shortly after, the mob threw a number of baggage cars across the track, since when no mail trains have been able to move. I am unable to disperse the mob, clear the tracks, or arrest the men who were engaged in the acts named, and believe that no force less than the regular troops of the United States can procure the passage of the mail trains or enforce the orders of the Court. I believe people engaged in trades are quitting employment to-day, and in my opinion will be joining the mob to-night, and especially to-morrow, and it is my judgment that the troops should be here at the earliest moment. An emergency has arisen for their presence in this city.

J. W. ARNOLD
United States Marshal

[1] Appendix to Annual Report of the Attorney-General for 1896, p. 65.

We have read the foregoing, and from that information
and other information that has come to us believe that an
emergency exists for the immediate presence of the United
States troops.

> P. S. GROSSCUP, Judge
> EDWIN WALKER
> THOMAS E. MILCHRIST
> Attorneys [1]

As is well remembered, a detachment of regulars immediately moved into the city.

The whole business had, of course [said Olney in the
Memorandum] been the subject of much anxious consultation between the President and the Attorney-General, and
to some extent with the other members of the Cabinet.
The Secretary of War [Lamont] and General Schofield
were in constant communication with the President and
the Attorney-General, and the Secretary of State [Gresh-
am] — who was a resident in Chicago — was of course
very much interested. He was, however, not impressed
with the plan pursued by the Department of Justice in the
first instance, and doubted whether the bill in equity as
filed was not fatally bad because amounting to an attempt
to enjoin against the commission of a crime. The President,
however, relied upon the Department of Justice, and in the
use of the United States troops, was perfectly content to be
able to justify himself on the ground that they were
employed merely to enforce judicial processes. . . .

From June 26th, Debs and the other officers and agents
of the Union had urged on the strike at every possible
point by speeches, telegrams, and personal exhortation.
By July 3d they had brought about what Carroll D.

[1] Appendix to the Annual Report of the Attorney-General for 1896,
p. 66.

Wright, the Chairman of the Special Commission which later reported to the President, described as "a practical insurrection of all the labor employed on the principal railroads radiating from Chicago and some of their affiliated lines...whose influences were felt all over the country."[1] They also attempted to induce a sympathetic walkout of all the unionized trades in Chicago; but at this point the American Federation of Labor brought its influence to bear and no general sympathetic strike occurred. The idle and lawless elements, which were especially numerous about Chicago during the year following the World's Fair, seized upon the occasion, however. "Riots, intimidations, assaults, murder, arson, and burglary" attended the boycott. Counting marshals, deputies, militia, and police along with the two thousand regulars the total force which was employed in restoring order amounted to more than fourteen thousand men.[2]

The injunction crippled the activities of Debs and his lieutenants, however. It forbade everything they most needed to do in order to convert their plan into action. It commanded the defendants named

and all persons combining and conspiring with them, and all other persons whomsoever, absolutely to desist and refrain from in any way or manner interfering with, hindering, obstructing or stopping any of the business of any of the following named railroads;

and, after specifying and amplifying in detail and at length, it explicitly enjoined all persons "from ordering, directing,

[1] C. D. Wright, *The Battles of Labor* (Philadelphia, 1906), 134-35.
[2] *Ibid.*, 139.

aiding, assisting or abetting in any manner" the acts of interference already forbidden.[1] It was issued in duplicate in the other jurisdictions in which there was trouble, and it threw on the strike organizers a burden of responsibility which was too great for them to carry. Unless they got the injunction dissolved — which they did not even attempt to do [2] — their every command to their striking men was an open defiance of the courts; and, though they tried for a few days to continue defiantly, the telegrams they sent out — often addressed to agents who had been likewise served with an injunction — no longer compelled obedience. "It was not the soldiers that ended the strike," Debs testified at the subsequent inquiry; "it was not the old brotherhoods that ended the strike; it was simply the United States Courts that ended the strike." [3]

Olney wrote to Richard Watson Gilder (September 22, 1897), à propos of General Schofield's book, "Forty-Six Years in the Army":

It has therefore occurred to me since I last wrote you that perhaps you would be glad to have a hint how the General's account of the strike impresses me. It impresses me —I am frank to say—unfavorably. From reading it the natural inference is that the army was the sole instrumentality employed to deal with the strike and that the military power of the Government was resorted to at once — from the beginning — and perhaps without sufficient justification.

Such an idea ought not to gain currency — would pro-

[1] *In re* Debs, 158 U.S. 564, at 570, 572.
[2] See Appendix I, at p. 203.
[3] Sen. Ex. Doc. 7 (53d Cong., 3d Sess.), 143.

duce a bad effect generally — and would be most unjust to President Cleveland.

The military arm was invoked with the greatest reluctance — only after all less drastic means had been employed — and only upon the strongest representations of the acuteness of the crisis by those in whose judgment the President had a right to place implicit reliance.

On the 10th of June, the grand jury which Milchrist had summoned at the beginning of the trouble indicted Debs and others for obstructing the mails. They were arrested and gave bail. On the 17th they were arrested again, this time for contempt of the court's injunction. It had become apparent that the strike was disintegrating, that public opinion was against it, that it was doomed to failure. The Union had already made an unsuccessful effort to open negotiations for a return to work on favorable terms. So, when the leaders were arrested this second time, they declined to give bail and elected to go to prison while the strike petered out, and to litigate the validity of the injunction by *habeas corpus* proceedings.

The Federal troops were withdrawn from Chicago on the 20th.

Of course, there were voices to cry out that disorders increased during the few days which followed the army's entry into Chicago, to argue that the troops were not needed, and that their presence did more harm than good. Governor Altgeld, of Illinois, protested that the President had no power to send them to the city. But when the military are called out to prevent trouble there are always some people who persuade themselves that any subsequent disturbances have been occasioned by the precautions. No impressive evidence has ever been offered to prove that the regulars caused violence in 1894. On the contrary, it seems certain that their arrival in Chicago put a check upon the disorders which had begun, and that their use in that city had a distinct moral effect in other places as well. Altgeld overlooked the fact that, from the Administration's point of view (and from the general public's), Illinois was merely one scene of disturbances which extended throughout the West, Mid-West, and Southwest; that the Government had to select a strategic point for a show of firmness, and that its choice could not be made to wait upon the diverse preferences which local authorities might entertain about local situations. He seems also to have evolved an indefensible theory that, since the Constitution expressly authorizes a Governor to call on the President for troops, it compels the President, by implication, to wait for such a requisition before employing them.

In using the army to suppress disorder in 1894, Cleveland and Olney may be said to have confirmed a correct construction of the Federal Government's powers, rather than to have enlarged them. But undoubtedly they surprised the country, and made the deeper impression on it accordingly. They acted before the popular mind saw what was coming, and without waiting for anything like a popular mandate. Then, too, their action jostled rudely against a supposition which was still commonly made in 1894. Among the convictions which the Civil War had embedded in the country's political consciousness, and which nothing had yet shaken, was the idea that the Democratic Party must champion the States against the power of the Federal Government on every occasion. Yet here were Cleveland and Olney not only throwing Federal troops into Illinois unbidden by her authorities, but keeping them there in spite of her Governor's protest and regardless of the fact that Illinois had contributed largely to the Democratic victory in 1892. As if to emphasize this abandonment of tradition, they relied upon a statute, among others, which had been passed in Grant's Administration as a measure of reconstruction. (R.S., sect. 5299.) What was more, they went ahead and discharged their duty to the country in that wise without vouchsafing so much as a word of regret or explanation for the Democrats, departed or still living, who had declaimed, fought, and protested about "States' rights" for two generations. Their action announced the end of a political era more convincingly than the most eloquent proclamation could have signalized it — announced that the theory of States' rights as Altgeld invoked it was now a discarded shibboleth, and that (with respect to anything like an Altgeldian political philosophy, at any rate) the Democratic Party was escaping from bondage to its memories of the Civil War. No language could have been more Federal in spirit than Olney's: "the soil of Illinois is the soil of the United States, and for all United States purposes the United States is there . . . not by license or comity, but as of right." One sentence which he issued to the press must have struck former secession Democrats as a truly brutal sentence for a Democratic Attorney-General to utter:

"The notion that territory of any State is too sacred to permit the exercise thereon by the United States Government of any of its legitimate functions never had any legal existence, and, as a rule of conduct, became practically extinct with the close of the Civil War." [1] Had words been needed when actions were so clear, none could have breathed the Administration's faith in the country's integrity more reassuringly than those in which Cleveland was said to have exclaimed, "If it takes every dollar in the Treasury and every soldier in the United States Army to deliver a postal card in Chicago, that postal card shall be delivered." [2]

Apart from the fact that the Administration's conduct set an example of the very highest value, there resulted from the action taken at Chicago one new judicial precedent of which the importance cannot be measured even now, and of which the latter-day implications are too complex for treatment here. The equity powers of the courts had never been invoked in this way. The end of the Chicago strike popularized a new weapon for use in industrial disputes, and Judge Woods's injunction was bitterly criticized by the labor organizations.

The reader will remember that Debs, committed to jail for contempt of the injunction, brought *habeas corpus* proceedings to test its validity. Of the progress and outcome of those proceedings an account can be given in Olney's

[1] See Appendix I, at p. 205.
[2] Rhodes, VIII, 425; repeating a quotation by Miss Agnes Repplier.

own words. The case went against Debs in the Circuit Court, was appealed, and was argued in the Supreme Court on March 26th and 27th, 1895.

The Chicago equity bills [says the Memorandum] had rested the Government's case on two grounds, first, on its general equity powers to interfere by injunction in a perfectly clear case of threatened irreparable injury, and, second, upon the provisions of the Sherman Anti-Trust Law of 1890. While not abandoning this second ground of jurisdiction, I made no argument about it and left the brief and the oral discussion of that part of the case to my assistant, Mr. Whitney. I argued the case solely upon the first point — telling the Court at the outset that I desired the case decided, if possible, with reference to it and not by reason of an experimental piece of legislation like the Act of 1890.[1] As is shown by the report of the case, the Court took my view, eliminating the Act of 1890 from consideration, and, what seldom happens when a new and grave constitutional question arises, unanimously deciding for the Government on the grounds stated by Mr. Justice Brewer in delivering the opinion. The case for Debs was ably and passionately presented by Judge [Lyman] Trumbull and Messrs. [S. S.] Gregory and [Clarence S.] Darrow, of the Chicago Bar. Their efforts surprised me, however, and I think the Court also, by their rather obvious avoidance of the crucial legal problem involved and their resort to heated declamations about individual liberty, the right to trial by jury, etc., etc. It was not possible, however, to doubt the sincerity of at least two of Debs's counsel. Judge Trumbull, an Illinois United States Senator during the Civil War, for many years an eminent Republican leader and statesman and the author [?] of "The Fourteenth Amendment to

[1] The court below had "decided rightly enough, but on the wrong ground — namely, the Sherman Anti-Trust Act." (Olney to Cleveland, January 14, 1902. Olney Coll.)

the United States Constitution," was in the eighties in 1895, and while he spoke with great feeling, argued from sentimental rather than legal premises. His colleague, Mr. Darrow, did the same, although a young man, somewhere between thirty and forty, who had been counsel for one of the leading railroads centering in Chicago — I think the Illinois Central — and who had thrown up his job because of his interest in the wage-earner and his desire to side with him rather than with the capitalist on the various issues arising between them and daily becoming graver and more difficult of settlement. From a strictly legal point of view the best argument was made by Mr. [S. S.] Gregory, who had been city solicitor of Chicago, and who, as I understood, unlike his associates, who acted gratuitously and from sympathy, was professionally retained and paid.

The evening of the day when the cases were argued, I gave a large dinner to which I invited the Debs counsel, Mrs. Trumbull, and any other ladies who had come with them to Washington. They accepted and were quite surprised as well as pleased at the attention, as they had apparently got the notion that, as the representatives of Debs, they would not be considered within the pale of respectable Washington society.

Olney added: "My part in the proceedings which put down the Debs conspiracy made me the recipient of numerous threatening letters from anonymous writers, some of which I preserved as curiosities, but most of which were destroyed as soon as received. Threatened men proverbially live long, and I doubt if I ever wasted a moment's anxiety on them." He also preserved in his files two letters which — for healing contrast with the violences which have been chronicled — may be used to close this chapter.

From Eugene V. Debs (May 16, 1895)

HON. RICHARD OLNEY
    Attorney-General of the United States
        Washington, D.C.
DEAR SIR:
    I am desirous of procuring a copy of your brief and that
of your assistant, Mr. Whitney, before the Supreme Court
in our case with your autographs attached, for binding in a
souvenir volume, and if you will be kind enough to forward
the same to my address I shall be greatly obliged to you.
    I will also thank you to send me a copy of your last
Annual Report for the year ending December 1st, 1894.
Thanking you in advance, I am
                    Very truly yours
                    (Signed)   EUGENE V. DEBS

P. S. While in Judge Trumbull's office at Chicago a few
days ago he showed me a copy of your oral argument
which I would also like to have for the purpose indicated.
The case is that of our petition for writ of *habeas corpus*,
etc.

From the Secretary of the Interstate Commerce Commission
                (January 30, 1908)
    ... By the way, Mr. Olney, Eugene Debs was in the
office a few days ago, and has repeated what he said before.
"He esteemed you as an absolutely honest man, and in
sending him to prison you only did your duty as the laws
existed." He said you did him the courtesy of sending him
your brief with an autographed presentation which he
cherishes most highly.
                With great regard and respect
                    (Signed)   EDW. A. MOSELEY

VI
OPPOSING DISCRIMINATION AGAINST
UNION LABOR

OLNEY was often described as a "railroad lawyer" by his political opponents. When he was appointed, they predicted that he would be biased in favor of capital and would play into the hands of the railroads. The circumstance that his principal clients at the Bar had been railroads was evidence enough to lead the New York "World," for instance, to complain of him on this score before he could have had time to acquaint himself with the docket of his Department. After the Chicago strike it was to be expected that people who were displeased should call him a "tool of the railroad interests"; and so they did —loudly. Some members of Congress rose to the rhetorical superlative which is irresistible for an angry Congressman, and talked about impeaching him. Olney paid no attention at the time, and it is unnecessary to discuss loose accusations and epithets now. He was never, either in or out of his profession, one of those men who deserve to be called courtiers in the opprobrious sense of the word because they play the part of intellectual lackey to their clients and friends. On the contrary, his defects were of an opposite order, and cast him for a rôle of almost quarrelsome independence in every relationship of life. The epithet "tool" fitted him as little as it fitted Grover Cleveland. Yet it is history that these things were said about him constantly, and mention of them serves to heighten the interest of two incidents which it is now time to touch upon.

Both these incidents were sequels of the Chicago strike. One was a labor dispute which arose in the Pennsylvania courts and in which Olney intervened. The other concerned an attempt to enact an industrial arbitration law. With both, that broad-minded and far-seeing public servant, Edward A. Moseley, who then held the position of Secretary of the Interstate Commerce Commission, had much to do.

Confessedly, Olney's injunction had in no wise touched the merits of the dispute at Pullman out of which the Chicago strike had sprung. Yet the railroads had lost, directly, more than five million dollars. One hundred and some odd thousand employees had lost nearly a million and three quarters in wages. The indirect losses inflicted on railroads, employees, and general public had been incalculable.[1] The security and welfare of one of the country's chief centers had been put in jeopardy. — And all to what purpose? It had been shown that the Government could put down violence and might incidentally break a strike; but this was likely to "leave whatever injustice there was in the situation to rankle, uncured and unconsidered." [2]

Even before the strike, Moseley had been concerned to find ways of preventing such crises, and had gone to work with some of the labor leaders to draft an industrial

[1] Sen. Ex. Doc. 7 (53d Cong., 3d Sess.), xviii.
[2] Morgan, *The Life Work of Edward A. Moseley in the Service of Humanity* (Macmillan, 1913), 147.

arbitration bill. Although this bill had been side-tracked in Congress, he had not stopped working. He knew Olney already and trusted him, and now he went about to enlist his interest. He carried a question to him concerning which Olney's Memorandum may be quoted:

The Receivers of the Philadelphia & Reading [Railroad] having notified certain of their employees that they must either resign from a labor union or lose their places on the railroad, they stated their case to Grand Master [S. E.] Wilkinson, who was the head of the Brotherhood of Railroad Trainmen, of which this particular labor union was one of the constituents. Wilkinson stated the employees' case to Moseley, who in turn stated it to me, and asked me what I thought of the legal merits of the situation. It seemed to me that the employees had a case which they could fairly present to the Court — whose officers the receivers were — that, while an ordinary employer was and ought to be entirely free in his choice of his employees, a court of the United States would not allow its officers[1] to discharge a competent and faithful servant for no other reason than that he was a member of a perfectly legal association formed for the protection of the interests of himself and other employees of the same kind. Without taking any responsibility in the matter, therefore, and stating my entire inability to act either as Attorney-General or as private counsel for the employees, I suggested that the proper and expedient course for the latter was to employ counsel and bring the matter to the attention of the Court for its consideration. I suppose Moseley communicated this suggestion to Wilkinson. At all events, it was acted upon, and Messrs. Day and Montague of Washington, and Francis Rawle of Philadelphia, were retained for the employees and

[1] Laymen should perhaps be reminded that the receivers who were operating the road were the Court's officers.

appeared and instituted the proper proceedings in the United States Court before Judge Dallas. Before the hearing in the matter came off, Wilkinson came to Washington and at Moseley's suggestion I had an interview with him. He appeared well, took a reasonable view of the situation, and, whether the proceeding before Judge Dallas eventuated for or against the employees, was satisfied it was the only reasonable and straightforward course to pursue.

Our conversation on that subject was brief — something that he said about the Chicago strike attracted my attention, and to my surprise he had a good deal to say on that subject of which I had had no previous knowledge. According to his statement, the strike was greatly hampered by the action of his own organization which as such declined to join the Debs movement. Wilkinson himself shaved off his whiskers so as not to be recognized and shouldered a musket against the rioters. After the collapse of the strikers, his organization disciplined as many as twenty thousand members — I think he so stated — by suspension or expulsion for having joined in the strike contrary to the decision of the Brotherhood.[1]

Wilkinson's account interested me both during the interview and afterwards and made me keep in mind the case of his employees. The more I thought of it the more ill-advised, if not illegal, the proposed action of the receivers seemed. After reflection it occurred to me that, on public grounds, there would be no impropriety in my filing a brief as *amicus curiæ*, provided that course was first suggested to and approved by Judge Dallas. I accordingly wrote to him

---

[1] Wilkinson has died. I have submitted the foregoing to Mr. W. G. Lee, President of the Brotherhood, who writes me that the statement is "substantially correct," except that Wilkinson did not carry a gun against the strikers, and that the organization lost nine thousand members, and that "it could hardly be correctly stated" that that loss was the result of disciplining. The difference concerns Wilkinson rather than Olney.

upon the subject, and upon his answering in the affirmative filed a brief.

As I expected, my interference was severely criticized by the receivers' attorneys. On the other hand, I was somewhat surprised and disappointed that views which I had convinced myself were sound were not concurred in by the Court, which decided in favor of the receivers, putting the decision, it is true, upon doubts as to certain facts assumed by me to exist, but at the same time disapproving generally the main positions of my brief. The suit and its incidents gained a wide notoriety and resulted in legislation, both in Pennsylvania and by Congress, adverse to the positions taken by the receivers and Judge Dallas.[1]

It is probable that Olney had never given a great deal of thought to industrial questions, or to the ways and means of preventing and settling labor disputes, but his mind was now fully alive to the gravity of such controversies and Moseley brought him excellent material for reflection. "He induced representatives of the working-men to go with him to see the official whom they had come to regard as their able and unrelenting foe . . . and the labor men found him ready to discuss matters in a spirit of fair-

[1] The case before Judge Dallas was Platt *vs.* Philadelphia & Reading Railroad, 65 Fed. 660. It was decided on the ground that the men named as complainants had not shown that they had been injured and were therefore not in a position to call upon the Court for aid. The question to which Olney addressed himself was therefore not reached. The report omits the arguments of counsel, and consequently all reference to the brief, for Judge Dallas ruled that he could take cognizance of it only if it were offered as part of the argument of counsel. A full report of the proceedings can be found in the *Railway World* for November 17, 1894, pp. 915-17. The brief was also printed in the *Philadelphia Press*, November 9, 1894.

The legislation referred to was the Erdman Act (see the following pages of the text), and Pennsylvania Act no. 98 of 1897. (See Pennsylvania Laws of 1897, p. 116.)

ness." [1] When Moseley asked Olney to help with the draft
of a new industrial arbitration act, he readily took the
matter up. Again his Memorandum can be quoted:

Probably I should not have been called upon but for my
action in the Philadelphia & Reading Receivers' case and
but for the impression thereby produced upon the employees that I could see their side of the case as well as the railroad company's side. At all events, Moseley again applied
to me — stating that the employees were before Congress
for an arbitration bill — that one had been drawn which
was not satisfactory — and that I should do them a great
favor if I would put the crude draft of a statute then before
the Committee on Labor into some shape that would make
it acceptable to all parties concerned. I accordingly took
hold of the matter, retaining as much as I could of the existing draft, but amending in various instances by entirely
new sections containing new provisions. While myself in
favor of compulsory arbitration, I did not venture to propose it in terms, being satisfied that then neither the companies nor their employees would agree to it. The general
scheme, therefore, after embodying a preliminary plan for
the settlement of controversies by mediation or conciliation,
provided for voluntary arbitration — each party to select
its arbitrator and labor organizations concerned being expressly recognized as being proper parties. An award resulting from such arbitration was to continue in force for a
definite period before there would be another arbitration
on the same subject and could be enforced by the United
States Courts. While avoiding any express provision for
compulsory arbitration, I endeavored to reach the end in
view by provisions of the act which should bring an indirect
but powerful pressure upon both parties in favor of arbitration. The provisions in question were to the effect that

[1] From *Life of Moseley*, 148.

when a controversy between a railroad company (engaged in interstate or foreign commerce, of course) and its employees was not and apparently could not be settled by either mediation or arbitration, and the antagonism reached such a point that the public interests were threatened through the hindrance or stoppage of traffic and transportation over such railroad, the Attorney-General of the United States might file a bill in equity in a United States Court and thereunder get receivers appointed to run the road until proper relations between its owners and its employees were restored.[1] This section of the bill was novel and was favored by Moseley. On the one hand, however, his immediate clients looked at it askance, as in the contingency contemplated it practically took the strike weapon out of their hands. On the other hand, the railroad companies were also opposed, since in the same contingency it practically took the roads out of their hands. In short, it put both the contesting parties under the strongest bonds to settle their differences either by agreement or by arbitration. It was natural, I suppose, for each of them to shrink from parting with any of its power; at all events each did — and that part of the bill failed while the rest of it was enacted substantially as drawn by me. Its very presence on the statute book has had a salutary effect, though at this writing I do not recall any instance in which its provisions have been actually availed of.

The law whose early history Olney thus outlined was passed later, in 1898, and is commonly called the Erdman

[1] "He also," says Moseley's biographer, "added a proviso that the use of the courts should not be allowed to the private individual in such disputes, but that action should be taken only by the President of the United States. In other words, the Executive could employ the peaceful method of the Court, as he now under similar circumstances uses the military forces of the country." (*Life of Moseley*, 151.)

The clause referred to by Olney was Sect. 10 of H.R. 8556 (53d Cong., 3d Sess.).

Act (30 U.S. Stat., p. 424). Though its provisions were not immediately "availed of," they were frequently called into operation after 1901 — which was the date of Olney's Memorandum. In the year 1910 there were sixteen applications for mediation under the Act. Up to December 31, 1911, a total of forty-eight disputes were brought to the mediators, and of these twelve were sent to boards of arbitration. The decisions of the boards were accepted in every instance. The Erdman Act was a milestone in the history of industrial arbitration. In 1895 Olney had hoped that there would not be enough disputes with the interstate carriers to require the existence of a standing board of mediation or a standing arbitration commission, and had advised against setting up either. But after thirteen years it became clear that a permanent board of mediation and conciliation was needed to relieve the Commissioner of Labor and the Chairman of the Interstate Commerce Commission; also that larger boards of arbitration were needed; also that the board of mediation ought to be given authority to take the initiative and proffer its services. These were just such changes as were to have been expected in course of time. In 1913 the railroad managers and employees united to embody them in the Newlands Law along with many provisions of the Erdman Act.[1]

Clause number 10 of the Erdman Act, which Olney used to speak of as the fruit of the Chicago strike and the Reading decision, and which forbade carriers engaged in

[1] See *Life of Moseley*, 154–57; also Sen. Doc. 493 (64th Cong., 1st Sess., 1916); *Report of U.S. Board of Med. & Concil., etc.*, and *Federal Arbitration Legislation*, by L. E. Hoffman, in 69 *Annals of Am. Acad. of Pol. and Soc. Sci.*, 223, from which I have taken the figures given above.

interstate commerce to discharge employees for belonging to a union, was eliminated from the Erdman Act in 1908, when the Supreme Court held, in the Adair case (Justices McKenna and Holmes dissenting), that it was unconstitutional.

A compulsory receivership such as Olney proposed would have been a mild measure compared to the action which Roosevelt contemplated during the anthracite coal strike. Olney would have given to the courts a power of temporary direction over an industry — the transportation of interstate commerce — over which control is granted to the National Government by the Constitution. Roosevelt looked to a sort of military receivership to be carried on under Executive authority in an industry which is not interstate commerce, although it may be a national necessity.[1] So many and such diverse experiments in State control of basic industries have been set going by the World War that the possibility of such interference with the free play of industrial forces as Olney suggested has become a matter of everyday discussion. But in the nineties it was novel.

His attitude toward organized labor is to be inferred, not from his conduct in the Chicago strike or in the Reading case, or from his draft of the Arbitration Act, but from all three taken together, and is to be appreciated by remembering that the body of conservative opinion which would not recognize the truths he saw was very much more massive in his time than it is to-day. He wrote to

[1] Roosevelt, *An Autobiography* (1920), 496–99. Rhodes, *The McKinley and Roosevelt Administrations*, 242.

Moseley, November 5, 1906, about the attacks upon the tenth clause of the Erdman Act (which ended in the Adair decision):

... human beings are among the instrumentalities of interstate commerce as much as cars, locomotives, automatic brakes, and other inanimate things. The character and qualifications of the persons engaged in such commerce are most important, both as regards its efficient conduct and as regards the safety of travelers. In the non-discriminatory rule under consideration, Congress must be held to have had precisely those considerations in mind. It must be taken to have thought that national carriers could not exclude from employment union laborers without detriment to the service — without barring out a class of employees who might be and probably would be among the best fitted for the work to be done.[1]

And again, in criticizing the Adair decision, he said:

It is archaic — it is a long step back into the past — to conceive of and deal with the relations between the employer in such industries and the employee as if the parties were individuals.[2]

[1] Printed anonymously in *Life of Moseley*, 168.

[2] "Discrimination against Union Labor — Legal?" *American Law Review* (March–April, 1908), 164. See also another paper by Olney, "Labor Unions and Politics," in *The Inter-Nation*, November, 1908.

VII

THE INCOME TAX CASES

BESIDES the Debs case, the Income Tax cases were the only ones which Olney argued before the Supreme Court while he was Attorney-General.

What would now be called a moderate tax of four per cent on incomes exceeding $4000 had been incorporated in the Wilson Tariff Act to compensate for reductions of import duties. The Administration and Congress, and the legal profession generally, had assumed that such a tax was constitutional, whether levied upon the income drawn from real estate or from other investments; for the Federal Government had raised large sums by means of an income tax during the Civil War and up to 1872 — could be said, indeed, to have brought the war to a conclusion by the help of such a tax — and the Supreme Court had then approved the procedure.

But the financial interests affected by this clause of the Wilson Act were so great that eminent counsel were straightway engaged to test the law. The cases which were started took the form of suits between individuals and banks, but, when they came up to the Supreme Court, the Department of Justice intervened. If there was any question at all, it was certainly a most serious matter, for the suits not only threatened havoc to the Administration's fiscal programme, but cast doubts upon the Government's power to raise money by a simple and fruitful method. Obviously such an occasion required the personal appearance of the Attorney-General.

The intricacies of this litigation need not be considered here. Questions of law and procedure, questions about the political economy of taxation, and still others about the meaning commonly attributed to certain words during the eighteenth century were complex and intertwined, and there was much ingenuity of reasoning during a solid week of argument. In the array of counsel who attacked the law were ex-Senator George F. Edmunds, Clarence A. Seward, W. D. Guthrie, Victor Morawetz, and Joseph H. Choate. To Olney and to James C. Carter, who represented interests which supported the Act, it seemed indubitable that the Constitution sanctioned the taxation of incomes by the Federal Government. They held the view that the Court had settled the point in a number of cases, and that the only question open to serious argument was whether the Wilson Law had been framed so as to satisfy the constitutional requirements about "uniformity." Olney's argument at the first hearing was accordingly directed broadly to a defense of the uniformity of the Act.

At this first hearing Justice Jackson did not sit, and the Court therefore consisted of eight judges. When opinions were rendered on April 8th, it appeared that the eight had divided over the question whether the Wilson Law sought to impose a "direct" tax, like a poll tax, such as the Constitution requires to be levied by apportionment among the States in proportion to population. Six of the Court held that a tax upon the income from real estate must be regarded as a "direct" tax, and that the law must be called unconstitutional with respect to rents. All eight who sat at the first hearing agreed in declaring the law invalid with respect to income from State and municipal bonds. But four thought the law was constitutional respecting all other income. This left it in force as to income not derived from real estate or public obligations. Thus the following intolerable situation was created: One part of the law remained in force, because an evenly divided Court does not upset an Act of Congress, although it may shroud it in a fog of constitutional questions; the two judges who thought that a tax on rents must be called a "direct" tax, while a tax on income derived from shares of stock or money at interest must be considered as something else, had not disclosed their reasoning; the grounds on which four of the Court upheld the Act were left in obscurity; it was to be feared that what remained of the law would fall as soon as it could be challenged before a complete Court with the ninth judge sitting; and finally, the question upon which six judges had aligned themselves against the Act had not really been argued either by the Government or by Mr. Carter.

Counsel opposed to the law moved promptly for another hearing on the questions left open by the opinions of the divided eight. But Olney urged that if a rehearing was to be granted it ought to cover all the constitutional questions involved, not merely those upon which the Court had been split evenly. He thus assumed the burden of re-contesting the rent question upon which six of the judges were already against him.

The meaning of this is easy to perceive and shows what

Olney reckoned to be his line of duty. Conceivably he might have succeeded in holding on to his winnings by surrendering the tax on rents without a fight and arguing that income from other sources of investment was really, as four judges seemed to think it was, a quite different sort of income — that is, by separating the question on which six judges already stood against him from the question on which four were already favorable to the Government. That would have been the way to rescue a partial victory for himself in the particular cases at bar, and to save one portion at least of the Wilson Act. But he could not bring himself to see any sound or valuable distinction between rents and other income as subjects of taxation; and, as he saw things, it would be better to thrash out the whole group of issues upon which a clear decision was needed, even if the outcome were to be a judgment condemning all the income tax provisions of the Wilson Act, than to save a few of its clauses by obfuscating the fundamental law. His client was the country; in the long run the country can do without any particular bit of legislation, but a lucid interpretation of the Constitution is a national necessity.

So the cases came on for complete reargument on May 6th. Justice Jackson, bearing the visible marks of a severe and, as it soon proved, fatal illness on his thin countenance, was in his place. He was at one end of the long row of nine judges, but the crowded courtroom felt that where he sat was the center of the stage. Each side was given five hours and was allowed to speak through two counsel. Mr. Guthrie and Joseph Choate spoke for the opponents of the law. On the Government's side James C. Carter did not again address the Court, and the one commanding figure was the Attorney-General's. He entrusted the presentation of briefs and an historical discussion about the meaning that had currently been ascribed to the words "direct taxes" when the Constitution was adopted to Assistant Attorney-General Edward B. Whitney,[1] and, instead of filling the two hours that were open to him, addressed the Court for just forty-eight minutes. Compression, candor, disregard of everything but the point which he thought ought to be recognized as the nub of the case, anxiety to bring out its full significance, marked this argument just as they had marked his arguments at the first hearing and in the Debs case. This was characteristic of the man and his methods at their best, and revealed him in such contrast to his principal opponent that if the hearing had been a scene in a theater and Olney and Choate, as principal actors, had been cast for rôles in which each was to play foil to the other's genius, their opposition could not have been more dramatic. For three hours Choate skirmished over and contended for the whole field. Olney struck one blow with all his might and sat down. Choate was all thrust and agility. He had begun at the first hearing by comparing Carter's argument to the thundering of Jupiter "all around the sky," and by likening himself to Mercury creeping out after the storm, "knowing it was only stage thunder, to reassure gods and men." At the second

---

[1] Later an able judge of the Supreme Court in New York, and now deceased. Whitney was in no way connected with Olney's family. Mr. Brisbane's repeated references to him in the New York *World* as Olney's "son-in-law" appear to have been gratuitous and stupid insinuations of nepotism.

hearing he abounded from beginning to end in felicities, persuasions, and urbane audacities as well as in real eloquence. His pleasantries wreathed the faces of the courtroom with smiles. He was wily — "nine times as deep as any Boston lawyer . . . deeper and more wily than most serpents." He was dextrous: his very manner was engaging. On the other side Olney's figure stood sturdy and almost immobile. His head, set down into his shoulders, and a little forward, could neither bow nor incline. His jaw stuck out pugnaciously. Under his heavy eyebrows his sharp eyes did not change. He was in earnest, portentously concentrated, and a little bitter; for the main issue had perhaps been predetermined against him. Having a definite view of that issue to present, and believing in it sincerely, he spent no time on other people's remarks. He attacked the rent question without skirmishing and, with an agreeable voice and enunciation, carried his reasoning through. He did not speak fast, but his every word mattered, so that he seemed to be driving ahead. There was a touch of fervor about it all. His thought was so knit that it would have been impossible to take any sentence out of its context. He offered his hearers no 'hits' or fine flights with intervals for relaxation between. Such arguments do not lend themselves to quotation. They must be heard or read as a whole.

But the ability of this argument did not save the day. To be sure, Justice Jackson, about whose opinion both sides had been most anxious, decided for the Government; but Justice Shiras, who had been with the Government after the first hearing, changed over; and all of the income tax provisions of the Wilson Act were consequently declared unconstitutional by a Court divided five against four. The result was enough to make the statesmanly spirit of John Marshall groan in heaven. It was a shock to the country, and has been much criticized. The majority's opinions rested largely on historical reasoning. The dissenting minority spoke, notably through the mouth of Justice Harlan, in a tone of moral indignation which was both impressive and unusual. No one could pretend that the majority, which would not have been a majority but for the one judge who changed his position between April and May, had spoken with authority. If the Supreme Court could allow itself to overthrow an Act of Congress concerning which the minds of its members were so evenly balanced that they seemed to oscillate at a breath, then it appeared to be a less trustworthy institution than the country wanted to suppose it. "Politically," as Mr. Rhodes says, "the decision was a gross error." [1]

Olney's belief in both the legality and the political expediency of an income tax never changed.

[1] Rhodes, VIII, 423.

VIII

TRANSFER TO THE STATE DEPARTMENT

ON the 28th of May, 1895, Gresham, the Secretary of State, died. If Cleveland was to fill his place by an appointment from within the Cabinet, it might have been in order for him to transfer Carlisle from the Treasury. But the laws which rank the Secretary of the Treasury after the Secretary of State have little bearing on appointments, and there could be no question of shifting the great responsibilities which Carlisle was carrying through that period of fiscal distress. There was no surprise when Olney was made Secretary of State.

The new Secretary, who took office on June 10th, was very much better qualified to head the Cabinet than he would have been two years before, when he first arrived in Washington. But, being one of the happy mortals whose capacity for development lasts through life, he had grown in two years. His mind had been forced into new channels; his acquaintance with men had been greatly widened. Even what is called "Society" had counted for him. Previously, in his home in Forest Hills or on Commonwealth Avenue or at Falmouth, he had revolved in the smallest of circles, limiting himself out of office hours to his own family and a few neighbors. His busy, concentrated professional days in Court Street had brought him various contacts and associations, some with business men from other parts of the country, to be sure, but all of much the same order. Boston, with due respect, had given him only Boston, after all. But in Washington he had plunged into a highly variegated little world, and had responded to its stimulations. In that little world, much smaller before the Spanish War than now, nearly everybody was concerned with the Government, and each man's affairs somehow touched elbows with every other's. That and the semi-official character of the city's continual dining and receiving had made it the easiest of active social *milieux* for a man of Olney's rather formal manners and great reserve to drop into naturally. He had taken everything seriously and enjoyed it all hugely. He liked giving and accepting dinners and entertaining public men, both American and foreign, in a manner that befitted his official position — it being understood that his wife always took the trouble to make the arrangements. Fortunately, he had a wife who understood very well how to help him 'hold his end up' in these matters and who was blessed with the tact and ready sympathy which was rather wanting in him. Their house became one of the "interesting" houses to go to. Washington was still cleft by the social chasm which had divided Democrats and Republicans since before the Civil War, but the Olneys brought men of both sides together round their table — especially at dinner on Sunday, which was nobody else's 'day' in that city of 'days.' [1] Olney was an interesting host. He liked

[1] "While I was Attorney-General, I each year in December invited the Chief Justice and the Justices of the Supreme Court to meet the President and members of the Cabinet — and I think my successor has done the same. But the function is of course voluntary. It was my custom while Attorney-General to give rather a large dinner at least once a week. I need

RICHARD OLNEY AT HIS DESK IN THE STATE DEPARTMENT

to keep the talk driving along. It was observable that he hated to be bored; that in a mixed company he was more apt to be absorbed in conversation by a clever woman than by a man, and that he preferred a Republican who had something to say for himself to a dull Democrat of no matter what position or political influence. But he was scrupulous about official proprieties. His unconventional common sense was affronted by the way in which any *attaché* of a European legation was likely to be given more consideration than the representatives of the Latin-American States, who were usually the ablest men their countries could send out; and accordingly he was at pains to be particularly courteous to the latter. In many respects he had presented an agreeable contrast to Gresham's saunterings in hotel corridors, shirt-sleeve appearances in the State Department, and generally uncouth personal idiosyncrasies. In short, he had made an excellent impression on Washington as well as on the country, and Washington, in return, had stretched him in a score of little ways.

These things were all of no slight interest and significance, but the great matter was that the Attorney-General had 'arrived' at being much more in the estimation of the public than a Massachusetts lawyer on whose ability and character the President was willing to gamble. During the Chicago episode his energy, decision, and courage had impressed the whole country. He had, in fact, attained

not have done so. But the recent Cabinet has not been particularly strong on the entertaining side and I have felt bound to do what I reasonably could to help out in that direction." (Letter to a correspondent who was considering an invitation to enter McKinley's Cabinet, February 12, 1897.)

such public stature that his transfer to the State Department would help the Administration's prestige. To be sure, he was known to be no politician, but he was regarded as a true member of the Administration's party—which Gresham had never been; and, that point being clear, an air of detachment from party politics would become him in his new post. Besides, the consular and other offices in the gift of the Department had already been subjected to so violent a panning and washing that nothing remained to be done with them. What the country might have been glad to know, and what Cleveland certainly realized, was that Olney had been a close observer of a great deal that went on outside the Department of Justice. His conception of his duty in the Attorney-Generalship was that he must be prepared before all else to assist the President as his legal adviser. He had kept an eye on any major problem with which the Administration was wrestling. Thus he was at work over the Venezuela *dossier* when Gresham died, and he had been drawn into the State Department's field before that.

IX

A GLANCE BACK AT THE HAWAIIAN CASE

AN example of this — undoubtedly the most important one — had been his participation in the Hawaiian affair. That complication had engaged the Administration's anxious attention in 1893, and might have been mentioned earlier in this record in mere deference to chronology; but it seemed better to defer it until this point in the story where other questions of foreign affairs are about to be taken up. Now it may be touched on.

The affair may be considered, for present purposes, as beginning during the last weeks of Harrison's term. Hawaii was then an independent sovereignty to which the United States accredited a Minister. Its Government was an unsatisfactory compromise between modern constitutionalism and the rule of a native dynasty. The Islands had no cable connection with the rest of the world as yet; news from Honolulu reached San Francisco by ship and was thence posted or telegraphed to Washington and other parts of the world. For many years the white population of the Islands, mostly American by origin, had been increasing and prospering, while the natives had been falling off in numbers.[1] The racial balance having become

[1] In the course of the previous sixty years the natives had decreased from about 130,000 to less than 40,000. White settlers had already acquired most of the land. For a brief review of the broad features of the Hawaiian question, see A. C. Coolidge, *The United States as a World Power* (New York, 1908), 319, and chap. xvii, *passim*.

predominantly white, the misrule of the Polynesian Queen, Liliuokalani, had become insupportable. So on the 19th of January, 1893, a self-styled Committee of Safety, composed largely of American settlers, brought about Liliuokalani's abdication, and assumed control. The news of this *coup* or 'revolt' reached San Francisco when a vessel from Honolulu debarked there a deputation of commissioners from the Committee of Safety on the 29th of the month. The deputation hurried on to Washington, was received by John W. Foster, then Secretary of State, and negotiated a treaty of annexation with him in the course of the next eleven days. President Harrison sent it to the Senate on February 15th along with a message in which he urged immediate ratification.

So far as public opinion was informed, the action of the Harrison Administration looked precipitate.[1] Nay, more, as details trickled into the newspapers, there appeared to be ground for suspecting that our Minister in Honolulu, John L. Stevens, of Maine, had bungled into such active coöperation with the Committee of Safety as to implicate the United States in the overthrow of Liliuokalani. Harrison's term was closing and the Senate let the treaty lie over.

Judge Walter Q. Gresham, whom Cleveland invited to take the portfolio of State in his new Cabinet at the very

[1] "Before the people of Oahu had a chance to pronounce upon their desire for the change, before the other Islands could even hear of it, before the new régime could demonstrate its capacity for fulfilling the obligations of the State, before it had gained possession of all the Government buildings and proved its power, its recognition was granted by the United States." (Theodore S. Woolsey in *The Yale Review*, February, 1894, vol. II, 348.)

moment when the papers were full of the news of what had happened in Honolulu,[1] has often been charged with harboring such feelings of personal jealousy and dislike toward his former political rival, Harrison, that he could not review any of Harrison's policies without bias. Be that as it may, he was a lawyer by training, a Middle-Western politician and Federal judge by recent experience, and his natural tendency was to take a legalistic view of the Hawaiian case.

Cleveland estimated his own grasp of foreign affairs very modestly, and was predisposed to espouse the native side in the Hawaiian Islands by both his temperamental generosity toward the under dog and his previous experience in protecting Indian tribes from spoliation. He and Gresham were shocked by the haste with which Harrison's Administration had proceeded. Thus from the beginning each must have found and confirmed in the other an impulse to halt the annexation programme. They discussed the situation at a conference to which the President-elect called Gresham, Lamont, and Carlisle at Lakewood in February (before Olney had been invited to join the Cabinet), and probably decided then on their first official step.[2]

For an incoming Administration to disavow the foreign engagements made by the State Department under a previous Administration was, for obvious reasons, extraordinary, but it was constitutionally possible and not with-

[1] Mrs. Gresham, describing the day when Cleveland's emissary called on her husband, says: "The papers had maps and pictures of tropical life. They told how the queen had been deposed. . . . A woman in trouble! My husband would certainly side with her against the power, greed, and lust of man." (*Life of Gresham*, II, 741.)

[2] *Life of Gresham*, II, 744.

out precedent. One such precedent had been made by Cleveland himself during his first term. Now, three days after his inauguration, he withdrew Foster's Hawaiian treaty from the Senate and dispatched a special agent, Congressman James H. Blount, of Georgia, to Honolulu to make an investigation. As Blount's reports came in during the spring and summer, Cleveland and his Cabinet became convinced that President Harrison had been misinformed when he told the Senate that "the overthrow of the monarchy was not in any way promoted by this Government," [1] and that, really, it had been accomplished with the "active aid of our representative," and "through the intimidation caused by the presence of an armed naval force of the United States which was landed for that purpose at the instance of our Minister." [2] One sentence in the dispatch which Stevens had sent to Washington on the critical day when the marines landed in Honolulu impressed the mind of every reader as soon as it was published and seemed to confirm the Administration's interpretation of what had happened. "The Hawaiian pear is now fully ripe, and this is the golden hour for the United States to pluck it." Gresham accordingly made up his mind that it was the duty of the United States, under the circumstances, to restore Liliuokalani to the throne. He seems to have thought at first that force should be used if necessary to accomplish her reënthronement. [3]

[1] In the message recommending the treaty to the Senate for ratification. (Richardson, IX, 348.)

[2] The words in which Cleveland subsequently stated his conclusions of fact in his annual message of December 4th. (See Richardson, IX, 441.)

[3] It appears to the writer that this is the necessary inference from

The Hawaiian question came before the Cabinet at the beginning of October, and shortly thereafter Olney sent a letter to the Secretary of State in the course of which he said:

In my judgment, the honor of the United States is hardly less concerned in securing justice and fair play for the Stevens Government [that is, the Provisional Government which the United States Minister had helped into the saddle] and its members and adherents, than in the restoring to power of the Queen's constitutional Government. It must ever be remembered that the Stevens Government is our Government; that it was set up by our Minister by the aid of our naval and military forces and was accorded the protection of our flag; and that, whatever be the views of this Administration, its predecessor practically sanctioned everything Minister Stevens took upon himself to do. Under such circumstances, to permit the men who were Stevens' instruments in this setting up and carrying on of the Stevens Government, and who undoubtedly acted in good faith and in the sincere belief that Stevens correctly represented his Government — to permit these men to be hung or banished, or despoiled of their estates, or otherwise punished for their connection with the Stevens Government, or to leave them exposed to the risks of any such consequences, would, it seems to me, be grossly unjust and unfair, and would deservedly bring the Government of the United States into great discredit both at home and abroad.

The practical conclusions I arrive at from the foregoing are these:

(1) All the resources of diplomacy should be exhausted to restore the *status quo* in Hawaii by peaceful methods and without force.

Gresham's report to the President (p. 86, below); Olney's letters to Gresham and Mrs. Minot (Appendix III); and the *Life of Gresham* (pages cited below).

(2) If, as a last resort, force is found to be necessary — by force I mean an act or course of acts amounting to war — the matter must be submitted to Congress for its action.

(3) In addition to providing for the security of the Queen's person, pending efforts to reinstate the Queen's Government and as a condition of making such efforts, the United States should require of the Queen and any other legal representatives of her Government, full power and authority to negotiate and bring about the restoration of her Government on such reasonable terms and conditions as the United States may approve and find to be practicable.

Among such terms and conditions must be, I think, full pardon and amnesty for all connected with the Stevens Government who might otherwise be liable to be visited with the pains and penalties attending the crime of treason.[1]

On the 18th, Gresham made a written report to the President, in which he summarized the history of the episode at length and closed with the following vague proposals:

A careful consideration of the facts will, I think, convince you that the treaty which was withdrawn from the Senate for further consideration should not be resubmitted for its action thereon.

Should not the great wrong done to a feeble but independent state by an abuse of the authority of the United States be undone by restoring the legitimate Government? Anything short of that will not, I respectfully submit, satisfy the demands of justice.

[1] For the whole letter, see Appendix III. "It assumes rather than argues," Olney wrote to his daughter in sending her a copy of it on November 24th, "that the United States put the Queen off the throne by force and fraud and is directed to the practical question what the United States ought to do on that assumption." (See, also, Appendix III.)

Can the United States consistently insist that other nations shall respect the independence of Hawaii while not respecting it themselves? Our Government was the first to recognize the independence of the Islands and it should be the last to acquire sovereignty over them by force or fraud.[1]

The reader will observe that this final and formal recommendation from the Secretary of State to the President was clear on one point, but quite indefinite otherwise. The Harrison annexation treaty was to be discarded; but what did Gresham propose in its place? The "restoration of the legitimate Government." But on what terms and by what means? If nothing "short of that" could "satisfy the demands of justice," then the white planters and settlers who had set up a new Government in Liliuokalani's place must make way for her to return to power. What means of prevailing upon them to make way for her return could the United States employ?

It is easier to see the elements of the case in proportion and perspective to-day than it was to estimate them all in 1893, and Cleveland and his advisers appear to have overlooked what now impress us as the most important aspects of the situation. In a community in which the native element was decreasing absolutely as well as relatively, political power had passed, formally as well as in substance, from its feeble grasp into more competent hands. Beside that fact, the manner of its transfer was a detail, even though an embarrassing detail. If any lesson could be read in the histories of other transfers of power from

[1] For the entire letter see *Life of Gresham*, ii, 746–52.

race to race, it certainly spelled a warning that the well-organized whites would not willingly give back the reins of government to the Polynesians, nor admit for a moment that the United States had any right to order them to give up what they deemed essential to their own protection. A compromise government which had been outgrown had fallen; an opera-bouffe court had ceased to exist. All the king's horses and all the king's men couldn't put Humpty-Dumpty together again. Furthermore, there were naval and commercial reasons, obvious in any sound estimate of our Pacific interests, for bringing the Islands under the flag of the United States. But all these evolutionary and selfish considerations belonged in another category and quite a different realm of thought from the moral and legalistic reasoning to which the Cabinet seems to have confined itself. Gresham, to whom it is probably right to attribute the initiative, approached the matter as if he were a court of appeal charged with the duty of restoring an injured party to her rights. He forgot that the previous Administration was not an inferior tribunal which he was to review, and did not see for himself that the Administration in which he was serving had, in some sense, stepped into its shoes and might not ignore certain obligations that it had incurred toward the Provisional Government. President Cleveland, for his part, distrusted compromises between moral principles and what are, by contrast, called considerations of expediency. In a maze from which no perfect exit offered, it was his generous impulse to lay a straight course by the Eighth Commandment and fight his way through. His indignation over the apparent indiscretions of Stevens might have blinded him to the possibilities of wrong that were involved in Gresham's proposal; but he differed from Gresham in that, when his attention was once called to those possibilities, he appreciated their seriousness immediately.

If he also saw how difficult it would surely be to reconcile the Provisional Government to Liliuokalani's reënthronement under any form of constitution, then his approval of the course which Gresham took should be recognized as a conspicuous illustration of his loyalty to his subordinates and his moral sincerity. It would have been so easy simply to pigeonhole the tainted annexation treaty, to adopt a policy of hands-off in the Islands and wait until a Government should have time to establish itself there as self-sustaining and independent of American intrigue before reopening negotiations for annexation. On the other hand, to try and restore the *status quo ante*, while at the same time resolving not to use any compulsion, was to court failure for conscience' sake. It was to walk into what might prove to be and did turn out to be an *impasse*.

A Cabinet meeting was held on the same day that Gresham sent his recommendation to the President. It was undoubtedly the meeting to which these sentences of Olney's Memorandum refer:

When the matter was mooted in the Cabinet, Mr. Carlisle and myself, perhaps others, took the ground that what had been done had been done at the instigation of the American Minister supported by the naval forces of the United States, that however wrongful their action might have been, they could not be left to the possible vengeance of the Hawaiian Government and Queen, and consequently that, in taking any steps toward reinstating her Government, care must be taken for the rights and interests of American citizens and other residents of the Hawaiian Islands who had joined in the movement against the Queen in reliance upon the United States as apparently represented by its Minister, Mr. Stevens.

After this Cabinet meeting Gresham dashed to the end of his diplomatic tether. He sent a new Minister named Willis to the Islands with a letter of credence addressed to the Provisional Government — also with instructions to seek an interview with Liliuokalani. Willis was to assure her that Cleveland would not send the annexation treaty back to the Senate; was to convey to her the President's "sincere regret" for the "reprehensible conduct" of Minister Stevens which "had obliged her to surrender her sovereignty, for the time being, and rely on the justice of this Government to undo the flagrant wrong"; and, finally, was to inform her that the President expected her to adopt a "magnanimous course." [1] Olney's suggestion had been that diplomacy should begin strongly at the point at which Gresham's instructions 'petered out'; namely, that the United States should require of Liliuokalani "full power and authority to negotiate and bring about the restoration of her Government on such reasonable terms and conditions as the United States may approve and find to be practicable" as a preliminary condition of making

[1] The instructions will be found in *Life of Gresham*, II, 752–55, with an account of the speed with which Gresham composed them. Also in "Affairs in Hawaii," Appendix II, *Foreign Relations of the U.S.*, 1894 (Exec. Doc. 1, Part 1, 53d Cong., 3d Sess.), 1189.

any effort to reinstate her. In other words, as she was known to be an unreasonable and benighted sort of person, she must submit to leading-strings or we would not embroil ourselves for her any further.

Obeying the actual instructions, Willis delivered his letter of credence to the Provisional Government. A letter of credence certainly warrants an assumption that the Government — de facto or de jure — to which it is addressed is recognized as the entity with which the envoy is to deal. But Willis gave the Provisional Government no indication of the policy he had been directed to follow. Instead he procured a private interview with Liliuokalani and conscientiously conveyed to her his President's assurances and regrets. Then, having flattered her pride and puffed up her self-confidence, he asked whether she would grant complete amnesty to all persons connected with the Provisional Government. Liliuokalani hesitated a moment and then slowly and calmly answered:

There are certain laws of my Government by which I shall abide. My decision would be, as the law directs, that such persons should be beheaded and their property confiscated.[1]

Decision appeared to be one royal attribute which the ex-Queen still possessed. Willis reported ruefully:

Views of the first party so extreme as to require further instructions.[2]

Gresham promptly ordered him to explain to the Queen that the President could not use force in her behalf without

[1] "Affairs in Hawaii," etc., Foreign Relations (1894), 1242.
[2] Ibid., 1243.

the consent of Congress, and also to tell the Provisional Government, in case it inquired whether Cleveland would compel the Queen to observe her promises, that, "acting under the dictates of honor and duty as he had done in endeavoring to effect restoration," the President would "do all in his constitutional power to cause the observance of the conditions he had imposed." [1] It was thus soon clear to everybody in Honolulu that the Administration could not enforce the policy which it still avowed and could not compel the Provisional Government to accept its unsolicited and unwelcome mediation. Clearly the Administration could then do no more with the Hawaiian question except 'pass it along.'

After receiving Willis's account of his first interview with Liliuokalani, Cleveland seems to have known that he had come to the end of his resources. The situation gave him "much anxiety," says Olney's Memorandum, and his conclusion was that he would lay the whole matter before Congress for such action as Congress might think advisable under the circumstances. He called on Gresham to draw up a message for him, and then on Olney, and, finally, using much of Olney's draft, [2] he wrote out his special Hawaiian Message of December 18, 1893. The result was a document both eloquent and curious. Its moral appeal was impressive.

---

[1] "Affairs in Hawaii," etc., *Foreign Relations* (1894), 1192.

[2] Mrs. Gresham's assumption that her husband must have written this message is not borne out by the evidence in Olney's papers, which supports the above statement. For instance, Mrs. Gresham (p. 763) quotes the message and remarks that "it was said at the time" that such sentences "were the utterances of a judge" (Gresham having been a judge). A great part of what she quotes is to be found in Olney's draft. (See Olney Coll.)

I suppose [it began in words which were Cleveland's own] that right and justice should determine the path to be followed in treating this subject. If national honesty is to be disregarded and a desire for territorial extension or dissatisfaction with a form of government not our own ought to regulate our conduct, I have entirely misapprehended the mission and character of our Government and the behavior which the conscience of our people demands of their public servants.

It then reviewed evidence that Stevens had helped to upset the old Government in Hawaii, at greater length than was done in Olney's draft, and dismissed Harrison's treaty of annexation as impossible to accept without dishonor: "The control of both sides of a bargain acquired in such a manner is called by a familiar and unpleasant name when found in private transactions." But it offered no alternative and dumped the whole affair upon "the broader authority and discretion of Congress."

Thus Cleveland invited Congress to 'give a lead' to the Executive in its conduct of foreign affairs — an astonishing invitation for a President who was jealous of his prerogatives to extend. In fact, he admitted his bewilderment in a way that would have been impossible to a President of Cleveland's forceful temper who did not at the same time possess Cleveland's sturdy honesty. Congress debated, but of course it was powerless to proceed beyond the point at which the Executive had halted.

In January, 1895, the Senate finally passed a resolution approving the Administration's policy of non-intervention in Hawaii and left the whole matter there. The country had been saved from a treaty which Cleveland considered tainted, but in the process the Administration had "black-guarded" the foreign policy of its predecessor before the world, had allowed things to reach an *impasse*, had finally turned its back and walked away in embarrassment; all this because it had embarked on an ill-considered policy and had pursued it without skill.

The *de facto* Government in the Islands, seeing that annexation was indefinitely postponed and that Hawaii must look after itself, reorganized itself as a republic on a basis which could be permanent, was recognized by the United States while Gresham was still Secretary of State, and conducted its own affairs successfully until the Spanish War brought the propitious moment for its annexation during McKinley's first term.

What Olney would have done had Hawaii been entirely his responsibility it is impossible to say. He was called upon at two stages of the imbroglio; once when the Cabinet considered Gresham's recommendation, later when the President wanted a particular message drafted. Only two things are clear. The first is that he 'went with' the President on the legal-moral issue, not only loyally but willingly. The second is that he helped to persuade the Administration to heed a wider range of facts and equities than were at first considered. The official documents already quoted leave no doubt on this point. They are confirmed by a private letter which Olney wrote to his daughter, Mrs. Minot, at the time, and which will be found in Appendix III, and in the course of which he said: "I wrote that letter to Judge Gresham because I thought that, while wholly right as to the wrong done by the

United States in the deposition of the Queen, he did not fully realize the practical difficulties that might attend the attempt to restore her. As I like to get what little consolation I can out of my being in my present office and must get it by realizing that I now and then do a little good, I don't mind saying to you that the letter was timely and I think kept the Administration from making a serious mistake. . . ."

It is also probable that reflections on the unwisdom of a diplomacy which proceeds without thinking out its whole policy at the start were present to his thoughts when he took up the Venezuelan case. To that it is now time to turn.

X

VENEZUELA — THE DISPATCHES AND THE PRESIDENT'S MESSAGE

THE details of what had happened in the Venezuelan case during upwards of half a century preceding 1895 are voluminous and involved and need not detain any one to-day. The essential features of the story as it concerned the United States are simple.

Doubt or dispute had existed over the boundary line between the territories which have come to be known as Venezuela and British Guiana ever since 1814. The ancient Spanish and Dutch records, to which both sides might appeal, were indefinite and confusing. Most of the disputed territory lay in the unreclaimed and little known tropical hinterland two to four hundred miles in from Demerara. Venezuela on her side had been guilty of the folly of laying claim to two thirds of what is now British Guiana, but she had shown a disposition, as time went on, to reduce her extravagant demands and to seek an arbitration of everything in controversy. On the other side, Great Britain had stated more moderate geographical pretensions, but had been more arbitrary in insisting on them, and appeared, as time went on, to be inclined to enlarge them.

In 1840 England took a step which must be mentioned in the briefest summary of the case. She sent an engineer named Schomburgk to run a tentative line, and his orders and his skill were such that the boundary which has finally

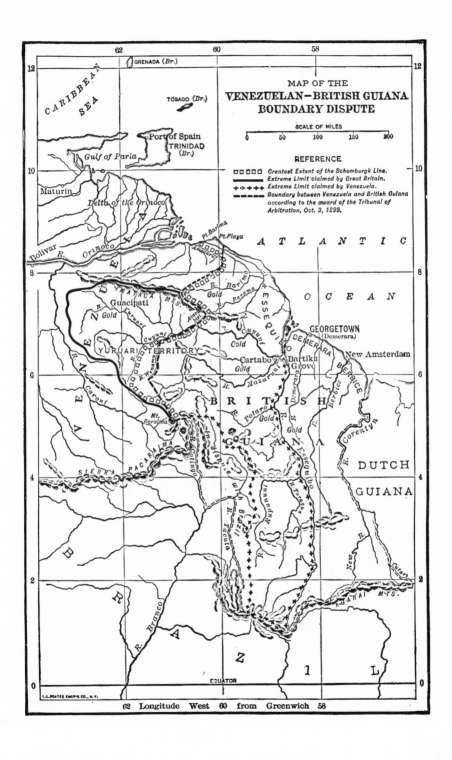

MAP OF THE
VENEZUELAN—BRITISH GUIANA
BOUNDARY DISPUTE

SCALE OF MILES

0   50   100   150   200

REFERENCE

□□ □□□   Greatest Extent of the Schomburgk Line.
————   Extreme Limit claimed by Great Britain.
+-+-+-+   Extreme Limit claimed by Venezuela.
- - - -   Boundary between Venezuela and British Guiana
          according to the award of the Tribunal of
          Arbitration, Oct. 3, 1899.

GRENADA (Br.)

TÓBAGO (Br.)

CARIBBEAN
SEA

Port of Spain
TRINIDAD
(Br.)

Gulf of Paria

Maturin

Delta of the Orinoco

A T L A N T I C

O C E A N

Pt.Barima
Pt.Playa

Bolivar

R. Orinoco

Guacipati
Gold

R. Barima
Gold

R. Yuruari

MATACA MTS.

YURUARI TERRITORY

Cuyuni

Cuyuni
Cold

Cartabo
Gold

Bartika
Grove

ESSEQUIBO

DEMERARA

GEORGETOWN
(Demerara)

New Amsterdam

BERBICE

R. Mazurini

R. Potaro
Gold

Mt.
Roraima

B R I T I S H

G U I A N A

Gold

R. Essequibo

R. Corentyn

DUTCH

GUIANA

SIERRA PACARAIMA

R. Caroni

R. Branco

B

R

A

Z

I

L

EQUATOR

R. Takutu

R. Tacuta

R. Rupununi

R. Torassu

ACARAI MTS.

R. New

R. Quari

L.L.POATES ENGR'G CO., N.Y.

62 Longitude West 60 from Greenwich 58

been established by arbitration gives to British Guiana most of what the "Schomburgk line" assigned to her. Venezuela denounced this line immediately, and Lord Aberdeen replied that Schomburgk's survey was only a preliminary measure intended to assist his Government in preparing to discuss the boundary question, and that it was not to be regarded as an indication "of domination and empire on the part of Great Britain." On the Venezuelan side, there developed subsequently a not unnatural disposition to argue that the Schomburgk line had established the maximum extent of England's pretensions in 1840. On the other side, England was careful not to admit that the Schomburgk line cramped her in any way so long as the boundary question remained unsettled. So the Schomburgk line, though tentative, oriented much of the later discussion.

After 1840 Great Britain took no very energetic measures to close the dispute. Time went on. Gold was discovered in the disputed region — not much, to be sure; but a little was enough to give rise to the reflection that more gold might make trouble. The British Foreign Office assumed a stiffer attitude as British settlements spread out, and in January, 1880, Lord Salisbury, then Foreign Secretary, stated a claim to very considerable territory beyond the Schomburgk line.[1] In 1886, Lord Salisbury, being then Prime Minister, the British Government made an an-

[1] *Parl. Papers*, vol. xcvii (1896), Cnd. 7972, page 295, and map opp. page 413. Mentioned in *Presidential Problems*, 197, 198. This seems to have been the extreme British claim shown on the map (page 96). It is fair to add that Salisbury said Great Britain would waive a portion of what she considered to be her "strict rights" if Venezuela would renew negotiations in a similar spirit.

nouncement which was tantamount to a declaration that she would consider nothing on her side of the Schomburgk line as discussable any longer.[1] Venezuela seems to have interpreted this as implicitly sanctioning British settlements up to the Schomburgk line. She accused England of discarding an agreement by which she had undertaken in 1850 to avoid settling disputed territory — an agreement concerning which it is probably fair to say that neither side had respected it to the satisfaction of the other — and discontinued "friendly relations" with Great Britain and withdrew her Minister from London in 1887. This diplomatic rupture continued as long as the dispute remained open; that is, until after 1895.

The British Colonial Office List and the Statesman's Year-Book, which are understood to draw their information from official sources even though they are not "official publications," enlarged their estimates of the area of British Guiana.[2]

The case was also influenced by factors which lay outside the four corners of the British and Venezuelan diplomatic documents. Taking them into account one surmises with confidence that Venezuela was so torn by internal dissensions and revolutions during a large part of the period covered by the controversy that she could not present herself to the vision of British statesmen as having a Government with which it was worth their while to arrange anything. She may have appeared to them as a

---

[1] *Presidential Problems*, 217–18. The proclamation to which Cleveland refers is in *Parl. Papers* (above), at 372; and comp. 354.
[2] See Adee to Bayard, *Foreign Relations* (1895), 562.

neighboring country later appeared to Roosevelt when he said, "You could no more make an agreement with the Colombian rulers than you could nail currant jelly to a wall — and the failure to nail currant jelly to a wall is not due to the nail; it is due to the currant jelly." [1] In the almost unknown hinterland nobody's title was so clear that England need have charged herself with infringing upon her neighbor's territory if she occupied right up to the Schomburgk line; and it was also true that Venezuela's strength was so insignificant that it never seriously jeopardized the security of the few British colonists and prospectors who penetrated the interior. Under such circumstances it was natural for England to let the matter drift and safe for her to assume that time and the pushing British settler, who has often advanced and has seldom receded, would determine the solution. To attribute to her any deep and deliberate design would seem gratuitous. So little was at stake that her public was never concerned to demand a quick adjustment. Venezuela might call for arbitration; but England had too many half-civilized neighbors about the borders of her scattered empire for her Ministers to want to make precedents for the arbitration of territorial claims that were largely unreasonable. Firmness and patience had usually resolved such disputes to her sufficient satisfaction.

Meanwhile Washington had been looking on with feelings which gradually changed from mild and benevolent concern into genuine anxiety.

[1] *Life and Letters of John Hay*, II, 328.

President Cleveland said later, "The appeals of Venezuela for help . . . were incessantly ringing in our ears." [1] In 1884, Secretary Frelinghuysen had instructed the American Minister in London, à propos of a Venezuelan mission to Great Britain, to "take proper occasion to let Lord Granville know that we are not without concern as to whatever may affect the interest of a sister Republic of the American Continent and its position in the family of nations." In 1885, similar instructions had again been sent to London, and in 1887, Secretary Bayard had adopted a more direct tone and had made a formal offer of mediation and arbitration. Lord Salisbury had declined this offer on the ground that the attitude of the Venezuelan President precluded Great Britain's going to arbitration before any third power.[2]

In 1890, Blaine, who had taken the portfolio of State under Harrison, had instructed our Minister in London to use his good offices to bring about a resumption of diplomatic intercourse and to propose to Great Britain an informal conference of representatives of the three powers — the United States participating solely as an impartial friend of both litigants — either in Washington or in London. But again nothing had come of the American suggestions.

[1] *Presidential Problems*, 247.

[2] Phelps to Salisbury, Feb. 8, 1887; Salisbury to Phelps, Feb. 22, 1887; *British Parl. Papers*, vol. xcvii (1896), Cnd. 7926, pages 1, 2. *Presidential Problems*, 236. Reference to Bayard's note to Phelps in 1888 has been omitted from the text, because, though it was quoted by both Olney and Cleveland, it seems that it was never delivered to the Foreign Office and that they were not aware of that circumstance. (See, for a more complete statement, Appendix IV.)

Thus, when Cleveland came into office for the second time he found that the Venezuelan situation was in no wise improved, and that the tenders of good offices which had been made during his first term and by the intervening Republican Administration had been of no avail.

His first Secretary of State, Gresham, sent two more dispatches to London, where Bayard — the same who had been Secretary of State from 1885 to 1889 — was now Ambassador. In these two dispatches he advised Bayard to urge arbitration upon Great Britain, but Bayard delayed about carrying out his instructions until after Cleveland — whether apprised of Bayard's inaction or not it would be interesting to know — had addressed himself to Congress on the subject and until Congress had taken up the suggestion. In his annual message of December 3, 1894, Cleveland said: [1]

The boundary of British Guiana still remains in dispute between Great Britain and Venezuela. Believing that its early settlement on some just basis alike honorable to both parties is in the line of our established policy to remove from this hemisphere all causes of difference with powers beyond the sea, I shall renew the efforts heretofore made to bring about a restoration of diplomatic relations between the disputants and to induce a reference to arbitration — a resort which Great Britain so conspicuously favors in principle and respects in practice, and which is so earnestly sought by her weaker adversary.

And on February 22d, Congress, acting on this hint, passed a joint resolution recommending the President's suggestion of friendly arbitration to both countries.

[1] Richardson, IX, 526.

Bayard thereupon called twice at the Foreign Office. According to the British advices to the British Ambassador in Washington, published at a later date, he said that the United States "would gladly lend their good offices" and "were anxious to do anything in their power to facilitate a settlement of the difficulty by means of arbitration." Lord Kimberley's report of the second interview ends with these words: "I reminded His Excellency that, although Her Majesty's Government were ready to go to arbitration as to a certain portion of the territory which I had pointed out to him, they could not consent to any departure from the Schomburgk line." [1]

Cleveland, looking back nine years later upon the position in which his Administration was thus placed, summed the matter up: [2]

It now became plainly apparent that a new stage had been reached in the progress of our intervention. . . . The more direct tone that had been given to our dispatches concerning the dispute, our more insistent and emphatic suggestion of arbitration, the serious reference to the subject in the President's message, the significant resolutions passed by Congress earnestly recommending arbitration, all portended a growth of conviction on the part of our Government concerning this controversy, which gave birth to pronounced disappointment and anxiety when Great Britain, concurrently with these apprising incidents, repeated in direct and positive terms her refusal to submit to arbitration except on condition that a portion of the disputed territory which Venezuela had always claimed to be hers should at the outset be irrevocably conceded to Eng-

---

[1] *Brit. Parl. Papers*, vol. xcvii (1896), Cnd. 7926, page 5.
[2] *Presidential Problems*, 252, 253, 254.

land. . . . Venezuela was utterly powerless to resist by force England's self-pronounced decree of ownership. If this decree was not justified by the facts, and it should be enforced against the protest and insistence of Venezuela and should result in the possession and colonization of Venezuelan territory by Great Britain, it seemed quite plain that the American doctrine which denies to European powers the colonization of any part of the American continent would be violated.

This was the stage that had been reached when Gresham died and Olney succeeded him at the head of the State Department in early June, 1895. What Gresham's preparations had been and what he had proposed to himself to do may be gathered from Mrs. Gresham:[1]

He said he believed he could make a statement of the facts and the controversy and advance conclusions that the British Government could accept, or come back and say, "You have suggested it — we will arbitrate." . . . He discussed the question not only with President Cleveland, but with members of the Senate and House and with newspaper men. . . . My husband was shaping his note for transmission . . . when . . . death intervened . . . there was to be no ultimatum as my husband had prepared it.

Olney had already, at the President's request, entered upon an examination of the *dossier*. Now he began "with characteristic energy and vigor," as Cleveland said, "to make preparation for the decisive step which it seemed should no longer be delayed."

---

[1] *Life of Gresham*, II, 794, 795. Mrs. Gresham strongly condemns the Venezuelan policy which she says was *not* her husband's. In imputing reasons and motives to Cleveland and Olney she seems to be a prejudiced guesser. But I assume that she gives a fair report of her husband's state of mind.

Perhaps (recalling the Hawaiian affair as he examined Gresham's memoranda) he asked himself whether there were not dangers to be avoided in the Cabinet as well as abroad. Must not the limits to which the Administration would go be ascertained at the outset? Arbitration had been recommended for years. Suppose another mild request to arbitrate were to be addressed to England, what then? If she still continued to put us off, what would be the effect on our case and our position in the world's eyes? What means did we have of compelling England's acquiescence? What hope of forcing the issue with her before the next American elections? What would become of the case if the State Department were to embark upon a lawyer's argument instead of insisting strongly that, apart from the merits of the boundary dispute, America had an interest in the manner and promptness of its settlement? For if the affair dragged on until a collision occurred in South America, the United States might have to choose between abandoning the Monroe Doctrine and leaping into a war.

People are wont to overlook this about diplomacy, that over and beyond mere arguments and arts of persuasion it commands only two real weapons, both of which are essentially hostile action: it may induce concession by making such alliances with third countries as will confront the Government-to-be-compelled with an inimical alignment before which it must seek to retire; or it may invoke, or threaten to invoke, force directly. Furthermore, it is to be borne in mind that the first weapon is generally unavailable to the United States, because it is her well-established

policy to keep out of European politics. In the absence of
international machinery for focussing, informing, and then
making palpable what is called the world's opinion — of
bringing to bear the irresistible pressure of the common
judgment of civilization, this is the state of things. Lacking some such machinery which a nation can set in motion
before it resorts to violence, it is frivolous to expect diplomacy to dispense wholly with the appeal to force. Diplomacy cannot *insist* — cannot insure itself against marking
time — except by invoking force. Therefore, a threatening message is not necessarily "undiplomatic diplomacy."
This is elementary and should be obvious; but it is well
to remind one's self of it in approaching the Venezuelan
episode. Given this fundamental truth about international affairs, given also Cleveland's addiction to bludg-
eoning methods in face of opposition or entanglements,
and given, finally, Olney's passion for disposing of a difficulty promptly, it seems now as if it might have been
foreseen in 1895 that the Administration would resort
to vigorous measures over the long-pending Venezuelan
affair.

Olney remained in Washington, buried in the voluminous record, until July 2d. Then he carried a draft of a
dispatch to Gray Gables. He reckoned that the Monroe
Doctrine, whatsoever might be its standing in the chancelleries of Europe, must have the validity and force of
law for an American Secretary of State. (He spoke of it
as "the accepted public law of this country" and as
"a doctrine of American public law," never as a "rule of
international law.") Although the dispatch which he

drew up was a diplomatic note in outward form, it was a lawyer-like argument in substance and spirit, a typical forensic review of record and authorities which ended in a hardly veiled threat to resort to extreme measures. It fell into two parts, the first of which he summarized in the following phrases:

1. The title to territory of indefinite but confessedly very large extent is in dispute between Great Britain on the one hand and the South American Republic of Venezuela on the other.

2. The disparity in the strength of the claimants is such that Venezuela can hope to establish her claim only through peaceful methods — through an agreement with her adversary either upon the subject itself or upon an arbitration.

3. The controversy, with varying claims on the part of Great Britain, has existed for more than half a century, during which period many earnest and persistent efforts of Venezuela to establish a boundary by agreement have proved unsuccessful.

4. The futility of the endeavor to obtain a conventional line being recognized, Venezuela for a quarter of a century has asked and striven for arbitration.

5. Great Britain, however, has always and continuously refused to arbitrate, except upon the condition of a renunciation of a large part of the Venezuelan claim and of a concession to herself of a large share of the territory in controversy.

6. By the frequent interposition of its good offices at the instance of Venezuela, by constantly urging and promoting the restoration of diplomatic relations between the two countries, by pressing for arbitration of the disputed boundary, by offering to act as arbitrator, by expressing its grave concern whenever new alleged instances of British

Page of the Pencil Draft of Olney's Dispatch
to Bayard of July 20, 1895

"It has been intimated indeed that by virtue of her South American possessions Great Britain is herself an American State like any other, so that a controversy between her & Venezuela is to be settled between themselves just as if it were between Venezuela & Brazil or between Venezuela & Colombia & does not call for or justify U.S. intervention. If this view be tenable at all, the logical sequence is plain. Great Britain as a South American State is to be entirely differentiated from Great Britain generally. If the boundary question for example is to be settled by force, British Guiana with her own independent resources and not those of the British Empire should be left to fight it out with Venezuela — an arrangement"

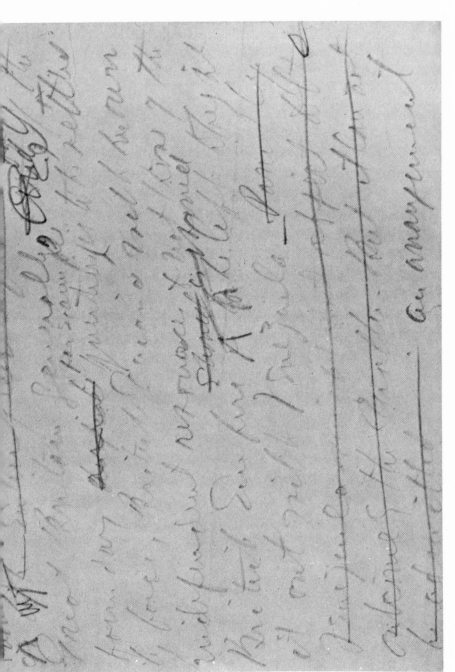

A PAGE OF THE PENCIL DRAFT OF THE VENEZUELA DISPATCH

aggression upon Venezuelan territory have been brought to its notice, the Government of the United States has made it clear to Great Britain and to the world that the controversy is one in which both its honor and its interests are involved and the continuance of which it cannot regard with indifference.

The accuracy of the foregoing analysis of the existing status cannot, it is believed, be challenged. It shows that status to be such that those charged with the interests of the United States are now forced to determine exactly what those interests are and what course of action they require.

Next Olney addressed himself to the law of the case and defined it with the help of precedents.

That America is in no part open to colonization, though the proposition was not universally admitted at the time of its first enunciation, has long been universally conceded. We are now concerned, therefore, only with that other practical application of the Monroe Doctrine the disregard of which by an European power is to be deemed an act of unfriendliness toward the United States. The precise scope and limitations of this rule cannot be too clearly apprehended. It does not establish any general protectorate by the United States over other American states. It does not relieve any American state from its obligations as fixed by international law nor prevent any European power directly interested from enforcing such obligations or from inflicting merited punishment for the breach of them. It does not contemplate any interference in the internal affairs of any American state or in the relations between it and other American states. It does not justify any attempt on our part to change the established form of government of any American state or to prevent the people of such state from altering that form according to their own will and pleasure.[1] The rule in question has but a single purpose and object. It is that no European power or combination of European powers shall forcibly deprive an American state of the right and power of self-government and of shaping for itself its own political fortunes and destinies.

The dispatch then went on to invoke considerations of public policy in support of the Monroe Doctrine. And here Olney said things which would have passed without comment if he had been hammering an opposing litigant in the heat of a trial, but which were startling in such a document. These extreme sentences must be quoted, too, for they account for much of the criticism that was directed against him:

The Monroe Doctrine rests . . . upon facts and principles that are both intelligible and incontrovertible. That distance and three thousand miles of intervening ocean make any permanent political union between an European and an American state unnatural and inexpedient will hardly be denied:

. . . whether moral or material interests be considered, it cannot but be universally conceded that those of Europe are irreconcilably diverse from those of America, and that any European control of the latter is necessarily both incongruous and injurious. . . .

The states of America, South as well as North, by geographical proximity, by natural sympathy, by similarity of governmental constitutions, are friends and allies, commercially and politically, of the United States. . . .

[1] At a time when the Republican Party was justifying its Central American policy by citing precedents from the Cleveland Administration, Olney said, "The truth is, as you must know, that the Monroe Doctrine was never so carefully defined and so narrowly restricted as by the second Cleveland Administration. In my notorious dispatch," etc., quoting the lines above. (Letter to Peter B. Olney, December 27, 1904. Olney Coll.)

To-day the United States is practically sovereign on this continent, and its fiat is law upon the subjects to which it confines its interposition. . . .

. . . with the powers of Europe permanently encamped on American soil, the ideal conditions we have thus far enjoyed cannot be expected to continue.

Olney then took the ground that Great Britain's position "in effect deprives Venezuela of her free agency and puts her under virtual duress . . ." — that it amounted to saying to Venezuela: "You can get none of the debatable land by force, because you are not strong enough; you can get none of it by treaty, because I will not agree; and you can take your chance of getting a portion by arbitration only if you first agree to abandon to me such other portion as I may designate."

He pointed out in conclusion that the United States must be understood as calling "for a definite decision upon the point whether Great Britain will consent or will decline to submit the Venezuelan Boundary Question in its entirety to impartial arbitration." And, finally, the note asked for a reply in time for the President to lay the whole subject before Congress in his next annual message. According to diplomatic usage, Lord Salisbury would, in the light of this last request, have been at liberty to take the note as an ultimatum.

Olney left this draft-dispatch at Gray Gables and went home to his house at Falmouth, near by, in a mood of great anxiety. He saw no hope of bringing the Venezuelan dispute to a prompt conclusion except by 'jolting' Great Britain out of her habit of profitable procrastination. She had paid no heed to repeated representations on the subject by his predecessors; something must be said or done to make her listen. But as jolts are unpleasant and strain good relations, no one could be sure what the consequences would be, although Olney might be confident himself that England would soon accept his contention. Even if Cleveland should agree that we could not expect to impress England with our earnestness except by inviting danger, he might well hesitate to take the extreme step. This was the first important matter upon which he had been called to act as Secretary of State. He was proposing to deal with it in very different spirit from that in which Cleveland's previous Secretaries of State had addressed Great Britain, and in a manner for which Gresham's "discussions" could hardly have prepared the President's mind. He was so firmly persuaded that his policy was the only workable one that he was ready to consider himself unfitted to continue as Secretary of State in case Cleveland should disagree. So, as he was not only proposing a policy, but testing himself and Cleveland by the proposal, he left it at Gray Gables without explanation or comment. The greatest nervous suspense he had ever experienced [1] was relieved by this letter three or four days later:

July 7, 1895

MY DEAR MR. OLNEY:

About five hours ago our family was augmented by the addition of a strong plump loud-voiced little girl. Mother and daughter doing well — also the "old man."

I want to thank you for the rubber gloves which came

[1] Personal statement repeated to the writer by Olney's daughter, Mrs. Minot.

last night. If the bluefish will hang around here a little while longer, I will test their effectiveness.

I read your deliverance on Venezuelan affairs the day you left it with me. It's the best thing of the kind I have ever read and it leads to a conclusion that one cannot escape if he tries — that is, if there is anything of the Monroe Doctrine at all. You show there is a great deal of that and place it, I think, on better and more defensible ground than any of your predecessors — *or mine.*

Of course I have some suggestions to make. I always have. Some of them are not of much account and some of them propose a little more softened verbiage here and there.

What day after Wednesday of this week can you come and spend a few hours with me that we can go over it together? Mrs. Cleveland sends love to Mrs. Olney.

Yours sincerely

GROVER CLEVELAND

The "suggestions" which were discussed at some time between the 10th and 17th were all minor matters or must have been dropped in discussion, for the draft copies among Olney's papers show no important difference from the final dispatch. At the President's suggestion Olney then took the document to Washington and read it to the other members of the Cabinet who were there — Carlisle, Harmon, Herbert, and Lamont. It does not appear that any of Olney's assistants in the State Department saw it. No change of any importance was made,[1] and on July 20th the dispatch was forwarded to Bayard in London.

[1] Authorities: Letter to the writer from Judge Harmon; interview with Mr. Adee at State Department, 1922; examination of drafts of the dispatch among Olney papers. The dispatch will be found in *Foreign Relations* (1895), I, 545.

The reader should remind himself, at this stage, that the position of the United States in the community of nations in 1895 was very different from what it has come to be since then. It was less than three years since Congress had provided the country with diplomatic agents of more than ministerial rank and since the first foreign ambassador had been accredited to the United States. The country's population was about forty millions less than it is to-day. For the United States to take a hand in ordering the affairs of the East or the Tropics, or of Europe itself, was too remote a possibility to have been generally considered. By comparison with England's naval strength that of the United States was almost negligible.[1]

To suppose that Bayard was perturbed by the instructions thus conveyed to him can hardly do him injustice. He was the first diplomatic agent of the United States to hold the rank of Ambassador, and had many reasons for considering himself a more experienced public servant, a more expert diplomatist and a better judge of the niceties of Anglo-American relations than the new Secretary of State who was instructing him. He had been a minority leader in the Senate during the bitter debates that grew out of Reconstruction and had won unfading honors as a champion of tolerance and good-will between North and South during that poisonous time. Then he had presided over the State Department during the four years of Cleve-

[1] In 1895 the United States had "an uncompleted system of coast-defense on the Atlantic, planned by Secretary Endicott's board in 1886, a regular army of little over 25,000, a national guard of varying degrees of unpreparedness, and one modern battleship, the Indiana...." (F. L. Paxson, *Recent History of the United States* [1921], 211.)

land's first term, and, although it had not been given him
to score any signal successes in that office, he had stuck
obstinately to a policy of conciliation in the fisheries dispute with Great Britain and had done something for the
form and tone of our diplomatic relations. His life's
achievements had thus been conciliations, protests against
intolerance and violence, words rather than actions. For
two years now he had cultivated English friendship dili-
gently, especially by going about to banquets in the city
and to other public functions throughout England. Tall,
handsome, portly, very much a gentleman and very fluent
as a speaker in an old-fashioned vein, he had proclaimed
his own and his country's good-will toward Great Britain
with unction and simplicity of heart. Now there came to
him what was practically an ultimatum, written by a man
whom he probably regarded as a sophomore in diplomacy,
and loaded with what Olney himself called "bumptious"
phrases. Into its peremptory spirit he was incapable of
entering. Every fiber of his polite being must have re-
belled at the business of presenting it to Lord Salisbury.

The Salisbury Government to which Bayard delivered
Olney's Venezuela dispatch had just come into office after
a general election. The Prime Minister had taken the
portfolio of the Foreign Office for himself. No Foreign
Secretary of modern times had brought to that office such
personal prestige both at home and abroad as Salisbury
enjoyed at the moment. Since Bismarck's retirement he
had been the recognized veteran of European diplomacy.
He commanded a greater Conservative and Unionist
majority than any majority that had supported a Govern-

ment in the House of Commons since 1833. His very
appearance, his massive old head, his big gray beard, his
ponderous body, seemed to announce the authority and
solidity of position. Salisbury had called Joseph Chamberlain to the Colonial Office, and that ambitious genius had
begun to make the better organization of the Empire an
important part of the Conservative programme. Although
no one had proposed to extend the Empire in South
America, it was predictable that any adjustment touching
a possession or dominion overseas would be approached in
such a spirit of solicitude for colonial susceptibilities
everywhere as had never complicated the movements of
the Foreign Office before.

When Lord Salisbury received Olney's dispatch from
Bayard, he remarked that it raised questions upon which
he must consult the law officers of the Crown before answering, and Bayard "commented upon the importance of
keeping such questions in the atmosphere of serene and
elevated effort." Disregarding the intimation with which
the dispatch closed, Salisbury let the autumn pass without
giving any indication of his answer. In Washington, as
December drew near and Cleveland began to prepare his
annual message, Olney sent word to Bayard to remind the
Foreign Office that a reply was being awaited. Meanwhile rumors had got abroad, much to Cleveland's and
Olney's annoyance, that an unusual exchange of views
with Great Britain was in hand. On December 2d, Cleveland included a paragraph in his annual message in which
he indicated the tenor of the note sent in July, stated that
it had called upon Great Britain for "a definite answer,"

Salisbury

and said that he would "probably" make a further communication to Congress when the answer came.

If, as seems to have been the case, Cleveland was laboring under the impression that England's Venezuelan policy was one of procrastination, this delay must have tended to confirm his peremptory mood.

When Salisbury's reply reached the British Embassy in Washington a few days later, Cleveland was away duck-shooting. He was subsequently accused of having run off at a critical moment, and was, with equal untruth, said to have carried the reply away to think it over in solitude. As a matter of fact he had written to Olney on December 3d:

You cannot receive anything from Bayard or Sir Julian before the early part of next week. Why can you not put the thing in your pocket, so that no one will know you have heard it read or at least that you have it in possession, until I return? In the mean time if its transmission should be accompanied by any particular message you can if you have time be blocking it out.

If I were here I would not be hurried in the matter even if the Congress should begin grinding again the resolution-of-inquiry mill.

On December 6th, Olney asked Sir Julian Pauncefote to bring the reply to him at his house the next morning, instead of to the State Department.

The reply fell into two parts: one dealing with the Monroe Doctrine, the other with the Venezuelan boundary. Salisbury's manner in both was as final as Olney's had been. He agreed that England had acceded in 1823 to President Monroe's contentions that "America was no longer to be looked upon as a field for European colonization," and that Europe must not attempt "to control the political condition of any of the American communities who had recently declared their independence." Although remarking that it was "intelligible that Mr. Olney should invoke, in defense of the views on which he is now insisting, an authority which enjoyed so high a popularity with his own fellow countrymen," he said that these principles of Monroe's afforded no support to Olney's claims, and restated that claim in his own words.

But the claim which he founds upon them is that, if any independent American State advances a demand for territory of which its neighbor claims to be the owner, and that neighbor is the colony of a European State, the United States have a right to insist that the European State shall submit the demand, and its own impugned rights to arbitration.[1]

The British Government could not admit this and there was no sanction for it in international law.

The Government of the United States is not entitled to affirm as a universal proposition, with reference to a number of independent states for whose conduct it assumes no responsibility, that its interests are necessarily concerned in whatever may befall those states simply because they are situated in the Western Hemisphere.

In the second part of the reply Lord Salisbury reviewed the Venezuela dispute in a way to emphasize the consistency of Great Britain's claim to all she was now pretending

[1] See *Foreign Relations of the United States* (1895), 563-76, for the full text of Salisbury's reply.

to. The Schomburgk line had never been regarded nor referred to by Great Britain as the westward boundary of her territory, but only as a possible line of accommodation. The understanding of 1850 had been grossly violated by Venezuela. During the long years while Venezuela's unfortunate internal disorders and the extravagance of her claims had been keeping the dispute open, the country had naturally been developing.

As the progress of settlement by British subjects made a decision of some kind absolutely necessary, and as the Venezuelan Government refused to come to any reasonable arrangement, Her Majesty's Government decided not to repeat the offer of concessions which had not been reciprocated, but to assert their undoubted right to the territory within the Schomburgk line, while still consenting to hold open for further negotiation, and even for arbitration, the unsettled lands between that line and what they considered to be the rightful boundary. . . .

In short, the whole reply said that Great Britain could not recognize the applicability of the Monroe Doctrine; asserted a complete title as far as the Schomburgk line; agreed to arbitrate "large tracts" beyond that line, but declined to admit or arbitrate

claims based on the extravagant pretensions of Spanish officials in the last century, and involving the transfer of large numbers of British subjects, who have for many years enjoyed the settled rule of a British colony, to a nation of different race and language, whose political system is subject to frequent disturbance, and whose institutions as yet too often afford very inadequate protection to life and property.

All this was said in a somewhat didactic tone, which does not seem very remarkable as one reads over the correspondence to-day, but was, in point of fact, resented in the United States. It seemed to Washington as if Lord Salisbury said, "Listen while I explain to you the law and the usages of nations, then you will understand your errors." Andrew D. White called it a "cynical Saturday-Review high Tory" style of communication. So dispassionate a judge as Mr. Rhodes evidently got the same impression.[1] Certainly Cleveland's nerves were rasped.

Lord Salisbury made no proposal, offered no solution, in no wise recognized the interest of the United States, and invited no further discussion. He seemed to intend and expect to close the incident as far as the United States was concerned. This impression was further confirmed by an inquiry which the British Ambassador sent to Olney on the 10th. Her Majesty's Government, he said, wanted to publish the correspondence — would the United States object?[2]

Olney's answer to this inquiry is not known, but its tenor may be inferred from the fact that the British Government did not publish. He had about finished his draft of a message to Congress. Characteristically he sent it to

[1] Rhodes, VIII, 447, where White is quoted. Rhodes also says (p. 449), "That Cleveland deemed England procrastinating and evasive in her negotiations with Venezuela is indubitable and he may further have thought her 'knavish' in that he believed she was encroaching upon and oppressing Venezuela. That idea being in his mind, Salisbury's cool reply was sufficient to produce an explosion."

[2] Pauncefote to Olney, December 10, 1895. (See Appendix IV.) Olney replied that the "contents of your note take me somewhat by surprise," and gave the Ambassador an appointment.

his Boston office, to be typewritten there, without letting any one in the State Department see it; and in Boston Miss Straw, his clerk, copied it off on the 13th. Cleveland got back to the White House Sunday afternoon, the 15th, and that evening Olney and also Lamont, the Secretary of War, spent some time with him.[1] The next morning Olney was again closeted with the President for several hours.

According to an account which Cleveland gave to Mr. Jesse Lynch Williams in a reminiscent conversation a few years later, he sat up into the small hours of Monday morning writing out what he wanted to say to Congress and then sent it to the printer without further consultations. Such was Cleveland's way, and the account is doubtless correct.[2]

The special message of December 17th gave to Congress and so published to the world, the correspondence between Olney and Salisbury. Recognizing the situation in which the British reply left the matter, it said that it now became "incumbent upon the United States" to determine the true boundary line "with sufficient certainty for its justification." So the President asked Congress to provide for the expenses of a commission which he would appoint to investigate and report. And he closed with these words:

[1] *Washington Star* of December 16th. Confirmed by Hon. C. S. Hamlin as to Sunday evening by reference to a private diary.

[2] On Tuesday morning there was a Cabinet meeting. The present writer asked Judge Harmon, who had succeeded Olney in the Attorney-Generalship, for his recollection of it. He replied that this meeting constituted the one exception he could recall to Cleveland's practice of asking the views of the Cabinet on important matters before acting. "On this occasion he simply said, 'I'm about to send this message,' read it and did not ask our views. It may be said, however, that it was hardly necessary to ask our views because he already knew them."

When such report is made and accepted, it will, in my opinion, be the duty of the United States to resist by every means in its power, as a willful aggression upon its rights and interests, the appropriation by Great Britain of any lands or the exercise of governmental jurisdiction over any territory which after investigation we have determined of right belongs to Venezuela.

In making these recommendations I am fully alive to the responsibility incurred and keenly realize all the consequences that may follow.

I am, nevertheless, firm in my conviction that, while it is a grievous thing to contemplate the two great English-speaking peoples of the world as being otherwise than friendly competitors in the onward march of civilization and strenuous and worthy rivals in all the arts of peace, there is no calamity which a great nation can invite which equals that which follows a supine submission to wrong and injustice and the consequent loss of national self-respect and honor, beneath which are shielded and defended a people's safety and greatness.[1]

[1] All sorts of presumptions have been hazarded as to whether these sentences were Cleveland's or Olney's or went entirely beyond Olney's intention. So it may be well to give the concluding sentences of Olney's draft in this place:

"When such report is made and accepted, it will then be the duty of this Government to communicate to Great Britain the boundary line thus ascertained and to give notice that any appropriation of territory or exercise of jurisdiction by Great Britain beyond that line (except with the consent of Venezuela) will be regarded by this Government as a willful aggression upon rights and interests of the United States which this Government cannot suffer to go undefended.

"In making these recommendations, I do not act without a keen sense of responsibility nor without a vivid realization of all possible consequences. It pains me inexpressibly even to imagine that the two great English-speaking peoples of the world can ever be other than friendly competitors in the onward march of a progressive civilization or ever be other than strenuous and worthy rivals in all the arts of peace. I am nevertheless firm in the faith — in which I doubt not to have the hearty concurrence of all the American people — that of all the calamities to which a

This was immediately taken by Congress to mean war in case England did not agree to arbitrate. Mr. Rhodes has described the effect on the country:

The message made a profound sensation. Congress at once gave the President the authority that he asked for. The press and the public mainly supported his positions, although there were some notable exceptions. The message was sent to Congress on Tuesday. On Friday the stock market reached the verge of panic with the result that Wall Street and certain large business interests condemned the message in terms such as had from the first been pronounced by some prominent journals. On Sunday the pulpit thundered against the President, treating his message as a threat of war to England. And the clergymen were right in their construction. No amount of explanation and justification after the event can alter the meaning of Cleveland's uncompromising words. That war was possible, even probable, as a result of the President's ultimatum to England, was the belief of most thoughtful men.

Perhaps the support of "the press and the public mainly" should be emphasized more than it is in Mr. Rhodes's sentences. The excitement which the message

great nation can subject itself none are more to be deprecated or more to be shunned than those which follow from a supine submission to wrong and injustice and the consequent loss of national honor and self-respect. That our request to Great Britain calls upon her for nothing more than justice and equity in her dealings with a weaker state, and that our honor and self-respect as well as our material interests are deeply concerned in her action upon such request, are matters which are fully set forth elsewhere and need not be here again discussed. I therefore invoke the earnest coöperation of Congress in support of the policy initiated by the Executive both through the specific measures already indicated and through such other additional measures as the wisdom and patriotism of Congress may dictate. Nothing will be wanting to the success of that policy, if Congress but rightly leads the way. In behalf of a cause which appeals to their sense of right, no loss and no sacrifice that may be exacted will be denied or begrudged by the American people." (Olney Coll.)

aroused in the United States was fairly to be described as clamorous. Cleveland and Olney had unquestionably reckoned that their policy would enjoy popular support. But they had foreseen nothing like the boisterous acclaim which their critics described as a popular outburst of jingoism. Within three days a bill appropriating one hundred thousand dollars for the expenses of the President's Commission was passed by Congress.[1] In the House not a vote was cast against it. The London Stock Exchange cabled to the New York Exchange (alluding sarcastically to the difficulties that had attended the recent international yacht races), "when our warships enter New York Harbor we hope that your excursion boats will not interfere with them." To which New York replied, "For your sake it is to be hoped that your warships are better than your yachts." The business world was finding fault with the Administration's 'tone,' but it could hardly be said that it set the Administration an example in fine manners.

As a matter of economic history it is now clear that the break in the market which followed this message registered a depression which was due to occur for other reasons and upon any pretext;[2] but it acted, none the less, like a dan-

---

[1] Peck, 425. This *ex-parte* Commission was pronounced by many people in England, and by some critics of the Administration in America, to be an impertinence and to be unrecognizable by Great Britain. Though Her Majesty's Government never directly recognized the Commission, it furnished documents for its use, upon request of the State Department, with amiability. (*Foreign Relations*, 1896, 242–44.) Olney's justification of the Commission is condensed into one sentence of dispatch no. 804: "Being entitled to resent and resist any sequestration of Venezuelan soil by Great Britain, [the United States] is necessarily entitled to know whether such sequestration has occurred or is now going on." (*Foreign Relations*, 1895, I, 560.)

[2] See Noyes, *Forty Years of American Finance*, 250–51.

ger signal to the country, and made the American public consider more soberly the fact that the English Foreign Office and the American Government had each expressed itself in a final manner. What step would be taken next and who could take it without sacrificing dignity?

The English press behaved with exemplary moderation and echoed the views which were expressed by the Parliamentary leaders of both political parties, namely, that a collision between the two countries over such a small matter was unthinkable and would somehow be avoided. Olney seems to have been surprised by the violence òf the explosion of jingo feeling and adopted the sensible course of saying no more until the storm could subside. Fortune favored him. Mr. Rhodes has made vivid what happened.

The interval between December 17, 1895, and January 2, 1896 [he says], was a gloomy period. . . . I remember that on the evening of January 2, I asked General Francis A. Walker what way there was out of the situation when each nation had practically given the other an ultimatum. "One or the other," he said, "must crawl, but the news in to-night's paper shows the resolution of the difficulty." This was the report of Dr. Jameson's raid into the Transvaal.[1]

The German Emperor's astonishing telegram of sympathy to President Kruger, following the Jameson Raid, effectively diverted the attention of the English public to the prospect of a falling-out with Germany.

On the 4th, President Cleveland appointed a commission to investigate the Venezuelan boundary under the law which Congress had passed for him.

[1] Rhodes, *History*, VIII, 450.

XI

VENEZUELA — THE SUCCESSFUL SETTLEMENT

THE first move in the direction of an adjustment was made by England. On the 12th of January, Lord Playfair, a former Liberal Member in the House of Commons who had recently been raised to the peerage in recognition of his many services to public philanthropy and education, a man of seventy-five years who had married an American wife and who was probably regarded as a promising agent because of his considerable personal acquaintance in the States, called at the American Embassy with certain suggestions from Salisbury and Chamberlain. The gist of these was that England found it difficult, first, to acquiesce vaguely in the large claims which had been advanced in the name of the Monroe Doctrine, and, second, to submit subjects who had established *bona fide* settlements to the jeopardies of an arbitration. Would the United States, Lord Playfair inquired, meet these difficulties by agreeing to a European conference on the Monroe Doctrine and to an arbitration of all disputed territory exclusive of "settlements"? A conference, to which the United States should invite all the European Powers who had interests in America, would, he 'urged, benefit the United States, for it would practically write a definition of the Doctrine into the law of nations. On the other hand, the exclusion of "settlements" from arbitration would enable England to stick to a policy which was obviously important to the Empire. Bayard immediately cabled a summary of this interview and expressed a strong personal endorsement of the conference proposal.[1] But Olney cabled back:

Suggestions coming through Lord Playfair highly appreciated, and desire for speedy, as well as rightful, adjustment of Venezuelan boundary controversy fully reciprocated. But the United States is content with existing status of Monroe Doctrine, which, as well as its application to said controversy, it regards as completely and satisfactorily accepted by the people of the Western Continents. It does not favor, therefore, proposed conference of powers.[2]

In this cable he also hinted that arbitration might be arranged on such terms that long-continued occupation of territory should be taken into account by the arbitrators.

Playfair and Bayard continued, however, to discuss the other half of the English suggestion, and on the 20th Bayard cabled that settlements were said not to overlap the Schomburgk line anywhere, and that the British contended, as a point of principle, that settlements ought to be excluded from arbitration. He further reported, or proposed, "Definition of settlements to be arranged." [3]

This narrowed the difference to a point at which Olney was invited to say, "Everything appears to be conceded except settlements; let's proceed to agree about settlements." But the difficulty was that Great Britain seemed to want to define them *out* of the arbitration; that is, to predetermine certain territory as settled and withhold it

[1] Bayard to Olney, Jan. 13, 1896. Appendix IV.
[2] Olney to Bayard, January 14. Appendix IV.
[3] Bayard to Olney, January 20. Appendix IV.

from further consideration, while the United States wished the arbitral tribunal to ascertain the facts as to any alleged occupation. Accordingly Olney replied by cipher cable dated January 22d:

With sincerest purpose to do so, am unable to comprehend the justice or pertinency of the proposition that mere occupation shall be decisive of title. The time, character, and all circumstances attending such occupation must necessarily be considered and must be interpreted and construed according to the principles of private and public law applicable thereto. Nor does the definition of settlements by agreement in advance seem to be feasible. Every one of the numerous elements involved in such definition would be subject of debate and of probable disagreement, while, as Venezuela must be consulted at every step, the inevitable delays would be interminable. As Great Britain desires the controversy should not drift, in which desire the United States heartily concurs, a resort to some form of arbitration which shall cover the real questions involved seems indispensable, since the moment it is agreed upon and the tribunal constituted, the controversy, so far as these two countries is concerned, is at an end.

But, as he did not mean to balk over a mere point of "feasibility," he also inquired how England would define "settlements," and on January 28th he cabled to Bayard again to suggest that a commission might report the facts about occupation under an agreement that the result, if not adopted, should go to arbitration. (See Appendix IV.) Over this question Bayard and Playfair between them were somehow so unfortunate as to let Chamberlain think the United States would assent to the exclusion of "settled districts." When, toward the end of February, the Colonial Secretary became convinced that such was not Olney's intention, he cut Playfair's colloquies short by a letter in which he practically said that he had been misled.[1] Time had thus been lost.

To ask Europe to define what a French writer called "la doctrine du feu Monroe" would have been to accept such European jurisdiction over the Western Hemisphere as it was the essence of Monroe's and Olney's policy to make impossible. One effect of the Playfair episode was that Bayard's ready endorsement of the conference proposal destroyed Olney's confidence in the Ambassador's comprehension of the American policy.

Meanwhile Olney had been trying another approach. When Playfair's first call was reported to him, he saw his 'cue to enter and speak' informally, and went about it to insure the fullest possible discussion. He was never content to rely on an agent whom he trusted less than absolutely, so on January 22d he told the First Secretary of the London Embassy, Mr. J. R. Roosevelt,[2] who was just then sailing for England, to win Mr. Bayard to the idea of transferring negotiations to Washington, and at the same time he took George W. Smalley, then the American correspondent of the London "Times," 'into camp.' Smalley, in turn, advised Mr. Buckle, the editor of the "Times," of the full extent of his relation with the Secretary of State, and straightway began a series of inspired dispatches. Mr. Buckle published many of these, and put himself in direct

[1] Chamberlain to Playfair, February 25, 1896. Appendix IV.
[2] Correspondence in Olney's private files. I am indebted to Mr. Roosevelt who has allowed me to examine papers in his possession. (H. J.)

communication with Lord Salisbury so that his editorial comments and his private cablegrams to Smalley were understood by Olney to reflect the views of the British Premier.

Undoubtedly this exchange, which Olney conducted through the columns of the "Times" while Bayard was discussing with Playfair, owed both its inception and its continuance largely to the satisfaction which Olney found in talking face to face with a man of Smalley's penetration and quickness, a man who also understood both countries and had access to the best sources of information about British opinion. It had the incidental advantage of informing the public on both sides of the Atlantic about the essential contentions of the two Governments, and of immediately linking a semi-official statement of England's concessions with the very friendly but more guarded references to the Venezuelan case which English statesmen — Balfour, Chamberlain, and others — were making in their public speeches.

In the course of the "Times" exchange Olney tried to feel London out on several points. As a result the "Times" made it clear that Great Britain would make two concessions — first, tacit admission of the United States's right to intervene; second, abandonment of the Schomburgk line. But in saying this, and in acquiescing in the idea of final arbitration, she stood firm for "settled districts." Having conceded so much, England said squarely that it was time for the United States to make some public avowal, preferably in the form of an official dispatch.[1] Here was a point of procedure. Salisbury's dispatches had, to be

[1] The *Times* leaders and its columns of American correspondence should

sure, not been answered except indirectly through Cleveland's message to Congress. But they had been so expressed as to close the door to discussion, and the feelings-out of the ground to which Lord Playfair and the "Times" had lent themselves had left one point to be cleared up still: no sufficient definition of settlements, nor formula for defining them, had been offered. It might have been fatal to resume correspondence in a formal way and arrive at a deadlock on this point. Olney accordingly moved to finish what remained to be done by personal conference with Sir Julian Pauncefote. The good pretext was that Venezuela had a representative in Washington, but none in London. Also the "Times" had suggested the transfer publicly. Olney, in a cable dated February 21st, drew these circumstances to the attention of Mr. Bayard whom Mr. Roosevelt had already prepared for the change. Salisbury assented to the transfer on the 27th, and apparently quite cheerfully, for Pauncefote quoted him as saying, "Now that the amateur diplomats have got through, perhaps serious negotiations can be set on foot." [1]

Salisbury's action in empowering Pauncefote to discuss with the Venezuelan representative, "or with the Government of the United States acting as the friend of Venezuela," has been described as conceding the main question at issue because "it tacitly withdrew the prior declaration

be consulted, especially from January 22d to February 21st inclusive. Its columns reflect the public aspects of the whole episode most helpfully, beginning December 10, 1895. The present writer's interpretation of *Times* matter has been corroborated by Smalley's private letters among the Olney papers. (Olney Coll.)

[1] Olney to Cleveland, March 6, 1901. See Appendix IV.

that American interference had no warrant in the law of nations."[1] But this is undiscerning, for Olney was not chiefly concerned to score such a showy but incomplete triumph for American diplomacy as was thus placed within his grasp. England had been willing all along to agree to a limited amount of arbitration, and could not have greatly objected to America's urging her to proceed with it. But she had not yet consented that "arbitration should have unrestricted application" to all the territory in question. Short of that, Olney saw, his contention would not have been clearly established.

To push a thing through from the *almost* stage to the *complete* stage is often the hardest part, and in this affair the "settled districts" proved to be a stubborn obstacle. Olney could discuss face to face with Sir Julian Pauncefote, however, and the two men were fitted to understand each other. Pauncefote had passed through a long and special experience, first as lawyer and judical officer in the Far East, and then as legal adviser in the Colonial and Foreign Offices in London before he came, at about the age of sixty, to his one diplomatic post in Washington. According to John W. Foster "he was methodical and attentive to business, a man of sound judgment, and he impressed every one who came in contact with him with his perfect sincerity and conscientiousness."[2] Furthermore — and this alone was enough to give him a claim on Olney's regard — he neither made public speeches nor gave out interviews to the press. The problem to be solved was a lawyer's prob-

[1] Peck, p. 434.
[2] *Diplomatic Memoirs*, II, 316.

Julian Pauncefote
Washington 1896.

lem. The Secretary of State and the British Ambassador canvassed it in personal conversations of which Olney's record is incomplete. But a cross-section picture of the situation which had been reached in June can be seen in an exchange of letters between Olney and Mr. Henry White, who was then in London unofficially. Before Mr. White went abroad in the spring, Olney had authorized him to explain the American point of view to any officials or influential persons in London and had asked him to send back confidential reports on the state of English sentiment. One of Mr. White's letters, which will be found in Appendix IV below, discloses the impressions he had gained after sounding the minds of Lord Salisbury, Sir William Harcourt, and Mr. Balfour (he also sounded Chamberlain, the Duke of Devonshire, Lord Rothschild and others), and shows with what freedom from personal animosity and with what anxiety to maintain good relations between the two countries the affair was considered by the men who were shaping England's policies. In July, Olney seized upon a statement of Salisbury's, that "the claim of Venezuela impeaches titles which have been unquestioned for many generations," to press again and more precisely the idea which he had broached in his reply to Bayard's first report of Playfair's advances.

. . . will Her Majesty's Government assent to unrestricted arbitration of all the territory in controversy with period for the acquisition of title by prescription fixed by agreement of the parties in advance at sixty years? [1]

This question led shortly to the satisfactory solution.

[1] Olney to Pauncefote, *Foreign Relations*, 1896, 253, 254.

At this point the correspondence went before the public in a British Blue Book, and was also published in the United States. With the help of Mr. Henry White, Olney had the preliminary brief of counsel who was representing Venezuela before the American Commission printed in London at the same moment.[1] It was politically necessary for the Salisbury Government to let public opinion declare itself, but nothing that came from the public after this publishing of correspondence and arguments indicated discontent with the concessions that were contemplated or anything but a general desire to have the matter disposed of amicably and soon. Pauncefote made a trip to London in August, and the report that he had been called to attend a Cabinet meeting was taken in Washington to be a promising sign.

Chamberlain visited the States in September, but did not influence the case. He arranged through his brother-in-law, Mr. William C. Endicott, to call on Olney one day when he was in his office on Court Street in Boston, and explained that he wanted to talk about Venezuela. The Secretary of State, being content to deal with Sir Julian, and having no mind to risk confusing that negotiation, asked right off whether Chamberlain had been empowered by Lord Salisbury to arrange matters. Upon his replying, in effect, that he was not particularly authorized, but that, being a member of the Cabinet, he considered that he was in a position to talk about it, Olney quietly turned the con-

[1] At Olney's suggestion, Venezuela had retained James J. Storrow, Senior, of Boston, as counsel. Storrow visited Venezuela. Olney's letter files show that he and Storrow communicated with each other constantly during the remaining stages of the negotiation.

versation and would not be brought to the crucial point in the case.[1] We have all been told that when an Irresistible Force encounters an Insuperable Resistance, the result is not "a terrible uproar," as a luckless schoolboy once supposed, but just *nothing;* and most of us have felt that the statement is not wholly satisfactory, because "nothing" seems, after all, to ignore too completely that the result is quite what the Resistance wanted. The interview between Chamberlain and Olney must have illustrated deliciously both the soundness and the incompleteness of the physicist's proposition.

On November 9th, Lord Salisbury, speaking at the Guildhall, announced that the two countries had composed their difference and likened the solution to Columbus's trick with the egg.[2] The accord which had thus been reached at last provided that an arbitral tribunal should ascertain all the facts necessary to a decision and should thus also determine the boundary line, no territory whatever being excluded from its consideration. It met the difficulty of the settled districts by agreeing upon three rules to be applied to the facts. The first and most important read:

Adverse holding of prescription during the period of fifty

[1] Statement to the writer by Mr. Endicott.

[2] Speaking at the annual Lord Mayor's Banquet in the Guildhall on November 9th, Salisbury said, "[I believe] that the controversy is at an end. It is always surprising by what very obvious arrangements problems of great difficulty are solved, and in the continent which Columbus discovered the tradition of Columbus's egg must be properly revered. . . . The question has been, not whether there should be arbitration, but whether the arbitration should have unrestricted application. . . . Our difficulty for many months has been to find how to define the settled districts, and a solution has been found." (London *Times*, November 10, 1896.)

years shall make a good title. The arbitrators may deem exclusive political control of a district, as well as actual settlement thereof, sufficient to constitute adverse holding or to make title by prescription.[1]

Although Olney had made the treaty, the parties to it were Great Britain and Venezuela. Cleveland remarked that "this was a fortunate circumstance, inasmuch as the work accomplished was thus saved from the risk of customary disfigurement at the hands of the United States Senate."[2]

The United States being concerned to bring about arbitration, rather than to establish any particular boundary-line, the ultimate decision of the Arbitral Tribunal had no importance for her. But it possessed a certain interest and a glance at the map on page 96 will show that the decision disappointed all Great Britain's claims beyond the Schomburgk line, and gave Venezuela a little of what Great Britain had begun by saying must not be arbitrated. On the other hand, it denied Venezuela's pretensions to a much larger area.

Abroad, the Venezuela messages stirred the Latin-American republics profoundly, and challenged the anxious attention of all the European powers who had territory in the Western Hemisphere or who sustained a creditor relation to the Latin-American states. None of them intervened in the discussion, at any rate so far as we know; but,

---

[1] For the full text see Appendix IV.
[2] *Presidential Problems*, 277. Great Britain and Venezuela signed in Washington on February 2, 1897.

standing by observantly, they saw England abandon an advantageous policy in South America in deference to the claim of the United States. If it was a fact — and nothing has come out that contradicts the appearances — that England did not remind other European powers of their community of interest with her, or invite them to support her against the United States, then her conduct certainly meant something else than that she did not care about the bit of territory in dispute. It meant that she was not averse to the enforcement of a substantial limitation upon European liberty of action in South America; and, also, it signalized her sense of a sort of solidarity between the English-speaking nations. For a difference which one arranges by making concessions and without consulting the neighbors who have something similar at stake is a difference settled in token of friendship. When Salisbury and other leaders of both parties in England said the matter was too small to quarrel over, they were not to be taken literally or to be interpreted as "condescending." What they wanted all the world to understand was that there would be no estrangement and no breach.[1] Their concessions were a portent. That they were so understood at the time may be illustrated by a quotation from the "Nineteenth Century" (London) for December, 1896, where an article summarized the Continental comments and noted in conclusion, "The best informed French and German journal-

[1] As this book goes to press, the *Life of Sir William Harcourt*, by A. G. Gardiner, has appeared. Pages 396–404 of vol. II include a number of Harcourt's letters about the Venezuelan affair and show how energetically he exerted his influence to bring about the adjustment that was accepted, and how genuinely an adjustment was desired by both political parties.

ists, ... though they acknowledge the equity and prudence of the compromise [to arbitrate] which has been reached, think it necessary to point out that it involves possibilities of considerable gravity, not merely to England and the United States, but also to the civilized world in general." The author also cited, as typical, the Cologne "Gazette," which "insists that a precedent has been established by the joint action of the two Anglo-Saxon powers, the effects of which are likely to be felt long after the British Guiana boundary question has been forgotten." [1] When Germany and England went to war in 1914 the American Ambassador in London wrote to Colonel House, "If Germany should win, our Monroe Doctrine would at once be shot in two." [2]

Once an American consul, who had acted vigorously without waiting to receive special instructions that were on their way to him, reported himself as assuming "that they were something pretty perpendicular containing a genuine American ring." Olney's dispatches must be admitted to have been of the 'perpendicular' variety. The arrogance of some of his phrases, which have been quoted already, stirred up an angry clamor in Canada and piqued the national susceptibilities of our Central and South American neighbors. Although Canada soon consented to forget them, the Latin-American peoples showed, as they have on other occasions, that they attend more to words and remember mere expressions longer than do the Anglo-

[1] Passages quoted, with others, in Foster, *A Century of American Diplomacy*, 474.
[2] *Life and Letters of W. H. Page*, I, 334.

PUNCH, OR THE LONDON CHARIVARI.—January 4, 1896.

"JUST OFF!"

Guard. "TICKET, SIR, PLEASE!"   Little New Year. "SEASON!"
Guard. "THANKEE, SIR! (Aside.) HOPE THE LAD WILL GET THAT LUGGAGE SAFELY THROUGH!"

PUNCH, OR THE LONDON CHARIVARI.—February 8, 1896.

"PRETTY DICK!"

"I should look forward with pleasure to the possibility of the Stars and Stripes and the Union Jack floating together in defence of a common cause sanctioned by humanity and by justice." *Mr. Chamberlain at Birmingham, January 25.*   "The time must come, when some one, some statesman of authority more fortunate even than President Monroe, will lay down the doctrine that between English-speaking peoples war is impossible." *Mr. Balfour at Manchester, January 15.*

TWO ENGLISH CARTOONS
Reproduced by special permission of the proprietors of *Punch*

Saxons. But what was done, as distinguished from what had been said during the doing, was the important matter and was something which they welcomed. Their weakness could not but cause them to rejoice when the United States gave proof of her willingness to come to their support — especially as she coupled with her action a disclaimer of any intention to interfere in their internal affairs.

The Venezuelan dispatch and message have been both panegyrized and severely condemned. Mr. A. C. Coolidge has said that the popularity of the Monroe Doctrine is partly due to the color of audacity which it wears. Olney and Cleveland appealed straight to this taste in the American public. The great majority of their countrymen, regardless of party, applauded them to the echo, and the applause still reverberates. It has even been said that they sowed the seeds of the "imperialism" which developed during the next ten years. It is more temperate, and wholly true, to say with Mr. Gaillard Hunt that the Venezuelan Episode had a profound influence upon our acceptance of international responsibility and international duty.

Only three criticisms seem to the present writer to have real force, and if they are stated along with certain other considerations the reader may be allowed to form his own conclusions.

Mr. Rhodes has said that a boundary dispute between two other countries should not have been allowed to involve us in the risk of war. This emphasizes the uncertainties of the Venezuelan boundary rather than the point Olney wished to establish, namely, that a European power must not force an overbearing policy anywhere in America.[1]

The best single statement that can be set off against this criticism is a note which Olney supplied to Mr. R. H. Dana (3rd) for inclusion in his recent edition of the Elder Dana's paper on the Monroe Doctrine.[2] Incidentally this note is interesting as being the nearest thing to an Explanation that Olney appears to have vouchsafed to anybody.

President Cleveland feared [that] if this matter were allowed to run on till open rupture came between England and Venezuela, we should be involved in the war. Diplomatic relations between England and Venezuela had already been broken off, and armed conflicts, followed by threats of war measures, had already occurred in the disputed territory. Should war have begun, in which it must appear that there was good reason to believe England's claim to territory had been increased so that her action would seem to be the forcible extension of territory, the American people would become aroused and force our Government to side with Venezuela. Then, Great Britain could not retreat with honor. Inevitably it would then be too late to get arbitration by mere suggestion of force, while, on the other hand, Cleveland, being a man of peace above all things, foresaw the great advantage of making this suggestion in the diplomatic stages of the controversy.

[1] "The line determined by the arbitral board differed very little from the Schomburgk line, which, at times during the dispute, England was willing to accept as the boundary and which at any time could probably have been secured by sage and fair diplomacy. Reduced to concrete terms, it was not wise to risk a war with England for a difference so small, especially when 'to cavil on the ninth part of a hair' was not for our own but for the behoof of a South American country." (Rhodes, VIII, 453.)

[2] *See Speeches in Stirring Times*, R. H. Dana (Houghton Mifflin Company, 1910), 336-37.

The Jameson Raid illustrated the possibilities referred to.

Another criticism is that of a psychologist. William James, writing privately during the moment of tension (January 1, 1896), and referring especially to the outburst of jingoism and anglophobia which was then at its height, said:

It has been a most instructive thing for the dispassionate student of history to see how near the surface in all of us the old fighting instinct lies, and how slight an appeal will wake it up. Once *really* waked, there is no retreat. So the whole wisdom of governors should be to avoid the direct appeals. This your European governments know; but we in our bottomless innocence and ignorance over here know nothing, and Cleveland in my opinion, by his explicit allusion to war, has committed the biggest political crime I have ever seen here. ... Every one goes about now saying war is not to be. But with these volcanic forces who can tell? ... Remember by what words the country was roused: "Supine submission to wrong and injustice and the consequent loss of national self-respect and honor." If any country's ruler had expressed himself with equal moral ponderosity wouldn't the population have gone twice as fighting-mad as ours? Of course it would.[1]

Clearly, Cleveland and Olney were not imaginative about what the French call "crowd-psychology," nor did they look upon popular emotion as a plastic matrix that no man may stir without thereby shaping prejudices and opinions which harden and endure. But it is fair to reiterate in the same breath that neither foresaw the explosion of jingoism which their action produced.

The third and commonest criticism has dwelt upon the

[1] *Letters of William James*, II, 31, 32.

rough language which Olney and Cleveland employed. On this obvious point Mr. Root remarked to the writer, "What one says in a court is of no consequence except as it impresses the mind of the judge. One need be concerned with no other mind; asides are not heeded; the audience doesn't matter. But a state paper is different; all the world studies it. Its effects on others than the Power to whom it is addressed are difficult to foresee; and often they are not considered." This, it will be noticed, seems to concede that the means used were fittingly chosen with a view to making a particular impression upon the Power to whom the messages were addressed. Olney himself seems to have adverted to the point once. In a letter to Secretary Knox, about an address on the Monroe Doctrine which Knox had just delivered before the New York State Bar Association, he said:

The point particularly interesting and gratifying to me, of course, is your just and comprehending view of the true ground upon which the second Cleveland Administration felt bound to interfere in the boundary dispute between Great Britain and Venezuela. The words you quote from the dispatch to Lord Salisbury have been severely criticized on both sides of the Atlantic. They were undoubtedly of the bumptious order — as are some other parts of the same communication — and were felt to be so at the time. The excuse for them was that in English eyes the United States was then so completely a negligible quantity that it was believed only words the equivalent of blows would be really effective.[1]

The words which Knox had quoted were those of the

[1] Olney to Knox, January 29, 1912. Olney Coll.

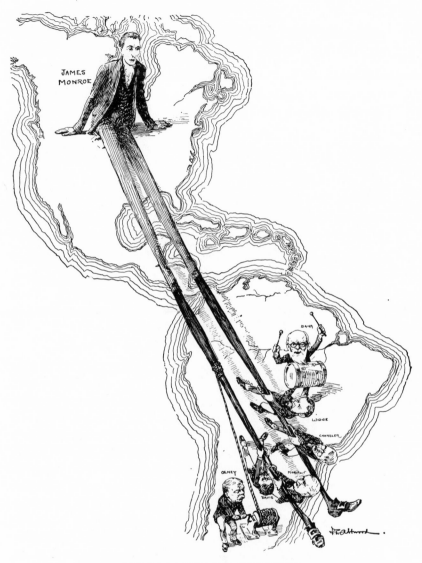

MAKING A LITTLE TOO MUCH OF HIM

"Vex not his ghost . . . He hates him
That would upon the rack of this tough world
Stretch him out longer."

AN ATTWOOD CARTOON DRAWN FOR "LIFE"

famous America's "fiat-is-law" sentence (see page 109 above) and Knox's "comprehending view" was probably that which he enunciated in this sentence:

The spirit behind these words contemplated, I am sure, no arbitrary exercise of sheer power, but a determined zeal in magnanimous consideration for the rights of other American Republics, a sincere sympathy with them in their trials, an insistence upon the right, that good might come to them, and that our own vital interests should not be menaced.[1]

Finally, after these criticisms have all been given full weight, the point to which one comes round is that diplomatic proceedings must be considered in the light of their results rather than by comparison with procedures which critics like to imagine as having been available alternatives. A more gentle diplomacy might have arranged the Guiana boundary in the course of time; but that it could have disposed of the Anglo-Venezuelan dispute about it so promptly, or before serious complications arose, is, after all, supposition. It could hardly have succeeded better in convincing Europe that the United States had a foreign policy which she was willing to insist upon. It could hardly have fixed the Monroe Doctrine so firmly in the consciousness of the American public. But for Olney, John Hay could not have asserted so simply that his foreign policy rested on the Ten Commandments and the Monroe Doctrine. Olney and Cleveland did much more than dispose of a discussion over a bit of tropical wilderness. They gave

[1] *Report of New York State Bar Association* (1912), 307. See also John W. Foster's remarks about criticisms on the language of Olney's dispatch in *A Century of American Diplomacy*, 470.

the United States a new standing in the eyes of other nations. To estimate their achievement by reckoning the value of a bit of territory in South America, or by saying "it was only a boundary dispute between strangers," is to ignore the fundamental purpose of their diplomacy and to miss the fruits of its boldness and tenacity.

XII

THE GENERAL ARBITRATION TREATY

NOTHING has been said about the general arbitration treaty with Great Britain, which was negotiated in 1896 and rejected by the Senate; but it grew out of the Venezuelan negotiation in a certain sense, and went along with that negotiation.

Pacific settlement of international disputes may be effected by negotiation, mediation, or arbitration. The first two are essentially diplomatic methods, while arbitration is genuinely judicial. In 1895 the movement to provide for the use of this method in advance of particular disputes — that is, in favor of "general" arbitration treaties — had reached this stage: Treaty projects had already been endorsed in more or less definite form by several international congresses, notably the Pan-American Congress of 1889–90, and had more recently been recommended to their Governments by the Congress of the United States, the House of Commons, and the French Chamber. Cleveland had spoken of them as desirable in his inaugural address. But except for certain agreements between South American states, no general arbitration treaties had been adopted or even negotiated.

When the Venezuelan affair threatened to halt in the spring of 1896, Lord Salisbury instructed Pauncefote to take up a project for such a treaty with the State Department. Undoubtedly he hoped to find a way of disposing of the Venezuela dispute by sweeping it into a larger scheme. He was also taking advantage of the public sentiment in favor of general arbitration which that dispute had aroused. Olney, speaking for the Cleveland Administration, responded cordially, but insisted that the Venezuela case and the project of a general arbitration treaty must be kept apart.[1]

The two Governments approached general arbitration with a common purpose, but with different views of the expediencies. Lord Salisbury was cautious. "A system of arbitration," said he, "is an entirely novel arrangement, and, therefore, the conditions under which it should be adopted are not likely to be ascertained antecedently . . . it would be wise to commence with a modest beginning, and not to hazard the success of the principle by adventuring it upon doubtful ground." Accordingly he proposed a treaty which was general and obligatory for limited categories of dispute, but which did not contemplate "universal" arbitration between the two countries, and he required that a court of six judges, three named by each country, should come within one of unanimity in order to render a decision on the more serious categories of question. Thus no award could be made against a state without the assent of a majority of its own representatives on the court. (If this limitation had governed the tribunal of six jurists who decided the Alaskan boundary question in 1903, their award would have left that dispute open.)

Olney conceived a different method of approach. To his

[1] See Cleveland's message of December 4, 1893; Richardson, IX, 442; Moore's *International Law Digest*, VII, 70-78; *Foreign Relations* (1896), 222, 224.

mind the main thing to achieve was a presumption in favor of arbitrating everything. So he wanted to make all disputes *prima facie* arbitrable, and whenever an exception was to be made he wished to have it depend wholly upon Congress or Parliament rather than upon the Executive or upon the tribunal's own view of preliminary questions. Accordingly he argued that arbitration should be "obligatory in respect of all questions . . . involving territorial rights, boundaries, sovereignty or jurisdiction, or any pecuniary claim or group of claims aggregating a sum larger than £100,000, and in respect of all controversies not . . . specially described," and offered a proviso that if Congress or Parliament should declare any particular subject likely to involve national honor or integrity, it should be withdrawn from arbitration. Such a scheme, said Olney in urging the merits of his proposal, would "put where they belong the right and power to decide whether an international claim is of such nature and importance as not to be arbitrable, and as to demand assertion, if need be, by force of arms . . ." and "if war and not arbitration is to be evoked [*sic*] in the settlement of an international controversy, the direct representatives of the people, at whose cost and suffering the war must be carried on, should be properly charged with the responsibility of making it." He did not want to leave it wholly to judges nor yet to diplomats to say whether a question should or should not be arbitrated.

Furthermore, the award must, he urged, be final. "There can be no arbitration in the true sense without a final award. . . . It may be better to leave controversies to the usual modes of settlement than to enter upon proceedings which are arbitral only in name and which are likely to have no other result than to excite and exasperate public feeling in both countries." "Precaution becomes excessive when the entire arbitration proceedings are made abortive unless the tribunal of six judges reaches an award by a majority of at least five to one." So Olney proposed that a tribunal of first instance should decide by a bare majority and that its decision should be binding unless one of the disputants protested it. In such event he suggested that a court of review should be convened which should be composed of six judges such as Lord Salisbury's proposal described, and which should also include three "learned and impartial jurists" to be selected in advance by the six judges. He recommended that a majority decision by the six should be final, but that if they divided equally, a binding decision should be entered by a majority of the three jurists.

To this Salisbury addressed a candid answer stating, among other things, why he feared to arbitrate territorial claims. Arbitration had never yet been obligatory, and obligatory arbitration was an untried device in more than one respect. A multiplicity of international litigation might be the result of making it easy and safe to present territorial claims, and might blight the prosperity of the border countries exposed to such claims. Furthermore, nobody had ever had to enforce an arbitral award in respect to territory, and nobody could say what difficulties enforcement would raise.

One reply to these objections was obvious, and was returned immediately; namely, that Lord Salisbury was thinking in terms of the disputes in which the diverse parts of the whole British Empire might be involved, whereas it was really irrelevant to discuss what could hardly be conceived as occurring between England and the United States. So argued Olney.

The final terms of the Arbitration Treaty were settled, as were those of the Venezuelan Treaty, largely in personal conversations between Olney and the British Ambassador. Only the chief points of difference were treated in formal communications, and the communications may be studied best where their full text can be examined. (It is given in Appendix V.) By the treaty which was signed, as a preliminary to ratification on January 11, 1897, the two countries agreed (without going into details) to submit "pecuniary claims ..." and "all other matters in difference, in respect of which either of the high contracting parties shall have rights against the other under the treaty or otherwise" to final arbitration, "provided that such matters in difference do not involve the determination of territorial claims." With respect to territorial claims it allowed for an appeal to a court of six, and an award was not to be binding if more than one member of the court of six dissented. It being thus evident that a territorial claim might not get itself finally arbitrated, the treaty further stipulated that hostile measures should not be resorted to until one or both countries had tried the additional expedient of inviting mediation by a friendly power. Another clause safeguarded national honor and integrity still further by saying that if the tribunal before which a dispute was pending should decide that it involved "the decision of a disputed question of principle of grave general importance" affecting "national rights" as distinguished from the "private rights" whereof a party contesting was "the international representative," such case should thereupon be dealt with like a territorial claim.

Thus Olney succeeded in embodying in the treaty his idea that arbitration must be automatic and must not depend upon a special vote or agreement in each instance; and he had carried as far as he could the principle that arbitration must be final.

Lord Salisbury seems to have realized better than did the Cleveland Administration the extent to which general arbitration bristles with difficulties. The doubts which he expressed indicated that he would not have agreed to such a treaty with any Continental power. His correspondence showed his belief that it would be hard for a country whose foreign affairs were as extensive as Great Britain's to make up a special court of unbiased umpires and judges for each special case as it came along. In view of the well-known tendency of arbitrators to hand down a compromise under the name of an award, he was cautious about binding England to litigate extravagant pretensions. The United States would doubtless be reasonable, but the treaty would make a precedent. It must also be admitted that twenty-five years of further experiment with arbitration proposals have shown that his misgivings corresponded to something skeptical and persistent in the political atmosphere. These facts, if facts they be, are worth appreciating, for they throw into relief the optimism with which Olney pressed his view and the altruism with which Salisbury finally subordinated his own misgivings and assented, as between England and the United States, to a broad presumption in favor of arbitration.

Parliament ratified the Olney-Pauncefote Treaty. President Cleveland sent it to the Senate on the 11th of January, saying, in words which Olney had given him, "It is eminently fitting as well as fortunate that the attempts to accomplish results so beneficent should be [initiated] by kindred peoples speaking the same tongue and joined together by all the ties of common traditions, common institutions, and common aspirations." It lay over until the Republicans came into office. President McKinley then recommended its ratification in his inaugural message, bu ton May 5th the Senate declined to consent to its ratification. So it passed into the limbo of rejected treaties.

Olney took great pride in this convention. He considered it a more important achievement than his Venezuelan victory, and he expressed himself bitterly over its rejection. In a letter to Mr. Henry White, which he expected Mr. White to show to certain public men in England who had supported the plan there, he ascribed its defeat, not to popular opposition to arbitration or popular dislike of England, but rather, first, to the anti-Cleveland animus which pervaded Congress at the time; second, to a Senate group, led by Mr. Lodge, whose policy it then was to harass and coerce England into considering a programme of international bimetallism; and, third and chiefly, to what he believed to be the Senate's definite intention to encroach upon the prerogatives of the Executive.

This resentful view of the Senate's action was natural enough at the time, but to-day it is possible to interpret what happened more charitably. The treaty was a novel departure in international affairs and very broad. It has been well said that our Constitution requires the Executive to lead in such matters and imposes upon the Senate the duty of keeping it from leading too fast for public opinion. Treaties depend more completely than do domestic laws on the sanction and support of the popular will. Public opinion is not clear about arbitration to-day, and it is obvious now that it was very little prepared in 1897. It would have accepted the treaty — of that there was no doubt — but it did not care enough to insist that it must be ratified. Unlike leaders of the Roosevelt and Lloyd George school, who combine diplomacy with direct appeals to popular interest, Olney and Cleveland did almost nothing to enlighten the public mind and to enlist popular backing before committing themselves to a policy. They tried to take a long stride in the first step. Less ambitious attempts that have been made with better success since have shown that it is well to exclude explicitly — for the present, at any rate — all disputes which involve national honor and integrity. These have come to be spoken of, indeed, as the "non-arbitrable" or "non-judiciable" cases. It is true that Olney expected a reasonable construction of the word "rights" — to confine the agreement to legal disputes, and thus to exclude questions of national honor and integrity; and that he also believed no reasonable interpretation of the word "rights" could possibly oblige the United States to submit the Monroe Doctrine to a tribunal; but it was too much to ask the Senate to trust the country's future to mere interpretation. Perhaps it would have been unwise to rely on interpretation in such vital matters anyhow. International conferences usually prove to persons who attend them that men of different nations have dissimilar mental habits and different ways of reasoning, and interpretation depends on reasoning. A more important point was probably the fact that the Olney treaty would have operated to send every dispute about "rights" to arbitration without any further action *ad hoc* by the Senate. In this it differed from the Root treaties of 1908, and from the Knox treaties which were drawn upon Mr. Root's model. Those all contained a provision which made each particular reference to arbitration dependent upon the Senate's advice and consent. The practical importance of the difference is easily seen, for if an arbitration programme is to be applied or ignored at the Senate's pleasure it may well come to very little. Mr. Root's theory was, seemingly, that it would be wise to build up public opinion by establishing a vague presumption in favor of arbitration, and a procedure, at the price of every certainty that it would be resorted to. By this policy he clearly conceded a precedent to the Senate which that body will be slow to relinquish. Olney's more heroic purpose was to carry arbitration across the Senate bar once and for all. Which was the better way, in the long view of things, will always be discussible, and will probably depend for an answer on how each one inclines to resolve the Protean question, whether it is better to sail out of harbor immediately, though in ballast, or to fight wind and tide with a full cargo. Olney never lost faith in the wisdom of his own project, as may be seen in an interesting paper on general arbitration treaties which he contributed to the "American Journal of International Law" for July, 1912.[1]

But what Cleveland and Olney did must be recognized none the less as a valuable diplomatic achievement. To commit Her Majesty's Government and the Executive Department of our Government to so complete a project was to lift arbitration out of the realm of academic discussion and make it a matter of practical politics. This marked a considerable gain. The episode added vigor to the movement for arbitration and nourished discussion. It helped to clarify the difficulties, the dangers, and the possibilities too; and made it easier for others to secure some definite results.

[1] See Appendix V.

XIII
CUBA AND SPAIN

THE Venezuelan affair was a sudden thunderhead in the heavens; but after rumbling out a couple of formidable-sounding mutterings, it passed away and left an atmosphere in which American diplomacy could draw its breath more easily and confidently than ever before. Cuba, by contrast, was a sultry storm-center on the line of the southern horizon, from which a cloud was spreading slowly but steadily and ever more darkly across the sky during the whole of the two years in which Olney was Secretary of State. Poor Cuba — and poor Spain too — was always with him.

When the Island's chronic discontent with Spanish misrule flared out into a new insurrection a few weeks before he became Secretary of State, the revolt was immediately reinforced by an active propaganda in the States, and by the more or less illegal shipment from the States of the wherewithal to carry on the struggle. American sympathy was generally with the rebels and began to assume the form of popular resentment against Spain and popular impatience over her harsh presence in the Antilles. But no cool head yet considered American intervention — and war with Spain as its probable accompaniment — as immediately thinkable. So the Administration's delicate part was to see that American sympathizers with Cuba respected Spain's rights and prerogatives in their actions if not in thought and speech.

In the discharge of this duty, it often seemed as if not only the *insurrectos*, but also the American public and Congress, were intent upon adding to its difficulties as much as they could, and Spain appeared to be less and less able to put an end to the trouble.

With regard to the public's attitude, Rear Admiral Chadwick has painted the picture in a few just strokes:

A great democracy, the education of whose mass usually ends with the public school, and whose library, later, is the newspaper, does not reason with a volume of international law in its hand or trouble itself, if the question takes form in its mind at all, with what seem to it minor distinctions which weigh not at all with its prejudices and sympathies. For a hundred years the American democracy had been in antagonistic contact with Spanish rule in Louisiana, in Florida, in Mexico, and it knew but one mode of settlement of the difficulties which had thus arisen; a mode which had swept Spanish authority from huge empires of territory which constitute to-day more than half the dominion of the Union. At the same time it had seen the same authority driven from the remainder of North America and from the whole of South America. It was to be expected that in such a question as that of Cuba, its base of reasoning would be the inherited views of these many generations, and that its starting-point would be that Spain was in the wrong. When to this was added the destruction of a great commerce, and a daily account, too often in overlurid form, of Cuban happenings, but which frequently in the calmest statement was deeply harrowing, it was impossible that American popular sympathy should not go to a people fighting for relief from a political system which some thoughtful Spaniards themselves believed unbearable.[1]

[1] Chadwick, *The Relations of the United States and Spain — Diplomacy* (Scribners, 1909), 432.

Congress reflected the popular state of mind. Its members moved resolutions and made speeches, not only in the House, but on the floor of the Senate; and considering that our foreign relations are supposed to be dealt with in a responsible way in the latter body, the carelessness and intemperance of some of its members were so extreme as to touch the low mark in the record of the Senate's failures to maintain its dignity and America's reputation for good manners toward other countries. Needless to say such debates exasperated Spain, excited the *insurrectos*, and made it harder than ever for the Executive to perform its duties.

The State Department watched the progress of the revolt in the Island very closely, especially with a view to discerning signs of the existence of an efficient revolutionary government. But even as late as the end of 1896, nothing was discernible which could warrant according a belligerent status to the *insurrectos*, and certainly nothing to justify recognizing the independence of the Island.

From every accessible indication [said Olney in his Report for 1896] it is clear that the present rebellion is on a far more formidable scale as to numbers, intelligence, and representative features than any of the preceding revolts of this century. Yet, so far as our information shows, there is not only no effective local government by the insurgents in the territories they overrun, but there is not even a tangible pretense to established administration anywhere. Their organization, confined to the shifting exigencies of the military operations of the hour, is nomadic, without definite centers, and lacking the most elementary features of municipal government. There nowhere appears the nucleus of statehood. The machinery for exercising the legitimate rights and powers of sovereignty and responding to the obligations which *de facto* sovereignty entails in the face of equal rights of other states is conspicuously lacking. It is not possible to discern a homogeneous political entity, possessing and exercising the functions of administration and capable, if left to itself, of maintaining orderly government in its own territory and sustaining normal relations with the external family of Governments.

Under these circumstances the course of the Executive was determined for it. In the first place, the State Department — with the coöperation of the Department of Justice and the Army and Navy — had to check filibustering and prevent the United States from being used as a military base by her rebellious subjects. The widespread sympathy with Cuba naturally added to the difficulty of detecting and intercepting gun-runners. Spain on her side did little to patrol the Cuban coast, although the physical task of guarding it was slight compared with that of watching the Florida Keys and the very much longer coast-line of the United States. In contending with its difficuties the Administration made a record of law enforcement which was highly creditable. It appears that "of the 71 expeditions of which there is report, but 5 were stopped on the coast of Cuba by the Spanish. The United States authorities stopped 33, the English 2; 4 were prevented by storms; 27 were successful. Nearly all the vessels were but small tugs of less than 100 tons." [1] Had the Spanish patrols exercised anything like the vigilance with

[1] Chadwick, 418.

which the United States watched for filibusterers, practically nothing would have got through.[1]

Then, too, there was all the while pouring into the State Department a stream of protests and complaints about outrages or injuries done in Cuba to the persons and property of *bona fide* American citizens and of other persons whom the Spaniards regarded as Cubans, but who claimed that they had been naturalized in the United States. The insurgents were attempting to paralyze the economic life of the Island and so harass and cripple the Peninsula party, and incidentally they were working on the theory that until their belligerency should be recognized it was to their interest to destroy plantations and other property belonging to foreigners, and let the foreigners hold Spain responsible under international law. The Spanish on their side were unable to police the Island successfully and were cruel and violent in carrying out retaliatory and punitive measures against persons whom they regarded as insurgents, and some of their officials pretended that martial law warranted them in ignoring treaty obligations and disregarding questions of citizenship. The result was a succession of petty emergencies in which the State Department had to intervene through its consular agents or protest to Madrid, and a still larger number of cases in which it had to claim compensation. Any one who had American papers had to be protected against illegal or cruel treatment, without delaying to decide at the moment whether his alleged citizenship was

[1] See quotation in Chadwick, 429, which shows De Olivart's recognition of the perfect correctness with which the United States used its endeavors.

unimpeachable; and in respect of damage to property that might belong to Americans, it was necessary to make a record such that indemnification could be insisted upon. In dealing with these cases the Department sought to keep Spain up to her maximum exertions by pressing it strongly upon her representatives that she would have to pay for injuries inflicted upon Americans by either side, and in doing so it had to avoid the discussions that might have served Spain's dilatory purposes "by judiciously withholding the special ground of liability in each case." It must be borne in mind, therefore, when one reads over the State Department's missives of remonstrance, that they were not "necessarily founded upon any well-formed conclusions as to [Spain's] obligations. They were often more or less *in terrorem* and often," Olney believed, produced the immediate result that was his prime object.[1]

But in addition to holding down filibustering and keeping the record clear, a Secretary of State might also use his diplomacy constructively. This, Olney did attempt to do. In March, 1896, as soon as it was apparent that he had got past the dangerous corner in the Venezuelan controversy, he took up the future of Cuba. He framed an elaborate note and presented it to the Spanish Minister in Washington, Señor Dupuy de Lome, on April 4th. This was kept secret at the time, and was not given to the public until Senator Foraker quoted it in the Senate after President McKinley's inauguration.[2]

[1] Letter regarding the extent to which these protests might be looked upon as legal opinions. (Olney to Geo. H. Olney, Esq., May 23, 1901. Olney Coll.)
[2] The letter will be found in Appendix V, and in *Foreign Relations* (1897),

ENRIQUE DUPUY DE LOME

It might well be deemed a dereliction of duty to the Government of the United States [this note began], as well as a censurable want of candor to that of Spain, if I were longer to defer official expression as well of the anxiety with which the President regards the existing situation in Cuba as of his earnest desire for the prompt and permanent pacification of that island. Any plan giving reasonable assurance of that result and not inconsistent with the just rights and reasonable demands of all concerned would be earnestly promoted by him by all means which the Constitution and laws of this country place at his disposal.

Touching then upon the history of the insurrection, Olney combined a candid admission with a significant assertion:

Whether a condition of things entitling the insurgents to recognition as belligerents has yet been brought about may, for the purposes of the present communication, be regarded as immaterial.

Spain must perceive that the United States was truly concerned in a much more practical question than that of the insurgents' ability to govern an independent Cuba.

That the United States cannot contemplate with complacency another ten years of Cuban insurrection . . . may certainly be taken for granted. The object of the present communication, however, is not to discuss intervention, nor to propose intervention, nor to pave the way for intervention. The purpose is exactly the reverse — to suggest whether a solution of present troubles cannot be found which will prevent all thought of intervention by rendering it unnecessary. . . . Thus far Spain has faced the in-

540–48. It was inadvertently omitted from the volume for 1896, which was prepared for the printer after Olney had retired, and has consequently often been overlooked.

surrection sword in hand, and has made no sign to show that surrender and submission would be followed by anything but a return to the old order of things. Would it not be wise to modify that policy and to accompany the application of military force with an authentic declaration of the organic changes that are meditated in the administration of the island with a view to remove all just grounds of complaint? It is for Spain to consider and determine what those changes would be. But should they be such that the United States could urge their adoption, as substantially removing well-founded grievances, its influence would be exerted for their acceptance, and, it can hardly be doubted, would be most potential for the termination of hostilities and the restoration of peace and order to the island. One result of the course of proceeding outlined, if no other, would be sure to follow, namely, that the rebellion would lose largely, if not altogether, the moral countenance and support it now enjoys from the people of the United States.

And Olney added, "It only remains to suggest that, if anything can be done in the direction indicated, it should be done at once."

No record of the conversations by which the delivery of this note was attended has been available, but later documents help to show in what manner Olney supposed that America's "influence might be exerted" to induce the Cubans to accept reforms from the hand of the Government in Madrid. A great part of the difficulty undoubtedly arose from the firm conviction of the Cuban patriots that Spanish *promises* of concessions in the way of local self-government, at any rate Spanish promises *to them*, were not to be taken seriously. So long as Spain did no more to meet their demands than say "Lay down your arms, and we will then deal with you as if you were good boys" — so long they must continue fighting and might count on sympathy from the States. Spain, on the other hand, knew, or should have seen, that she could not hope to perpetuate even a titular sovereignty over the Antilles unless she could allay American irritation. A proclamation or other act appropriately directed to putting a liberal measure of local self-government into immediate effect as a *fait accompli* might be expected to work a profound change in American sentiment. It would necessarily create an entirely new situation in Cuba. If such a proclamation could be linked with some formal transaction between Spain and the United States, it would take on the character of a reform solemnly inaugurated before an impartial witness whose good opinion both sides desired. It would be something very different and very much more than a mere promise by a capricious and fickle mother to a disillusioned and furiously rebellious child. Olney thought he saw a way of accomplishing something like this by drawing up a new commercial treaty with Spain and incorporating in its preamble a recognition of Cuban autonomy. This would, in effect, if not in form, have offered the Cubans an American guarantee of the new order of things, and it would have gained for the American Government such an international admission that the welfare of the Island was a matter of legitimate concern to it as would have placed it in a strong position *vis-à-vis* both Spain and the Cubans.[1]

[1] The note of April 4th was not made public until 1897, as has been said,

That Olney was not foolishly sanguine in advancing this plan is apparent. He and the Spanish Minister had done much business with each other by this time and understood each other well. They had begun dealings over the famous Mora claim for a million and a half dollars, which Spain had acknowledged to be payable nine years before, which the American Minister in Madrid, Mr. Hannis Taylor, had been pressing with ability and vigor, but for which no Spanish Government had dared to ask the Cortes to supply the necessary money. On August 10, 1895, a few weeks after he became Secretary of State, Olney had met the Spanish Minister in Boston, and at the end of the interview had borne away with him de Lome's signature to an assurance of cash-payment by September 15th. "Olney had a passion for finishing things," [1] and he knew how to make the other man in a negotiation realize

but in the meanwhile a passage in that part of the President's annual message of December 7, 1896, which dealt with Cuba, said: " The objection on behalf of the insurgents that promised reforms cannot be relied upon must of course be considered, though we have no right to assume and no reason for assuming that anything Spain undertakes to do for the relief of Cuba will not be done according to both the spirit and the letter of the undertaking. Nevertheless, realizing that suspicions and precautions on the part of the weaker of two combatants are always natural and not always unjustifiable, being sincerely desirous in the interest of both as well as on its own account that the Cuban problem should be solved with the least possible delay, it was intimated by this Government to the Government of Spain some months ago that if a satisfactory measure of home rule were tendered the Cuban insurgents and would be accepted by them upon a guaranty of its execution, the United States would endeavor to find a way not objectionable to Spain of furnishing such guaranty." (In the vigorous Cuban paragraphs of this message, Cleveland followed the thought and adopted a great part of the phraseology of a draft which was furnished by the Secretary of State. See Olney Coll.)

[1] Remark of Dr. Gaillard Hunt to the writer à propos of this achievement.

that the "zero-hour" had been reached. The encounter must have been a sharp one, and de Lome had so skillfully impressed his Government with the importance of the occasion that it had paid up by the extraordinary procedure of drawing upon the credit of the Ministry of the Colonies, without going first to the Cortes. During the seven or eight months which had passed since the meeting over the Mora claim, the Secretary of State and the Spanish Minister had touched upon every aspect of the Cuban trouble, and had come to regard each other with cordiality as well as respect. The Venezuelan matter had added greatly to the Administration's prestige in the chancelleries of the Continental powers, for it was already clear that the American contentions were going to be accepted by Great Britain. Finally Olney knew de Lome well enough to be sure that he appreciated the gravity of the situation and to feel that he could count on him to advise Madrid accordingly.

Although his dispatch spoke its warning as honestly as a bell-buoy tolling in a fog, its language presents an interesting contrast to that of the Venezuelan note of eight months before. It contains no defiant rhetoric, partly perhaps because this time Olney wished to persuade rather than startle, but perhaps also because he had already acquired enough of the diplomatic manner to address Spain on a matter which touched her Spanish pride and do it without giving her any excuse for taking offense. It has in fact transpired that when de Lome forwarded the dispatch to his Government he said:

When one considers the numerous resolutions of the two

houses of Congress, the popular agitation, the tide of public opinion, superficial but widespread, which has been inspired against Spain by our enemies, the attitude of the press and what it has been asking and is asking even to-day — nay, more, what has been demanded and is demanded even now of the President of the Republic — we can do no less than admire the high qualities of rectitude and honor, the fearlessness and respect toward the legitimate rights of Spain in this note addressed by this Government through me to the Government of His Majesty.[1]

When the Duke of Tetuan, then Minister of Foreign Affairs, received it, he and Campos were in favor of adopting its suggestion. But[2] different views prevailed. High-sounding but vague promises of liberal reforms in Cuba were included in an address from the throne to the Cortes, and the Spanish Foreign Office then sent a dispatch to Washington in which it pointed pompously to the royal pronouncements as if they must be taken to remove all occasion for further discussion. In one sentence it withdrew about everything which it promised in many others: "There is no effectual way to pacify Cuba apart from the actual submission of the armed rebels to the mother country."[3]

The Spanish reply, dated May 22d, was delivered to Olney early in June.

[1] Señor Enrique Dupuy de Lome, to the Spanish Minister of State, April 10, 1896, *Spanish Diplomatic Correspondence and Documents*, 4; quoted by Chadwick, 451.

[2] Statement of the Marquis de Olivart based upon "confidential information," quoted by Chadwick, 467. The Duke and Campos' successor seem to have returned to this view in October. See below, and de Lome to Olney, October 24th., in Appendix VI.

[3] See Appendix VI.

The Secretary of State, whom I have seen to-day [re-ported de Lome], has shown himself very reserved, under-standing that the note contains a courteous refusal to [by] the Government of His Majesty to accept the good offices of the United States, and showing an interest in being in-formed at the proper time of the discussion of matters con-cerning the Island, and the propositions of law which are presented to the Cortes, because he believes that the situa-tion here and in Cuba must be bettered.[1]

...I regarded the Spanish Minister's letter [said] Olney] ... as intended to postpone the matter somewhat indefinitely, but so that the subject could be renewed at any time. That was the purport of various conversations I had with Mr. Dupuy de Lome soon after his letter was re-ceived in June. He went, immediately thereafter, to Lenox for the summer — early in July I went to Falmouth — and the question was not taken up again between us until after my return in October. ... The Spanish Minister either said to me or wrote to me early in October that his Government had come to the conclusion that it would like to act in the line of the suggestions made in mine of the 4th of April. He had previously asked me how the United States was to guaranty the execution of any administrative reforms which the Spanish Government might grant to Cuba. I had told him that I thought it could be done by a new com-mercial treaty between Spain and the United States, the preamble of which should recite the Cuban reforms as part of the inducement to the United States to make the treaty. That mode of working the scheme out seemed to him feas-ible, but at this time — October — he also desired that the treaty should include some provisions respecting natu-ralization — the idea being to put a stop to fraudulent naturalizations of Spanish subjects. My response to that suggestion on his part was that the insertion of any natural-

[1] *Spanish Diplomatic Correspondence* (1896–1900), 13; quoted by Chad-wick, 465.

ization provisions into the treaty would, in my judgment, insure its rejection by the Senate — that while our naturalization laws ought to be amended in the manner suggested it would be no use to make the effort while the present contest in Cuba was going on. My impression is that there were two or three conversations between us on the subject of the treaty and the proposed naturalization clause — the grand result being that nothing was accomplished.[1]

Olney's note, remarks Chadwick, "was, indeed, the turning-point of the affairs of Spain. Its rejection meant, could only mean as a finality, the forcible intervention by the United States, and war." Perhaps it is too dramatic to say, as Chadwick does, that the Spanish answer "sounded the knell of Spanish dominion in Cuba." But Spain's rulers certainly failed to face the meaning of the facts and to seize the moment to forestall disaster. "Canovas, with mind cast in the same mould with that of Philip II, was determined to first assert the authority of Spain over the insurgents, as Philip was determined to assert the authority of a unified religion over all races of the Peninsula, whatever the cost to Spain. Ruin followed the policy of the one as of the other."[2]

> "By sloth and lust and mindlessness and pelf
> Spain sank in sadness and dishonor down."

From this on there were but two alternatives open to diplomacy: (1) some form of interference which would have precipitated war, and (2) the continuance of a patient policy of doing nothing more than should be neces-

[1] Olney to J. Walter Blandford, May 29, 1897. (Olney Coll.)
[2] Chadwick, 465, 466, 467.

sary to suppress filibustering on the one hand and to maintain the rights of American citizens on the other. The Cleveland Administration had been desirous of maintaining peace all along. By July it was placed in a position in which it had no business to embark the country upon a new policy even if it wanted to. In that month, at the Chicago Convention, the Democratic Party repudiated its old leaders so completely that they could regard themselves as nothing but a hopeless minority during the remainder of the Administration's term of office. A vigorous foreign policy was thenceforward impossible. As the months went by, the agony of the unfortunate Island became more acute, and its disorders more desperate. Popular sympathy for Cuba rose higher in the States. Spain realized dimly that its only hope lay in some such adjustment as had been proposed. De Lome seems to have clung to his faith that something might happen, and to have carried his hopes to the State Department with almost innocent optimism. He was right if he believed that Cleveland and Olney would still have welcomed a peaceful solution that Congress could have been expected to accept. But the mood of Congress had been waxing more aggressive every day. Finally de Lome reported to his chief, with evident disappointment: "I should not conceal that I note a certain tendency to inaction on the part of the Secretary of State during the little time that remains to him in the discharge of his office." [1]

The debates about Cuba which occurred in Congress

[1] De Lome to the Spanish Minister of State, February 13, 1897, *Spanish Dip. Cor.*, 24; quoted by Chadwick, 488.

during this time have been alluded to. On the whole they need not be examined here; but one episode which grew out of them produced an instructive collision between Olney and the Senate's Committee on Foreign Relations. In December, 1896, that Committee let it be known that it was proposing to report out the so-called Cameron Resolution, recognizing the independence of the Republic of Cuba. The President was away on a shooting or fishing trip. Olney gave an interview to the Washington "Star" in which he said:

It is, perhaps, my duty to point out that the resolution, if passed by the Senate, can probably be regarded only as an expression of opinion by the eminent gentlemen who voted for it in the Senate, and if passed by the House of Representatives, can only be regarded as another expression of opinion by the eminent gentlemen who vote for it in the House.

The power to recognize the so-called Republic of Cuba as an independent state rests exclusively with the Executive.

A resolution on the subject by the Senate or by the House, by both bodies or by one, whether concurrent or joint, is inoperative as legislation, and is important only as advice of great weight voluntarily tendered to the Executive regarding the manner in which he shall exercise his constitutional functions.

The operation and effect of the proposed resolution, therefore, even if passed by both houses of Congress by a two-thirds vote, are perfectly plain. It may raise expectations in some quarters which can never be realized. It may inflame popular passions, both in this country and elsewhere; may thus put in peril the lives and property of American citizens who are resident and traveling abroad, and will certainly obstruct and perhaps defeat the best efforts of this Government to afford such citizens due protection.

But except in these ways, and unless the advice embodied in the resolution shall lead the Executive to revise conclusions already reached and officially declared, the resolution will be without effect and will leave unaltered the attitude of this Government toward the two contending parties in Cuba.

This appeared on the 19th of December. None the less Senator Cameron's Committee reported his resolution on the 21st. But it had been made obvious that it could serve no good purpose beyond calling attention to sentiment in favor of pacification in Cuba, that it had done that much already and that it would never pass, so it was allowed to sleep on the Senate's calendar as peacefully as a bellicose and inflammatory resolution can be supposed to sleep anywhere. Senator Lodge, who was a member of the Committee which reported it, says, in his history of "The War with Spain," that the stock-market fell when the Cameron Resolution was published, and adds, "the financial interests had their way. Mr. Olney announced in an interview," etc. This not only imputes undue deference to Wall Street to the Secretary of State without any sufficient justification, but also quite ignores an objection to the resolution of which Senator Lodge could hardly have been unaware.

I suppose you see the connection between the two cases, [Venezuela and Cuba—wrote Olney on the 24th]. Once we had recognized Cuba as independent, the Monroe Doctrine iust established by this Administration would require us to at once declare war against Spain — to prevent her acquiring territory on this continent by force. Neither this nor the next Administration could help itself — after the pronounced stand taken in the Venezuela case. It was the conviction that such was the scheme that made me step on it as hard as I knew how, and without waiting to consult or ask anybody to help share the responsibility.[1]

Thus, what was accomplished in respect to Cuba was on the whole a negative result. But it was none the less a real achievement. The Cleveland Administration enforced the laws of neutrality, bequeathed an efficient machinery for carrying on that work to its successor, and kept the country from being drawn into war. It pursued a policy which consulted the dignity and honor of the United States before all else, and, amid many difficulties, pursued it with skill. As time goes on the judgment of history seems to bestow upon it more rather than less praise.

[1] From a letter to Miss A. M. Straw, December 24, 1896.

CLEVELAND AND OLNEY ON THE VERANDA AT FALMOUTH

XIV

ADMINISTRATION OF THE STATE DEPARTMENT

THE Cuban record has brought this narrative to the spring of 1897, when Cleveland's Administration went out of office, and that point of time invites a glance at Olney's management of the State Department in general. He had an excellent chance to devote his time to the foreign business on the Department's docket. The unusual political isolation into which Cleveland and his official family fell during the last part of the term, combined with Olney's own reputation for not letting politicians and reporters "hang around" and with that something which made most people a little afraid of him anyhow, relieved him from a large portion of the distractions and interruptions which ordinarily harass a Cabinet officer. Within the Department the Secretary was a synonym for punctuality and dispatch. He was naturally an orderly and a rapid worker himself, and his habit of deciding things as they came along facilitated and expedited the labors of his assistants (among whom he was lucky enough to have men of such experience and ability as Alvey A. Adee, William W. Rockhill, and E. Uhl). For some minds the questions which come before a Secretary of State are freighted with fascinating provocations to embark upon historical research, philosophical and political reflection, or experiment with the refinements of language. But Olney was interested in nothing except what tended to bring things to a conclusion. He could fill his room with books and papers till they covered all the tables, work over them alone until the case and his own decision on it were clear in his mind, then dictate for an hour and make few revisions in what he had dictated. It seems that his lack of technical experience did not abash him, for he felt himself competent to make the essential decisions. When he had got into the draft of a dispatch the substance and general form of what he wanted there, he would turn the paper over to Mr. Adee or some other experienced assistant and tell him to put it into "the lingo." (Although this was not his procedure in the case of the Venezuela note.) "If he had been in the Department for a few years he would have got the docket cleared for once." Thus, although his dispatches lacked the style and the sweep of political vision which distinguished Mr. Root's, he is said to have disposed of more business in a day that ended regularly on the stroke of four than even his great successor disposed of by working at all hours.

In fact it used to be said in Washington that at four o'clock precisely every day you could see the Secretary of State come streaking down the Department steps with everybody else following at his heels. It suited his pleasure and his constitution to play tennis or walk every afternoon. He had stuck to the hour of tennis during the hot week at the end of June, 1894, when the Chicago strike kept him at the Department of Justice or the White House night and day, and no equal crisis occurred to interfere with his regular habit while he was Secretary of State. Also it belonged to his view of the order of things that if the working day was supposed to end at four o'clock in the departments, everybody's work should go on until then and stop at that hour. Once, as he was striding from his own room to the elevator, the tall figure of Sir Julian Pauncefote appeared before him. "Mr. Ambassador," said the Secretary of State, "it's now four o'clock and the Department is closed; so I must ask you to call again to-morrow." And he passed and left Sir Julian standing agape in the corridor.

It sounds arbitrary and a little inconsiderate, perhaps; but busy men appreciate an efficient worker and too seldom find such an one as Olney in the Government's offices to do anything but smile over such an incident. Olney's relations with the members of the diplomatic corps were, indeed, excellent. His handling of the Mora claim and the Venezuelan case excited their respectful attention at the very beginning of his secretaryship, and his courtesy, his intelligence, his downrightness, and his industry all commanded their growing esteem.

Within the Department questions of personnel were nothing to what they would have been at the commencement of a presidential term. But so far as they did arise they were simplified by an order which made a date in the history of the consular service. This was issued under the Civil Service Act and provided a merit system for the appointment of consuls having salaries of more than $1000 and less than $2500. Olney recommended such a measure. Cleveland was eager to improve the consular service in such a way and signed the order on September 20, 1895.[1]

[1] Correspondence (Olney Coll.) indicates that this had been a topic of conference when Cleveland was at Gray Gables and Olney at Falmouth

It remained in force until the next Administration came into office.

That order, and the examinations held under it, along with other events of the year, diplomatic and departmental, and a few recommendations, including one that our representatives abroad should be housed by Government, are mentioned in a "Report of the Secretary of State" which is printed at the beginning of "Foreign Relations" for 1896. It is an interesting report because it is the only annual report that any Secretary of State has ever made. It was like Olney to think that there was no reason why he should not account for his Department once a year just like any other Department head, and to start a precedent accordingly. But it was natural that his successors should prefer the earlier practice of letting the President review our foreign relations in his annual message. Brief as the report was, it has given us, along with the diplomatic correspondence in "Foreign Relations" for 1895, 1896, and 1897, an unusually complete survey.

In these volumes lie the stories of numerous incidents which were, in their special ways, of real moment. They could not be treated with satisfactory amplitude in this place. Students and scholars will go to the records and special histories, anyhow. It must therefore suffice here to have pointed to them generally and to pass on.

earlier in September. Olney's formal letter of recommendation of September 17th was preceded by a note in which Cleveland referred to "our civil-service scheme" and said, "You will see I have blundered away at the order you drew . . ."

XV
THE LAST YEARS

AFTER March 4, 1897, Olney took no part in the responsibilities of government again. The spectacle of such a retirement is in itself a commentary on American politics, for he lived almost exactly twenty years longer, and the numerous unofficial public services which he performed while still carrying on a law practice showed that he continued to exercise all his faculties and powers. He said once, with a conviction of manner which impressed his hearer strongly, that "a man who splits his party assumes a great responsibility." It was certainly true that one of the most unfortunate consequences which flowed from the Democratic disruption of 1896 was that many men whom the nation needed were forced out to the side-lines. The Chicago Convention — surely one of the most extraordinary conventions in the history of the Republic — condemned Cleveland's sound-money policy, his fiscal arrangements, the Debs injunction — in fact everything important that his Administration had fought for except the Monroe Doctrine. It refused to mention the name of the President who had been the party's only successful standard-bearer since the Civil War in either its resolutions or its platform, and it even cast aside a motion which contained a vague *pro-forma* endorsement of the honesty, economy, courage, and fidelity of Cleveland's Administration. It crowned its work by choosing Mr.

Bryan to lead the party into the desert, and in November it sank down in defeat at the polls. In Massachusetts, the people who had followed Cleveland and William E. Russell and nad won victories for them in a constituency that was normally Republican, soon gave over the reins of party control to local free-silverites and to a near-Tammany element in the city of Boston. Everywhere the Democratic machine fell into the hands of men between whom and Olney there was too little sympathy for effective collaboration to be possible. So his experience and ability and influence, which ought to have been useful to the nation for another ten or fifteen years, went largely to waste.

He had made too great a name for himself to be forgotten by the public, however. Certain consequences of that could not be avoided. As he continued to call himself a Democrat,[1] he had to appear in public sometimes when the dignity of the occasion required a parade of the illustrious. Before each election his statement of how he meant to vote and why, usually very carefully prepared, excited a good deal of comment and was widely read. It seemed to the public that his opinions represented, more genuinely than those of any but a very few men of public standing, something that was powerless but still vital. His detachment from the race for office inspired confidence in his sincerity. And he was listened to with rather more than less attention when it was seen that his convictions could be recon-

---

[1] He supported the Bryan ticket publicly in 1900 and again in 1908 — in what frame of mind may be seen below. (Letter to S. B. Griffin, Appendix VII.) He appears to have remained in Washington on election day, 1896.

ciled with a steadfast allegiance to his party. As he never "took the stump" and did not go into print often, he seemed — on the rare occasions when he gave his views to the world — to be speaking from somewhere above the dust of the arena. In Massachusetts, and in other parts of the country as well, he was frequently mentioned as a presidential possibility. Considering his record and his abilities, that was inevitable. But he never prompted the suggestion himself, and it never advanced very far. If ex-Governor W. E. Russell had not been alive and active and the favorite of the Massachusetts delegation in 1896, Olney might have received the compliment of being put forward by his native State at the Chicago Convention in that year; but obviously the compliment could have led to nothing there. In 1903–04 when it looked as if the sound-money element would wrest the leadership from Bryan's grasp, all presidential "timber" on the conservative side was surveyed with care. Olney's name was brought forward in many parts of the country. The work of organizing the pre-convention arrangements was in the hands of men who were most of them a generation younger than Olney. In Massachusetts a group, in which General Patrick A. Collins, Mr. Ira C. Hersey, and Mr. Charles S. Hamlin were prominent, tried to boom him and carried his name through the State Convention successfully.[1] They also wanted to prevent Hearst from winning Massachu-

---

[1] April 21, 1904, the State Convention pledged the delegates at large whom it elected to support Olney's nomination. Later, in the Congressional District Conventions, twenty-two out of twenty-eight delegates chosen were favorable to Olney. Under the unit rule the thirty-two votes which Massachusetts sent to St. Louis were therefore instructed for him.

setts to support his candidacy. Olney sympathized with this purpose. Naturally too the endorsement of his own State was gratifying to him, and there is evidence that he was human enough to let his ambition be titillated. The men who wanted to put him forward found him friendly. But also they found him skeptical and exceedingly reserved. They got an impression that he would not refuse a nomination if it were handed to him, that he would rather like to have one handed to him in fact; but he never said so, never sanctioned their efforts in any explicit way, never "came out" or bestirred himself in his own interest at all. Apparently Cleveland would have been glad to see him nominated at St. Louis, and in the National Convention there the Bay State delegation was held together in his name until it was clear that Judge Parker's nomination was going through. But this did not mean that there was any strong expectation that Olney would be nominated. State delegations to a nominating convention are the better in many ways for being "tied up" in the name of a "favorite son" at the outset. Olney quite understood this, and did not let himself be excited by people who wanted to use his name, nor disturbed by the collapse of the "boom" they started for him. At no moment did he think of himself as a probable nominee or as a possible winner at the polls.[1]

[1] Since these sentences were written a letter which Olney wrote to his brother Peter on May 5, 1903, has come under my eye. In it he said, "As for my supposed candidacy, there is absolutely nothing in it — a draft might of course fetch me — it would, I suppose, any man — but nothing else. As for Parker's general character and his political standing and merits, my talk with you in your office entirely satisfied me, and I have ever since taken occasion to say that he seemed to me the best and most available candidate in sight."

He continued to be a constant and interested observer, however. He liked to be called on and consulted by men whom he trusted and who were active in public affairs. He made suggestions about points of policy or such matters as party platforms to them, and sometimes gave much thought and time to the preparation of these recommendations. Clearly, these occasional and undisclosed advisings, and his periodical utterances on campaign issues could hardly be said to amount to active participation in politics. But his loyal attachment to that something which always existed for him as the true Democratic Party, in spite of the habiliments it sometimes assumed and the vagaries in which it indulged too often, came out clearly in a letter about Cleveland's relation to the party during his last years. Indeed, when one considers how many ties of association, confidence, and regard bound the former Secretary of State to the chief who had died only a few months before, there is a sad sincerity about this lament. (The reader will be glad to go through a few personal sentences in order to have one of Olney's letters in its entirety.)

My DEAR PETER [so he wrote to his brother on March 24, 1909], Thank you for your last favor. I was a pretty much used-up man in New York the other day and am still the same, though I don't know that the New York visit did me any special harm. The doctor who operated on me protested against my taking the journey, and consented at last only upon condition of his assistant accompanying me and taking care of the by no means small hole in the back of my neck. I felt bound to go if I were alive both for the Cleveland celebration and because of a special meeting of the Trustees of the Peabody Education Fund which I had instigated Chief Justice Fuller to call.

The Republicans who fought and reviled Cleveland when he was in power have of late years sought to make him one of the assets of the Republican Party — with only too much success. He seems to me, perhaps unconsciously, to have done much to forward their purposes. He had a perfect right, if he so desired, to dislike and denounce Bryan and all his works, and certainly exercised the right very freely and publicly. But, while losing no opportunity to pour out the vials of his wrath upon them, why might he not have emptied them, occasionally at least, upon the Rooseveltians and their policies and proceedings? After 1904, however, he absolutely abstained from doing anything of the sort, and in all he said or did, in his connection with the insurance companies and with Paul Morton, and in all his apparent sympathies and affiliations, was, intentionally or otherwise, giving aid and comfort to the Republican Party. In the last election, as the platforms of the two candidates were practically the same, and the Roosevelt principles and policies adopted by Mr. Taft were every whit as obnoxious as those imputed to Mr. Bryan, he had not only every excuse, but every reason for giving the Democratic Party a much-needed lift. Yet, while the Broughton-Brandenburg letter is probably a forgery, the sentiments of the letter, especially those relating to Taft, are sentiments which it is said that Mr. Cleveland can be shown to have expressed to many persons. Hence, while I agree with you that the Cleveland Memorial Exercises were impressive, indeed exceedingly well designed and carried out, yet they made me rather sorrowful and rather resentful. There were excluded from them Cleveland's great merit as an opponent of all the distinctively Republican policies of the present day and his great achievement as the one presidential candidate who, in a period of nearly fifty years, has been able to shake the power of the Republican party. Indeed, the celebration seemed to me in some measure a celebration by his enemies, inspired by the belief that in honoring him they honored themselves and successfully appropriated a large part of the credit attaching to his great qualities and his great actions.

Did I mention to you when you were last in Boston a book called "Twenty Years of the Republic," by Professor Peck of Columbia College — covering the period from 1885 to 1905? You will find it, if you care to read it, a very vivid and entertaining, if not wholly reliable narrative. The characterization of Mark Hanna is specially graphic.

Begging to be remembered to all your household, I am
Sincerely yours
RICHARD OLNEY

Olney had gone to Washington for four years at considerable pecuniary sacrifice; for his single-handed law practice had not made him rich, and his professional income practically stopped while he was away from Boston. When he returned to his office in the Adams Building, he was not at all confident that a profitable practice could be resumed without a great deal of work. He and all Cleveland's associates were very much out of popular favor at the moment; and Boston was, of all American cities, the one in which his Venezuelan policy had aroused most critics. He was reassured very speedily. He found it easy to earn what he needed to maintain the standard of unextravagant comfort to which he had accustomed himself and his wife. So he rode his practice — not too hard — and did not let it ride him. It suited his tastes, and his sense of what was seemly for a man who had held his official position, to keep out of court and to confine himself to consultation and advisory work. In this he was happy and successful. His afternoons in the office became shorter than they had been before 1893; his summer retirements to Falmouth longer. He played golf and tennis quite regularly, or, in winter, walked daily in the new Charles River parkways.[1] He devoted more time to his wife and to his widowed daughter, Mrs. Minot, who lived with him; went to art exhibitions with her and used to drop in at picture dealers' shops. (He got interested in the outdoor work of the French impressionists and bought modern canvasses by such men as Maufra, Moret, and L'Oiseau.) Above all he read more, and read more widely, especially about what are called current events and tendencies of the times. "He used occasionally to ask me about some young writer who had appeared in the 'American Historical Review'—which one might have supposed to lie outside his field of interest," said Mr. Rhodes.[2] In short, he showed that he was not one of the majority for whom age is a process of settling ever deeper into a narrower and narrower groove, but one of the precious few whose field of consciousness goes on widening and enriching itself until the very end. Even in such a trifling matter as a hand at cards, the hero of this sketch showed that he was not attached to an "old-fashioned game."

[1] At Falmouth, Olney played tennis when he was eighty. "Until within a few years of his death he played a better game of tennis than did Mr. Balfour when he was in Washington during the Disarmament Conference" (statement of Richard Olney 2d, to the writer). For many years he got up an annual local tournament on his excellent green court and provided prizes. From the time when he was an undergraduate at Brown until his seventy-fifth year he never had a real illness. His physical strength and elasticity were always extraordinary for a man of his age.

[2] Statement to the writer.

He was keen to understand and try any innovation in bridge-whist.

It would be impossible to imagine Olney as an enthusiastic plunger into all sorts of philanthropies and causes, and it has been said that in his earlier years he took no great part in "good movements." After he had become a public character, he had to resist — and did resist — countless attempts to borrow his name for miscellaneous though doubtless worthy philanthropies and "causes." But Washington had quickened his interest in public service, besides making him famous; so now he accepted membership in several public boards in whose work he felt himself able to join helpfully. One of these was the Smithsonian Institution in Washington, for which he served as a regent from 1900 to 1908; one was the Peabody Education Fund to promote education in the Southern States.[1] Another was the American Society of International Law, of which he was a vice-president from 1906. Olney believed that progress toward a sound and self-consistent foreign policy for the United States — all progress depending upon a better general comprehension of international relations — was to be industriously worked for in the ways proposed by this association. Among its enterprises was the publication of the "American Journal of International Law," to which he occasionally made highly interesting contributions. Appar-

[1] Dr. Wickliffe Rose, then the executive officer of the Fund, says that Olney was one of the most attentive and helpful members of the board; and that his advice and assistance contributed largely to the success of the plan by which the Fund was converted into an endowment for George Peabody College in Nashville.

ently there was nothing to be hoped from a direct attack on
the mental apathy of the multitude about world questions.
But for that reason he was the more eager to inform and
clarify the minds of the small minority who are already
disposed to interest themselves in international affairs, and
he trusted that their ideas would filter out gradually into
the reservoir of popular belief.

There was also among these public trusts the Franklin
Union. Olney became as much interested in it as in anything else except our foreign relations. The "Union" grew
out of the fund of one thousand pounds which Benjamin
Franklin had left to accumulate for one hundred years and
then to be laid out (in part) in public works in Boston. In
March, 1904, Mr. Olney and seven others were appointed
"Managers" to act with the Mayor of Boston and the
ministers of three churches named in Franklin's will. The
Managers determined to found a trade school to give instruction to men already at work. It was seen that this
plan would fill a gap in the educational system of the community and also fit Franklin's purpose to help young "arti-
ficers." The fund with its accumulation was not sufficient
to carry this scheme into effect, so the Managers secured
an equal sum (it was something over $400,000) from a
public-spirited person, and erected a building on the corner of Berkeley and Appleton Streets. In 1908 they made a
corporation under the name of the Franklin Foundation,
and in the autumn of that year the school was opened,
with Mr. Olney as its president. Of the result Mr. Justice
Loring says:

The Union has been an extraordinary success. It gives to the workman the practical instruction necessary to enable him to become a foreman, and to the foreman the instruction necessary if he is to be a superintendent. When the school opened in September, 1908, it had thirteen instructors and three hundred and eighty-nine scholars. In 1917 (the last year of Mr. Olney's life) it had sixty instructors and two thousand and fifty-six scholars. During these nine years it had given instruction to eleven thousand five hundred different individuals. Mr. Olney conducted the affairs of the school with the thoroughness which was characteristic of his work at the Bar. He made himself familiar with the instruction given in the building from cellar to attic. In his report for the year 1917 the Director of the Union said: "By the death of the President of The Franklin Foundation, Richard Olney, Franklin Union loses a man who has given unreservedly of himself for its success. ... His office door stood open to the Director of Franklin Union, and he was ever ready with a word of counsel. Mr. Olney's democratic simplicity, his quiet humor, and his rugged strength of character have left a lasting imprint alike on Director, instructors, and students.[1]

Such public services were of no mean importance. They deserved recognition and have been more or less fittingly acknowledged in the records of the boards on which Olney served. But perhaps the unnumbered hours that he spent during his last twenty years in reading and jotting down his reflections on what he saw going on in the world are what impress one most, although their fruit cannot be plucked, counted, or weighed. The greater part of it fell to the

[1] Remarks at the Memorial Exercises of the Boston Bar Association, June 28, 1919. Pamphlet printed by Ellis & Co., Boston, p. 31.

ground — or into the waste-basket. He gave some of it out when occasion offered and when this or that bit ripened or was called for. But the spectacle recalls Lord Roberts's remark that for fifty years he had kept himself fit to serve his country in her hour of need. Olney's files abound in evidence that he kept reckoning and reappraising the changing currents of the time, and that he was continually reducing his thought to definite outline by working it over until it brought him to conclusions in which he felt confidence. Considering his "passion for finishing things," these painstaking and much revised memoranda show how strong was another passion in him — the passion to see things as they are and as they are going to be next, instead of as they were or as he might like them to remain.

The present rather than the past was what looked vital. His mind appears never to have turned willingly toward that orthodox occupation of old age — retrospection. Once, in compliance with repeated requests, he began to dictate a memorandum of reminiscence (it has been quoted in the earlier pages of this sketch); but he never revised what he dictated and never went on with it. Recollections fascinated him as little as explanations pleased him. This man who had spent four years in an Administration which met very rough weather took no pains at all to put up defenses against what somebody has called "the insolence of younger generations." Intellectually he never stopped living forward. Though Olney's ruminations resulted most often in brief statements to some newspaper à propos of a question of the moment, or in a few remarks at a banquet or other public occasion, he sometimes found opportunity for a full expression of his views. A few such utterances may be re-read with profit, for their message has not lost its meaning and has acquired an added interest from recent events. They deserve to be republished and it is to be hoped that they may be. For example, a paper which he gave to the "Atlantic Monthly" under the title, "The International Isolation of the United States," led Cleveland to speak of him as "a man who in my judgment is largely responsible through his 'Atlantic' article for the doctrine of expansion and consequent imperialism." [1] It began with an historical examination of the situation at which Washington was looking when he delivered the Farewell Address, and an argument about what Washington did *not* say. See, now, how aptly some of the concluding sentences — penned in 1898 — refer themselves to the present hour:

A noted Republican statesman of our day, a protectionist though not of the extreme variety, is said to have remarked, "It is not an ambitious destiny for so great a country as ours to manufacture only what we can consume or produce only what we can eat." But it is even a more pitiful ambition for such a country to aim to seclude itself from the world at large and to live a life as insulated and independent as if it were the only country on the footstool. A nation is as much as member of a society as an individual. Its membership, as in the case of an individual, involves duties which call for something more than mere abstention from violations of positive law. The individual who should deliberately undertake to ignore society and social obligations, to mix with his kind only under compulsion, to abstain from all effort to make men wiser or hap-

[1] Cleveland to Bissell, September 16, 1900. This letter will be found in McElroy's *Cleveland.*

pier, to resist all appeals to charity, to get the most possible and enjoy the most possible consistent with the least possible intercourse with his fellows, would be universally condemned as shaping his life by a low and unworthy standard. Yet, what is true of the individual in his relations to his fellow men is equally true of every nation in its relation to other nations. In this matter, we have fallen into habits which, however excusable in their origin, are without present justification. Does a foreign question or controversy present itself appealing however forcibly to our sympathies or sense of right — . . . The upshot is more or less explosions of sympathy or antipathy at more or less public meetings, and, if the case is a very strong one, a more or less tardy tender by the Government of its "moral support." Is that a creditable part for a great nation to play in the affairs of the world? The pioneer in the wilderness, with a roof to build over his head and a patch of ground to cultivate and wife and children to provide for and secure against savage beasts and yet more savage men, finds in the great law of self-preservation ample excuse for not expending either his feelings or his energies upon the joys or the sorrows of his neighbors. But surely he is no pattern for the modern millionaire, who can sell nine tenths of all he has and give to the poor, and yet not miss a single comfort or luxury of life. This country was once the pioneer and is now the millionaire. . . . There is such a thing for a nation as a "splendid isolation" — as when for a worthy cause, for its own independence, or dignity, or vital interests, it unshrinkingly opposes itself to a hostile world. But isolation that is nothing but a shirking of the responsibilities of high place and great power is simply ignominious. If we shall sooner or later — and we certainly shall — shake off the spell of the Washington legend and cease to act the rôle of a sort of international recluse, it will not follow that formal alliances with other nations for permanent or even temporary purposes will soon or often be found expedient.

The only danger in making such a quotation is that all preliminary reasoning is omitted. It is needless to say that in this paper, as in others, such as "The Growth of Our Foreign Policy" (1900), "The Development of International Law" (an address before the Society of International Law in 1907), and "Our Latin-American Policy" (1916), Olney spoke with a full sense of the care with which a former Secretary of State should pronounce himself. He knew that he was on debatable ground and took pains to make his reasoning clear.

One other series of papers which deserves particular mention might not have been expected from a man of his generation and lifelong associations. Ever after the Chicago strike — if not before — the so-called struggle between labor and capital was full of significance for him. Speaking broadly, his own walks and ways had been among the capitalists. In that environment the orthodox school of thought had reasoned that the freest play of economic forces is not only normal, but also most nourishing to the health and vigor of the community. It accepted the fact that society had long since substituted government for self-help wherever life and property were to be protected, but it would have perpetuated complete competitive individualism in business enterprise and the labor market. Olney thought the time had come to check and modify this in the very interest of individualism. "There is no right more precious," he said, "than the right of inequality — than the right of every individual to the use and development of all his faculties and to whatever deserved superiority over others may thus accrue to him. Nevertheless, this right of inequality, like every other, is subject to regulation"; and he elaborated the theme in several directions. It might do more good than harm, he thought, if labor unions entered politics. The experience would educate them and their influence would help to check the social inequalities which tend to flow from 'big business.' He had seen a great deal of 'big business,' in trade and industry, and was disposed to curtail its power.[1] Ways of imposing a greater measure of legal control must be worked out if society was to keep pace with the times. In closing the address to the Boston Merchants Club in 1913, which has just been quoted, he spoke in a tone of warning: —

The hoary axiom — "Competition is the life of Trade" — in the sense in which it has been heretofore understood and acted upon is, I believe, thoroughly discredited. The competition of the future promises to be a regulated competition — a competition regulated by law, so regulated as to be fair, and that it may be known to be fair, restricted to practices and methods that are open and honest and succeed only through superior merit. Competition in the future in all lines of business is likely to be governed by rules generally analogous to those now peculiar to public-service occupations — such as that of common carriers. They are forced to play the game with their cards on the table face up because the courts say a public interest attaches to their calling. But an equal, perhaps even greater,

[1] Address before the Merchants Club of Boston, 1913. Printed as a pamphlet. See also "Labor Unions and Politics," *The Inter-Nation*, December, 1906; "Modern Industrialism," *ibid.*, February, 1907; "Paternalism and Personal Freedom," *ibid.*, January, 1908; "Discrimination against Union Labor — Legal?" *American Law Review*, March–April, 1908.

public interest certainly attaches to the calling of the pro-
vision-dealer, the clothier, the shoemaker, the coal-dealer,
and to many other callings. If the carrier must sell transportation to all comers at the same price for the same service, what possible reason is there why the baker or the
coal-dealer shall not be compelled to sell bread or coal to all
customers on the same terms? . . . The advent of a new era is
not to be ignored. It cannot fairly be condemned by ap-
plying to it the standards of a bygone age. True conserva-
tism dictates that what it stands for be examined with an
open mind and be determined by such actual merits, if any,
as are found to exist. If none are found, condemnation
will of course be in order. But if merits are found, if government ought to be made in fact what it is in theory,
namely, government by the people; if government ought to
be utilized for the general welfare of society to a greater degree than ever before; if business enterprises and the mutual relations of business men ought to be regulated in the
interest of fair play, justice, and equality of opportunity
and treatment — such assuredly meritorious objects are
not to be refused recognition because not within the conception of the men of past generations. On the contrary,
the ends in view being found worthy, good sense and good
citizenship require them to be supported even if the cherished ideas and sentiments of a lifetime must go to the
scrap heap.

This was said, be it noted, when Olney was seventy-
seven, and before the World War forced all western civilization to hurry in the direction to which he was looking. As
one reads over the whole address one feels as if one were
hearing the old lawyer deliver his valedictory to the successful business world whose ways he had studied during
the legal battles and intimate consultations of more than
half a century.

After President Wilson's election had brought the Democratic Party into office again, Olney was twice invited to accept an important post. First the President asked him to take the London Embassy. Later, in 1914, Colonel House came to urge him to assume the office of Governor of the new Federal Reserve Board. When the ambassadorship was offered him, Olney was in his seventy-eighth year. His wife had become an invalid and needed his care at home. Although it was explained to him that the President wanted his name and prestige for the Reserve Board rather than great labors, he declined that position as well as the ambassadorship without hesitation. "An Ambassador is nobody in these days," he is said to have remarked, half jocosely; "he sits at the other end of a cable and does what he is told." The words have an authentic ring. Probably nobody who can imagine Olney at "the other" end of the cable with Secretary Bryan on this end; or who thinks of the patience and physical endurance which were required of our Ambassador in London when the war broke out, would deplore Olney's decision. But both offers were agreeably complimentary and they brought him expressions of confidence and good-will which could not but please him. One, from Joseph H. Choate, which includes a bit of testimony on the Venezuelan affair, must be repeated.

NEW YORK, *March* 14, 1913

MY DEAR MR. OLNEY:

I do hope, for the sake of the country, that you will accept the Ambassadorship to England, which has been offered to you by President Wilson. You will find it, in all respects, a delightful post, and one in which your robust

Americanism will be not only thoroughly recognized, but most heartily welcome. There is nothing they like there so well as a representative of the United States who stands very firmly for its rights, and I anticipate that in the next four years, the United States will have a much more effective voice in international affairs than it has ever had before, and if we keep up our Navy to the point to which I think it ought to be kept, our opinion will be eagerly sought, although I hope that we shall not unnecessarily meddle with foreign affairs in which we have no direct concern. But in all that concerns China and Japan, we do have a very direct concern and are entitled to have at London the best man that can be got, to make our views known and understood. . . .[1]

It goes without saying that you would be most warmly welcomed and all the more so from having stood your ground so well when you were Secretary of State in Mr. Cleveland's administration. I thought, at that time, that the snapper which Mr. Cleveland added to his message to Congress on the Venezuela matter was much too harsh, but my experience afterwards satisfied me that the strong position which you took had a startling and permanent effect, and that after that, we were looked upon as a nation always to be reckoned with in anything that fairly concerned us. . . .

I think that Mrs. Olney could measure her share in social life according to her strength, and would rarely be called upon to go beyond it, and I am sure that she would greatly enjoy the intercourse with the best people, which is always due to our Ambassadress.

What I fear is that, if you do not take it, it will be hard for the President to find any other adequate representative, and I venture to prophesy that if you do accept it, you will come home, after four years, as young as you went away.

[1] The omitted paragraphs discuss the expenses and the fatigues of the post.

I want the English to see, for once, the best that our Democracy can furnish.

Yours very truly

JOSEPH H. CHOATE

When, on a third occasion, Olney was asked to let himself be named as the American Commissioner of the United States to serve under the Bryan "Treaty to facilitate the Settlement of Disputes" with France, he accepted. No dispute was in sight, and none arose for the Commission of which he thus became a member to act upon, however.

It might have been supposed that when the World War broke out, Olney would have taken a share in the moulding of opinion. But when the President issued a prohibition against the moulding of opinion, Olney's code of loyalty to the Government tied his tongue, and the reserve which he imposed upon himself was complete.

I do not share your impression [so ran a letter to a correspondent who urged him to issue a statement about the Lusitania] that I could say anything at the present time which would be especially authoritative or influential. But the surer I were of that fact, the more cautious I should be and ought to be about saying it in advance of knowing what the Administration proposes. It has apparently settled upon its course. Not knowing what it is, I might unwittingly antagonize it, to my lasting regret and mortification. In an exigency like the present, the first duty of the citizen is to support the constituted authorities and, whatever his doubts or fears, to abstain from any act or speech which might tend to diminish public confidence in the wisdom of their efforts or the prospects of their success. . . .

That he was none too well satisfied with the country's course may be inferred both from the way in which he himself had handled our foreign affairs when he was at the head of the State Department, and from the fact that his loyalty to the Administration expressed itself chiefly by silence. And once in a while he fell into an expression which betrayed what was going on in his mind, as when he declined an invitation to speak before the Boston Economic Club, "for the reason that any peace demonstration at this time seems premature and possibly damaging" (January 19, 1915), or as when he wrote to an English correspondent the next day:

It is impossible for New-Englanders not to view with keen sympathy the severe trials and sufferings you of Old England are now undergoing. I note the anxiety and grief the war is causing you personally. At the same time I realize that you would be unwilling that you and your family should not assume their share of the inevitable burdens of a conflict which seems to put at issue all that English civilization stands for.

The war was always in his thoughts. When Theodore N. Vail urged him to protect his health by dismissing worry, Olney replied (February 1, 1917):

... But in these parlous times the desideratum is a practical recipe for carrying the advice into effect. Every member of your family wants to know what you think of this or that bellicose episode; every caller on business or pleasure, after a little time spent on the object of the call, plunges into the war and is willing to stay there indefinitely; even the doctor, called to combat your particular ailment, will dismiss it in a few sentences only to give you a lengthy discourse on when the war is to end and what is to follow. In these circumstances, not to think, not to demand to know the latest, not to worry about both the present and the future, is almost impossible.

Before this was written grave ailments had at length descended upon him. For a year his health had been failing. Without telling anybody — leaving the arrangement to be discovered after his death, in fact — he went out to the Mount Auburn Cemetery and chose and paid for a lot in which to be buried. By the beginning of 1917 it was certain that he was dying of cancer. "You'll never see him again," said his doctor to President Henry S. Pritchett; "I've never named his trouble to him, and he has never named it to me; but I am sure that he knows." His mind was clear. He had made a will in which he directed that his estate should ultimately be divided among his grandchildren — the four children of the daughter he had banished each to fare as well as the one child of his other daughter. But, though he now put with it a note telling his wife that he believed she would "approve" this disposition, and remarking also that she and Mrs. Minot would be able to help "any member of the family" from the life-income which he was leaving them, he never brought himself to say a word about this or any other arrangement that he was making. Whatever may have been his reflections about life, and his own journey, and death which was now waiting at his elbow, they remained locked in his breast. Like the stoic Roman he had always been, he dwelt still, in conversation at any rate, on what was happening around him rather than on what was about to happen to himself. Mr. Nathan Matthews tells how anxiously he watched the country's course until the very last.

On December 27, 1916, about two weeks before his last illness, in what was probably his last political conference, he expressed to me his apprehension lest our friends in France and England should misunderstand the real attitude of the people of this country. He rejoiced in the rupture of our diplomatic relations with the German Empire, because he knew that this meant war between that country and our own. In a [telegram] to the State Department written only one month before his death, he approved the action of our Government in arming American merchant ships "to enable them to defend themselves against lawless and hostile attack." During the next few weeks, when on his deathbed, he was much worried because the government appeared to move so slowly, and he frequently referred to the notice served on England in the Venezuela case as a precedent for action against Germany. Finally, a day or two before he lost consciousness for good, he was informed of the President's message to Congress urging a declaration of war on Germany. His rejoicing at this long-awaited news was tempered only by the regret that he would not live to see the end.

His own end was very near.

The unconsciousness into which he sank soon after hearing the news of the war message deepened. On the evening of April 8, 1917, in his eighty-second year, death came.

APPENDIX I

EXTRACTS FROM A MEMORANDUM DICTATED BY OLNEY IN 1901

[IN February, 1901, Olney began to dictate what was to have been a Memorandum covering his connection with Cleveland's second Administration. To this he added a few pages of pencil notes. The dictation and the few notes were typewritten, but he never revised them and never went on. What was thus put on paper touched nothing that occurred in Washington later than the argument in the Debs case. The Memorandum should be read with these facts in mind. But, although it is thus no more than a statement of recollections, dictated or jotted down just as they occurred to him six or eight years after the event, it contains much that is interesting. Several passages have been quoted in the text, other passages are given below.]

(*Regarding Hawaii*)

Immediately after his inauguration, Mr. Cleveland withdrew from the Senate the treaty for the annexation of Hawaii made by President Harrison. Having done so, he then appointed Mr. James H. Blount, of Georgia, special commissioner to go to the Hawaiian Islands and investigate on the spot the manner in which the Queen had been dethroned and the steps which had been taken as preliminary to annexation. Reports from Mr. Blount satisfied the President and his Cabinet that the case was one in which the dethronement of the Queen had been brought about by the United States Minister acting in conjunction with the Navy of the United States, and that the action of the Minister, backed up by the power of the United States, amounted to nothing less than criminal aggression upon the Government of a friendly state. In these circumstances, Mr. Cleveland proposed to restore the *status in quo* as far as was practicable. When the matter was mooted in the Cabinet, Mr. Carlisle and myself, perhaps others, took the ground that what had been done had been done at the instigation of the American Minister supported by the naval forces of the United States; that however wrongful their action might have been, they could not be left to the possible vengeance of the Hawaiian Government and Queen; and consequently that, in taking any steps toward reinstating her Government, care must be taken for the rights and interests of American citizens and other residents of the Hawaiian Islands who had joined in the movement against the Queen in reliance upon the United States as apparently represented by its Minister, Mr. Stevens. Consequently, Mr. Blount was instructed to advise the Queen of the President's desire and purpose to put things back as they were before the Stevens revolution, on the understanding and condition that she should proclaim a general amnesty in favor of all persons (American citizens [sic.]) who had taken part in the movement. Though instructions of this purport were promptly forwarded to Mr. Blount, he did not report his action thereon in time to enable the President to state the result to Congress in the annual message to Congress of December, 1893. Shortly after that message had been sent in, however, Mr. Blount's report of his action was received — when it appeared that the Queen refused to accept the conditions attached by the Administration to any effort to reinstate her in her Government. This condition of things gave the President much anxiety. His conclusion was that he would lay the whole matter before Congress for such action as Congress might think advisable under the circumstances, and in that view desired to send to Congress a special message upon the subject, which he asked Secretary Gresham to prepare. He did so, but, as the result did not cover the ground desired by the President, he asked me to see what I could do with it. I accordingly went over Mr. Blount's voluminous reports and all other papers on the subject and prepared a draft which was accepted by him and forms by far the larger part of the message actually sent to Congress on the 18th of December.

(Regarding the Chicago Strike)

The attention of the Department of Justice was first called to the [Chicago Strike] by representations from the Post-Office Department that the passage of the mails in various parts of the country was seriously obstructed. As a result, orders to the United States Marshals were sent to the designated places directing them to see that the regular passage of the mails was not interfered with, and to that end to use such force of special deputy marshals as might be required. Chicago was the center of the disturbance, but in a few days all the principal Western cities were involved. It soon became evident that the movement engineered by Mr. Debs was on an extraordinary scale and of a most threatening character, and might have to be met and dealt with by the Army of the United States. The Department of Justice, in order to be prepared for the exigency, took measures to put itself in the position which had induced the President to authorize the use of troops as against the Coxey movement. That is to say, the Department of Justice instructed the District Attorney at Chicago, and afterwards other District Attorneys, to file bills in equity enjoining certain persons by name and all other persons coöperating with them from any interference with the mails or with interstate commerce — the bills being filed both on general grounds and under the express provisions of what is known as the Sherman Anti-Trust Law. The first bill was filed in Chicago in the name of the Attorney-General, by the District Attorney, Milchrist, ancillary bills being also filed at the same time by the various railroad corporations. The Attorney-General's bill was very comprehensive and was so drawn as to inhibit all interference with any interstate commerce railroads running into Chicago. The bills as filed called for interlocutory injunctions and, upon being presented to the court, such injunctions were issued. They were not, however, at first respected. Although Arnold, the United States Marshal, had under his command at one time as many as three thousand special deputies, the field of operations of the strikers was very large, and he was generally outnumbered by the mob at any points where disturbances were going on. Though the injunctions were printed and pasted all over the city and were read wherever a gathering of strikers seemed to be meditating violence, no appreciable effect was produced. The marshal was hooted and his assistants overpowered, and though a few persons were taken in custody, the strike rather increased than abated in force.

In this situation of things, applications for the use of the United States troops were frequent, from the marshals, from lawyers, and from eminent citizens of Chicago. The President, however, deemed it best to follow strictly the precedent made in the Coxey case and not to move until satisfied that he must do so by proof that could not be resisted. In anticipation of such proof being furnished, however, the troops at Fort Sheridan were kept under arms, and a train ready to bring them to the city of Chicago was kept there with the locomotive fired up. Finally, Judge Grosscup, judge of the United States District Court, Mr. Milchrist, the United States District Attorney, and Mr. Walker who had been retained specially in the business on behalf of the United States, joined the United States Marshal in a telegram to the Department stating that the writs and processes of the court could not be executed by the marshal and any force of deputies that he could collect, and asking for the immediate appearance on the scene of the United States troops. The President thereupon gave the order and the troops then at Fort Sheridan went by rail to the city of Chicago. . . . [Here follows a paragraph which has been quoted in the text. Also some remarks about military dispositions which have no connection with what Olney did.]

The importance of the military demonstration in Chicago by the troops of the United States was, of course, very great. Yet it was the common opinion at the time — an opinion confirmed by the explicit declaration of Debs himself — that the action of the United States Courts enjoining the proceedings of Debs and his followers, and resulting so far as Debs himself was concerned in committing him to jail for contempt, really broke the back of the movement. It put the strikers in the wrong — in the position of rioters wantonly defying the law.

The President might have used the United States troops to prevent interference with the mails and with interstate commerce on his own initiative — without waiting for action by the courts and without justifying the proceeding as taken to enforce judicial decrees. But, as already intimated, it is doubtful — at least seemed doubtful to me at the time — whether the President could be induced to move except in support of the judicial tribunals. In the next place, assuming there was time enough to set the judiciary in motion, as it turned out that there was, it was unquestionably better to await its movements and make them the basis of Executive action. The injunctions were issued *ex parte* — and justifiably in view of the exigency and the irreparable character of the mischief going on and threatened. But, though issued *ex parte*, they were not final; the question of their legality and propriety was open and could have been raised at any moment by Debs or any parties enjoined by a simple motion in court for the dissolution of the injunctions. As law-abiding citizens — citizens who meant to respect the law — they were bound to take that course — and it always seemed to me unaccountable they were not advised so to do. In fact, they pursued exactly the opposite and a wholly indefensible course — Debs in particular proceeding after the injunctions as before and proclaiming at public meetings his intent to disregard the injunctions and urging his followers to do so likewise. He thus put himself hopelessly in the wrong.

The excitement at Chicago reached a great height — and the strikers were not the only parties who were carried away by it. After Debs's arrest on process for contempt — or at the time the process was being executed — his quarters were searched and all his papers carried off by the United States officers. As soon as I was aware of the fact, I telegraphed the special counsel for the United States — Mr. Walker — to make immediate restitution of everything that had been seized — which was immediately done. Mr. Walker rather resented my action as being a public censure of him and his acts. I replied that nothing of the sort was intended, and that

I had assumed that the ill-advised seizure was not due to him or to his counsels, but to the over-zeal of the marshal and his deputies. He afterwards recalled his first impulsive language — adding that I probably did not realize the intense local excitement nor the strain to which he personally had been subjected.

It probably should have been before stated — as one feature of the situation which to the Washington authorities seemed to make the use of United States troops at Chicago imperative — that both the Governor of the State (Altgeld) and the Mayor of the city (Hopkins) were known to be in sympathy with the strikers — so far at least that the Governor held himself aloof from the scene and made no effort to repress the disorders going on at the chief city of his State, while the Mayor, besides taking no active measures to prevent the violent and lawless interference with the running of interstate and mail trains and the lawless destruction of railroad property, even went so far as to openly wear the distinctive badge of the rioters. Both Altgeld and Hopkins were Democrats — largely by their efforts Illinois had been carried for Cleveland and the Democracy in 1892 — and some of the President's advisers, of whom Colonel Lamont was one, very much doubted the expediency of any action antagonizing or discrediting the Democratic Governor and Mayor. The President saw the point as clearly as any one, but never for a moment wavered in his determination to do what he believed to be his constitutional duty.

The advent of the United States troops in Chicago amounted, of course, to a reflection upon Governor Altgeld and his performance of his duties. He so regarded it and in an interview — or a letter to the President — he denounced the President's action as unconstitutional. The President took no notice of the missive except by a brief telegram — which did not, of course, deal with Altgeld's legal position.[1] It

[1] Olney's recollection was at fault. Altgeld's protests resulted in two telegrams. (See *Presidential Problems*, 110–13.) The second one contained little more than the often quoted words: " it seems to me that in this hour of danger and public distress, discussion may well give way to active efforts on the part of all in authority to restore obedience to law and to protect life and property."

seemed to me something on that aspect of the matter should emanate from the office of the Attorney-General, who was, of course, responsible for the legal attitude of the Government. I therefore broke over my rule against interviews or any communication with the press or its agents and sent for the reporters and gave them a statement.[1] It was meant to be brief so that it would be read — and to be non-technical in terms so that laymen as well as lawyers would comprehend it. At the time I was satisfied it had accomplished the object in view.

Governor Altgeld's letter — and perhaps other criticisms made at the same time— called the President's attention to the matter of an Executive proclamation in the nature of a riot act calling upon the strikers to cease from their unlawful courses, etc., etc. Such a proclamation did not seem to me necessary then and does not so seem now. No such step had been taken in any of the Coxey cases in which the President had used troops to enforce the orders of the United States courts. Yet such a proclamation could do no harm and might do good, and I advised making it. It was accordingly made, was posted about Chicago in the English language, and, I think, in German, and perhaps in other languages, and was said to have a most quieting and salutary effect.

As I now recollect, the United States forces in Chicago never numbered over five thousand men, if so many.[2] It would not have been easy to add much to that number without ordering out the State militia — the whole Regular Army of the United States amounting to only twenty-five thousand men and being distributed in garrisons and small detachments all over the United States. In dealing with the strike, and in recognizing the necessity of a demonstration by the United States Army, its size and situation had to be taken into account. It seemed clear that whatever was done should be done at Chicago, because that was the center and headquarters of the strike, and that, if smashed there, it would collapse everywhere else. For that reason and because the army was too small to permit of any considerable force being assembled at numerous points, such force as was available

---

1 See text at page 56, *ante*.   2 1936. Wright Report, p. xix.

should, it seemed to me, be sent to and used at Chicago. At the same time, it was necessary as far as practicable to avoid anything like an armed collision between the strikers and the United States forces, not only on general and obvious grounds, but because, by reason of the great disparity of numbers, it was entirely possible that the result might be to diminish rather than increase the wholesome respect of the populace in general for the regular soldiery. In accordance with these views, the strike was tackled at Chicago first; whatever regulars were readily available were sent there; by direct orders from Washington the force was kept together so as to be formidable wherever and whenever and in whatever direction it was called upon to act; while the actual use of the military against the rioters, being postponed until circumstances should compel it, proved in the end not be to required. The prestige of the United States, its readiness to act and its determination to act with its troops in support of the United States Courts should that course become necessary, brought the strike to an end in Chicago and its vicinity without a single individual having been wounded or killed by the forces of the United States.

The troops remained in Chicago until the [20th] of July, and with General Miles at their head were daily paraded through the streets of the city. During one of these parades an artillery caisson exploded, killing —— and wounding —— men, and inflicting the only loss sustained by the United States forces during the Chicago *émeute*. For some days prior to the [20th] July, the Administration at Washington were satisfied that the object of the presence of the troops in Chicago had been accomplished and that they should be withdrawn from the city. Several inquiries on that subject from [to?] General Miles eliciting nothing definite — he seemed to rather favor postponing the departure of the troops — explicit instructions from Washington directed their removal and they were removed accordingly.

The strike being ended in Chicago, the United States were in a position to send troops elsewhere for the same purpose if needed. But, as was anticipated, the termination of the strike in Chicago terminated it everywhere else, and, with one exception, the use of troops in connection with the strike was no longer required. The exception came in the cases of the Northern Pacific and Union Pacific Railroads. Both those roads were Government roads — were by their charters bound to carry for the Government men, supplies, munitions, and materials of all sorts — and were then required for such use and were then in actual use for those purposes except so far as such use was prevented by the strikers. It was impossible to open those roads to their customary functions by sending troops to particular points. The army was not large enough to cover all the points of disturbance, while at the same time the interruption of transportation, if prevented at one point, would be renewed at another, or, if prevented at one point to-day, would be renewed at the same point to-morrow the moment the United States troops had departed. In these circumstances, it was deemed best to send a force of United States Marshals and troops on the trains from one end of the route to the other. The expedient proved successful, and the Pacific roads, having once been cleared for travel, the attempts to close them were not renewed. Serious resistance of the troops at some California points — Sacramento in particular — was anticipated and prepared for. But, by the time those points were reached, the hopelessness of the Debs movement was recognized and practically no organized opposition was made to the opening of the roads for traffic by the United States authorities.

APPENDIX II

THE CLEVELAND ADMINISTRATION AND THE SHERMAN ANTI-TRUST LAW

[DURING the political campaigns of 1904 and 1908 Republican speakers accused the Democratic Party loudly of having failed to enforce the Sherman Anti-Trust Law while it was in power. These accusations seemed quite unwarranted and unjust to Olney and provoked him to write the following memorandum and letter. See also his "Reports of the Attorney-General" and the last page and a half of Cleveland's annual message of December 7, 1896.] [1]

Memorandum sent John H. Holmes, Editor " Boston Herald" — to be used as reply to New York "World" article — and published as editorial March 18, 1904

The New York "World's" recent statement that the second Cleveland Administration did nothing to enforce the Sherman Anti-Trust statute is a complete misrepresentation. The real facts, including the legal situation as Mr. Cleveland's Attorney-General found it, are as follows:

1. The Sherman Anti-Trust statute was passed in 1890.

2. In May, 1892, an indictment in the Massachusetts District against officers of the so-called "Whiskey Trust" was quashed by Judge Nelson. (50 Fed. Rep. 469.)

3. In August, 1892, an officer of the same Trust, being arrested in Ohio for removal to Massachusetts for a trial upon an indictment found under the Act of 1890, was discharged on *habeas corpus* by Mr. Justice Jackson, afterwards Judge of the United States Supreme Court — upon practically the same grounds afterwards adopted by the United States Supreme Court in the case of the United States *v.* Knight *et al.*, to be hereafter referred to.

[1] Richardson, IX, 744-45.

4. In October, 1892, an indictment against a combination of lumber dealers was quashed in the United States District Court for the District of Minnesota on substantially the same grounds as those set forth in the cases above referred to. (United States *v*. Nelson, 52 Fed. Rep. 646.)

5. In November, 1892, it was held in the United States Circuit Court for the Kansas District that the Act of 1890 had no application to common carriers — an adjudication afterwards affirmed by the Circuit Court of Appeals. (United States *v*. Trans-Missouri Freight Association, 53 Fed. Rep. 440; 58 Fed. Rep. 58.)

6. In March, 1893, a bill in equity was pending, which had been brought under the direction of Attorney-General Miller against the combination known as "the American Sugar Trust." This case was pushed to argument and decision with all possible dispatch, with the result that towards the end of January, 1895, the Supreme Court dismissed the bill on the ground that manufacture was not commerce and that, although the products of manufacture were intended to be sold and might be sold beyond the State of manufacture, no interstate commerce would be involved until the goods were actually *en route* to their destination beyond such State. (United States *v*. Knight *et al.*, 156 U.S. 1.)

7. Judge Harmon became Attorney-General in June, 1895.

8. In December, 1896, an appeal having been taken from the Circuit Court of Appeals to the Supreme Court in the case above referred to of United States *v*. Trans-Missouri Freight Association, Judge Harmon caused the case to be argued, with the result that on March 22, 1897, the Supreme Court (four judges dissenting) reversed the decision of the courts below and held the Act of 1890 to be applicable to railroads engaged in interstate commerce. (166 U.S. 290.)

It was a notable triumph for Judge Harmon inasmuch as before the argument the defendant Association had been dissolved, so that, besides the construction and the legal merits of the Act of 1890, an important question of jurisdiction was involved.

9. In 1896 or 1897, by the direction of Judge Harmon, pro-

ceedings were begun by the United States against the Addyston Pipe & Steel Company. (78 Fed. Rep. 712.)

It will be seen from the foregoing —

First, that during the seven years succeeding the enactment of the statute authoritative adjudications of the courts
had been against its application to the cases brought before
them;

Second, that industrial combinations for the purpose of
manufacture, no matter how large or monopolistic, were decided by the United States Supreme Court in 1895 not to be
within the purview of the statute — a decision which has
never been overruled and is still the law of the land;

Third, that the first important adjudication in favor of the
Act in its practical operation upon interstate commerce was
procured by Judge Harmon in the case of the United States *v.*
Trans-Missouri Freight Association, whereby the Act of 1890
was declared to be applicable to railroad companies engaged
in interstate commerce;

Fourth, that the decision in the Northern Securities case
simply applies the doctrine settled in the Trans-Missouri
Freight Association case; and

Fifth, that the notable Addyston Pipe & Steel Company
case, which has been thought to qualify in important respects
the previous decision of the Supreme Court of the United
States in United States *v.* Knight *et al.*, was initiated by
Judge Harmon.

Copy of the above memorandum was sent to various people in 1904, and in 1908 a copy was sent to the Editor of the
New York "World" accompanied by the following letter:

30 *September,* 1908

C. M. VAN HAMM, Esq.,
    Editor New York "World," New York, N.Y.

MY DEAR SIR:

The telegram of the "World" of the 28th inst. offering its
columns for any statement in refutation of President Roosevelt's charges against the Department of Justice during Mr.

Cleveland's second Administration, was received by me last evening.

The charges relate to the supposed delinquency of the Department in reference to the enforcement of what is known as the Sherman Anti-Trust Law.

I shall make no statement on the subject myself. But it seems to me that the "World" may well take this opportunity to do justice to the Department. In my judgment it has never treated the Department fairly — whether intentionally or otherwise I do not know and do not care. But it seems to me that it is due to the "World" itself that a paper of the influence and standing it has now achieved should put itself right on a question which seems to be of some importance in connection with the pending elections.

I enclose a statement of the facts which I believe to be entirely accurate, and which is a duplicate of a statement furnished to the "Boston Herald" in March, 1904, and published by it as an editorial. I do not ask its present publication on my own account. But members of the National Committee have written me suggesting that a reply to Mr. Roosevelt's accusations should be published.

You will, of course, treat the contents of this note as strictly confidential.

Very truly yours
(Signed)   RICHARD OLNEY

APPENDIX III

LETTERS ABOUT THE HAWAIIAN QUESTION

[THE letter to Secretary Gresham, here given in full, has been quoted in the text above. It has also been printed in the "Life of Walter Q. Gresham." It so happened that in December, 1893, Olney's daughter, Mrs. George R. Minot, was preparing a paper on Hawaii for a "discussion club." Part of a letter and a complete letter to her which follow it were written to coach her and have the particular interest of informal and confidential communications.]

Olney to Gresham

DEPARTMENT OF JUSTICE
WASHINGTON, D.C.
October 9, 1893

HON. WALTER Q. GRESHAM
    Secretary of State
MY DEAR JUDGE:

The Hawaii business strikes me as not only important, but as one that may require great delicacy in the handling.

There is no question, it seems to me, that a great wrong was done under the auspices of United States Minister Stevens when the regular constitutional Government of the Queen was supplanted and the present, so-called, Provisional Government installed in its stead.

There is no question either, I think, of the good sense, the statesmanship, and the sound morality of your proposition that this great wrong should be rectified, and that to rectify it the *status quo* at the time of its perpetration must as far as possible be restored.

The Queen's Government was overthrown by an exhibition of force — if it can be reinstated by a like exhibition of force without actual resort to it, there is not, it seems to me, any real ground for hesitation. Whether the exhibition of force in each case be or be not a technical act of war, the undoing of

the original wrong by the same means by which it was con-
summated would hardly be criticized in any quarter and
would probably be universally commended as an act of substantial justice. It would be the short and ready way out of
the complication if the Stevens Government were a thing of a
few hours' or even a few days' existence.

But the present situation is not so simple. The Queen has
been in our hands, and the Stevens Government has been in
authority with our acquiescence for many months. All parties have been awaiting the action of the United States. In
the interim the Stevens Government has had complete possession of the country and all its resources, and may have acquired such control of them and such ascendancy over the inhabitants that it can be displaced only by actual force and
after more or less loss of life and destruction of property.

In any event, and whether the Stevens Government will be
fought for or not, it has in this interval been receiving the
revenues of the country, collecting the taxes, administering
justice, and enforcing the laws, and generally exercising all
the functions of a legitimate Government.

This being the situation, let the worst be assumed, namely,
that, as a matter of fact, the Stevens Government cannot be
ousted except by the application of superior military force.
To that course there are, it seems to me, various formidable
objections. One is, that the resort to military force would be
clearly an act of war however righteous the cause, and would
be beyond the President's constitutional power. Another is,
that to hand over to the Queen's Government a country more
or less devastated, and a people more or less diminished in
number and alienated in feeling by a contest of arms, would
produce a result that would be but a poor substitute for that
peaceful control over an uninjured territory and undecimated
population which the Queen's Government enjoyed at the
time of United States Minister Stevens's lawless intervention
in its affairs.

Still another, and, to my mind, an insuperable, objection is
this. The Stevens Government will not be fought for unless
its adherents are sure of a strong backing, not merely in war-

like force, but in the intelligent public sentiment both of Hawaii and of this country. If such sentiment has grown up and now exists in Hawaii — and we know to how large an extent it prevails in this country — the Administration in undertaking to reinstate the Queen's Government by force of arms would be open to the reproach of sacrificing the interests of the country and its people to the interests of the Queen's Government and of her dynasty. It would not be sufficient to urge that the Queen's Government had been unlawfully deposed by the United States, and that they were merely endeavoring to right that wrong. The answer would be that the Queen and her Government were not the only and first things to be considered; that the paramount objects of our care should be the people of Hawaii and their interests; that we have no right to redeem the original wrong by the commission of another still greater wrong, to wit, the imposition upon Hawaii of a Government not wanted by its people; and that if through their experience of the Stevens Government, or otherwise, the people of Hawaii are now sincerely opposed to any restoration of the Queen's Government, the United States would have no right to insist upon such restoration, but must find some other means of compensating the Queen and all others immediately injured by the unlawful setting up of the Stevens Government.

The above suggestions are not made because serious resistance by arms to anything the United States may do in Hawaii is to be reasonably anticipated. It is wholly unlikely. At the same time it is the unexpected that proverbially happens in politics, and in shaping its present policy, the Administration ought, so far as it can, to take into consideration every contingency however remote. Let it now be assumed that any contest of arms by the Stevens Government is out of the question — the Administration in determining its course upon that theory, cannot, I think, properly lose sight of certain considerations of vital importance. The Stevens Government is the lawful Government of the country and has been and is recognized as such by the United States and by foreign nations. However illegitimate in its origin, it has since governed by the consent of all parties. It follows that its acts, unless shown to be *mala fide*, ought to be recognized as legal to all intents and purposes. It follows that all the officers of that Government, from the highest to the lowest, ought to be exempt from any loss or punishment or from any fear of loss or punishment in consequence of their official actions. In my judgment, the honor of the United States is hardly less concerned in securing justice and fair play for the Stevens Government and its members and adherents, than in the restoring to power of the Queen's constitutional Government. It must ever be remembered that the Stevens Government is our Government; that it was set up by our Minister by the aid of our naval and military forces and was accorded the protection of our flag; and that whatever be the views of this Administration, its predecessor practically sanctioned everything Minister Stevens took upon himself to do. Under such circumstances, to permit the men who were Stevens's instruments in this setting up and carrying on of the Stevens Government, and who undoubtedly acted in good faith and in the sincere belief that Stevens correctly represented his Government, to permit these men to be hung or banished, or despoiled of their estates, or otherwise punished for their connection with the Stevens Government, or to leave them exposed to the risks of any such consequences, would, it seems to me, be grossly unjust and unfair and would deservedly bring the Government of the United States into great discredit both at home and abroad.

The practical conclusions I arrive at from the foregoing are these:

(1) All the resources of diplomacy should be exhausted to restore the *status quo* in Hawaii by peaceful methods and without force.

(2) If, as a last resort, force is found to be necessary — by force I mean an act or course of acts amounting to war — the matter must be submitted to Congress for its action.

(3) In addition to providing for the security of the Queen's person, pending efforts to reinstate the Queen's Government and as a condition of making such efforts, the United States

should require of the Queen, and any other legal representatives of her Government, full power and authority to negotiate and bring about the restoration of her Government on such reasonable terms and conditions as the United States may approve and find to be practicable.

Among such terms and conditions must be, I think, full pardon and amnesty for all connected with the Stevens Government who might otherwise be liable to be visited with the pains and penalties attending the crime of treason.

(4) The negotiations above recommended would, I have no doubt, have a successful issue. It would be understood that the power of the United States was behind them, while there would be and need be no statement nor intimation of the necessity for the intervention of Congress, if it were found necessary to reinforce the negotiations by the use of the war power. The negotiations being in the hands of the United States, and it being known that it would insist upon fair dealing, not merely for the Queen's Government, but for all others concerned, the chief motive for standing out on the part of the adherents of the Stevens Government would be taken away. While in doubt as to the policy of the restored Queen's Government toward them, they would naturally be disinclined to consent to any change in the existing status. That doubt being dispelled and all apprehension of severe or vindictive measures toward them being removed, it is to be anticipated, I think, that they would readily follow the course recommended by the United States.

I trust you will not regard this as an unnecessary intrusion upon your time or an uncalled-for meddling with affairs especially in your care. Neither charge me in your thoughts with imagining that there is anything especially valuable in it or anything that would not readily occur to yourself. I write because of my general interest in the subject and because an expression of opinion from each member of the Cabinet seemed to be invited last Friday. Wishing I had something better to offer, I am

Very truly yours

RICHARD OLNEY

Olney to his daughter, Mrs. G. R. Minot, November 24, 1893. (Extract)

... I note the formation of that club and the subject to be discussed. I hope the members will not come to blows. As a little pabulum and perhaps because you will be a little interested, I enclose a little paper on the subject which I sent to the Secretary of State. It assumes rather than argues that the United States put the Queen off the throne by force and fraud and is directed to the practical question what the United States ought to do on that assumption. I don't know but I will send you also Blount's full report, if I can get a spare copy. ...

Olney to his daughter, Mrs. G. R. Minot, December 3, 1893

DEPARTMENT OF JUSTICE
WASHINGTON, D.C.

MY DEAR AGNES:

This is Sunday and I am not writing at my place of business — as the heading of this paper might indicate, but in my den, 2111 Massachusetts Avenue. Your letter came this morning which has enlisted my interest and my sympathy greatly. I reply at once — to be of any service I can before the next debate comes off. So far as that is concerned, I can do little more than answer your specific questions, because I am ignorant just what phase of the Hawaiian question is up for discussion. If the question is whether the Queen was rightfully dethroned, Blount's report furnishes you all the ammunition you can possibly need, and shows that she was deposed by a mixture of fraud and force to which United States Minister Stevens was a party and brought the aid of the naval and military forces of the United States. A greater outrage upon a weak nation by a strong one could hardly be imagined. If, however, the question is whether, having been wrongfully dethroned by the United States, she can properly be reënthroned by the same power, the matter is a much more complex one. I wrote that letter to Judge Gresham (a copy of which I sent you and which must be strictly *entre nous*) because I thought that, while wholly right as to the wrong done by the United States in the deposition of the Queen, he did not fully realize the practical difficulties that might attend the attempt to restore her. As I like to get what little consolation I can out of my being in my present office, and must get it by realizing that I now and then do a little good, I don't mind saying to you that the letter was timely and I think kept the Administration from making a serious mistake. However that may be — and to come back to our muttons — if the question before your club is what the United States may legitimately do to right the wrong that has been done, theoretically the course is clear — the Queen ought to be put in the same position she was in when Minister Stevens wrongfully intervened and brought about her downfall. While that is theoretically and logically as plain as possible, things may have changed so at Hawaii since the Queen's enforced retirement that to restore the *status in quo* is impracticable. Whether they have so changed or not is the question, and is just what Minister Willis is finding out before he makes any decisive movement. Because of the doubt whether there has been any such change, it is almost impossible to intelligently discuss the question of the United States's present duty in the premises. It may be the wrong done to the Queen and her constitutional Government is irreparable in the sense that the United States cannot put her back on her throne and in quiet possession of her kingdom and of the sympathy and support of her quondam subjects. That is possible — that may be found to be the true condition of things in Hawaii. If it is, then the United States will have to do the next best thing — will have to atone for the injury to the Queen in the most satisfactory manner that can be devised. The thing, if it comes to that, will probably take the form of some pecuniary solatium — just as many other wrongs to private persons, which cannot possibly be specifically redressed, are partially compensated for by pecuniary indemnities.

But the above is pretty rambling and I dare say will do you no good at all. Mr. Blount had served in Congress for a long time and of late years as Chairman of the House Committee on Foreign Relations, and was believed to be much better informed than people in general concerning international matters and the relations of the United States with foreign powers. Moreover, I found on inquiry that he had the reputation of being an able, clear-headed man, of resolute purpose and of absolute integrity. Whatever irresponsible penny-a-liners may say, no one in Washington pretends that his report is not the result of his honest convictions after as thorough and impartial investigation of the facts as he could make. His political foes as well as friends agree on that point. It was for exactly these qualities that the President sent him to Honolulu. The President wanted information — wanted to know exactly what the facts were about this remarkable revolution, the way it was brought about, and the wishes of the people as respects annexation. He believed at the start and believes now that Blount's investigation may be absolutely relied upon, and while Stevens and the Republicans are necessarily sore and worried, and will do all they can to discredit Blount for political purposes, I have yet to see myself the slightest piece of evidence going to show that Blount has made any mistakes or has been deceived. He was sent alone because there was only one man's work to do — namely, to get at and report the facts. Two men, even if honest, would have been in each other's way and would have been less efficient and expeditious than one. And the importance of all reasonable dispatch in the matter is only too obvious. The power of the Provisional Government has been consolidated while that of the Queen's has been correspondingly impaired by this long delay. If the morning after Stevens and his marines took possession and hoisted the American flag at Honolulu, the President could have been on hand and could have known all about the conspiracy, he could and would have put the Queen's Government in power again without the least difficulty, and all the world would have applauded.

But this letter has stretched out to most inordinate length. I shall forgive you if you tell me you haven't read it — indeed, as I look it over and realize how fast I have written and what awful handwriting mine has got to be, I don't believe you can read it and shall hardly credit you if you say you have.

By the way, for subjects for your club, if you really want one, I think you might find the subject of Chinese immigration interesting. If you care to think of it seriously, there is a most interesting and philosophical book I shall send you which for the first time led me to ask whether laws forbidding the Chinese to enter this country were not justifiable. But this must wait till another day. When does your club meet next? I want to hear of the encounter as soon as it is over. If it does not come on right off, and you think of anything — any point — upon which I may be able to give you a little light, don't hesitate to let me know.

With sincere regards to your husband and St. Francis [Mrs. Minot's child] with the game leg, I am as always

Yours

RICHARD OLNEY

Dec. 3d

Many happy returns of the day! Am sorry this is the only souvenir of the occasion you will have [from] me. It comports with my means, though not with my wishes. These will have to go unfulfilled till I get out of office.

APPENDIX IV

VENEZUELAN CORRESPONDENCE, UNPUBLISHED

[THIS appendix consists principally of letters which Olney kept in a personal file and which therefore have not found their way into the State Department's published collections of diplomatic correspondence. The full text of his original Venezuelan dispatch (No. 804, of July 20, 1895), of Lord Salisbury's reply, and of the President's special message about Venezuela may be consulted conveniently in "Foreign Relations of the United States," for 1895, vol. I, pages 542–76.]

Note as to Secretary Bayard's Venezuelan Dispatch of February 17, 1888

The earnest protest about the Venezuelan situation which Secretary Bayard sent to the American Minister in London (Phelps) on February 17, 1888, should not be allowed to occupy a false relation to the record any longer. So far as the present writer is aware, attention has never been drawn to the fact that it was not delivered to the British Foreign Office. The dispatch was printed in the State Department's official volume, "Foreign Relations" for 1888, as if it had been transmitted. Olney seems to have had no misgivings about its delivery when he quoted it in his No. 804.[1] Cleveland dwelt on it in his later history of the Venezuelan affair,[2] but it appears from an unpublished letter in the files of the State Department that when Mr. Phelps received this in London he wrote a letter [3] in which he said: "It seems obvious, therefore, that no further interference with that subject [Venezuela] by our Government would be either useful or consistent with its character, unless it is prepared to espouse and maintain the cause of Venezuela as against Great Britain. This is doubtless far from your intention, however

---

[1] *Foreign Relations*, 1895, Part I, 550.   [2] *Presidential Problems*, 243 *et seq.*
[3] Phelps to Bayard, No. 706, March 28, 1888.

friendly the feeling that happily exists between the Republic
of Venezuela and the United States. . . . Quite concurring in
the propriety of your instruction on this subject, No. 791, of
February 17, 1888, and fully intending to follow it whenever
the opportunity is offered, I do not understand it to go beyond the expression to the Secretary of Foreign Affairs of
the gratification an amicable settlement by arbitration or
otherwise between Great Britain and Venezuela would afford
the United States Government, and its readiness to do anything properly in its power [to] assist [to] that end." Bayard
apparently acquiesced in this without comment. But later,
when he himself was standing in Phelps's shoes and was instructed to deliver the dispatch of July 20, 1895 (No. 804),
he looked the matter up and wrote to Olney (August 9,
1895), saying, "I am not aware, however, that such an opportunity was ever availed of, nor that in any way was the
instruction of the State Department ever communicated to
Her Majesty's Government." [1]

The files of the State Department are so arranged that it is
difficult to examine together all the items of a long-drawn-out
negotiation. Before Secretary Root's time the difficulties
were, it is said, much greater. Phelps's letter might easily
have been overlooked.

The chief interest of Bayard's dispatch thus lies in the
impression which may have been made upon the minds of
Olney and Cleveland by the supposition that it had been
delivered to and ignored by Great Britain. But the importance of even that should not be exaggerated, for it is
clear that they based their policies upon the Venezuelan
situation as a whole rather than upon any single document. (H. J.)

Bayard to Olney

EMBASSY OF THE UNITED STATES

No. 492   LONDON, *August* 9, 1895
                          (*Rec'd Aug.* 19, 1895)

SIR:

. . . On the 1st instant, I had the honor to receive your
further instruction on the same subject (No. 804, dated

[1] See letter which follows.

July 20), and, as supplementary thereto, the Acting Secretary, Mr. Adee's No. 806, dated July 24.

I need not say that this important paper has commanded my instant and careful attention, commensurate with the magnitude of the interests which may be involved, and that, as soon as it was possible, I possessed myself of its contents, had it copied here, and an interview was arranged with the Marquis of Salisbury, who did not return to London until Wednesday, the 7th instant, when, in accordance with notes exchanged between us on the subject, I called upon him at the Foreign Office.

As introductory to the communication, and to impress upon his Lordship the long and steady continuance of effort on the part of the United States to induce a resort to mutual amicable and voluntary arbitration by Great Britain and Venezuela for the ascertainment of their true and just boundary line in Guiana, I recalled an instruction from the then Secretary of State (Mr. Bayard, No. 508, of February 17, 1888) to the then Minister of the United States at London (Mr. Phelps) in which the earnest and friendly advocacy of the United States in favor of "an amicable final and honorable settlement" of the dispute between the contestants was recited, and an expression of the "necessarily grave disquietude" which had been caused to the United States by the sudden unexplained increase of the claims for territory by the authorities of British Guiana.

This instruction had been accompanied by a map of the region in dispute, which had been communicated to the United States by the Venezuelan Representative in Washington.

And the instruction, together with a copy of the map, had been duly published in the volume of the Diplomatic Correspondence of the United States for the year 1888, at page 698, etc.

Upon reviewing the documentary history of the subject, I could find no trace whatever of any reply from Her Majesty's Government, nor any subsequent publication of the reply, to the State Department, by the United States Minister. I did, however, discover, on the files of this Embassy, a dispatch from Mr. Phelps, No. 706, dated March 28, 1888, acknowledging the reception of my No. 791,[1] of February previous, and stating his intention "fully to follow it, whenever the opportunity is offered." I am not aware, however, that such opportunity was ever availed of, nor that in any way was the instruction of the State Department ever communicated to Her Majesty's Government.

There were other questions pending for settlement at that time between Great Britain and the United States, the pressure of which tended somewhat to obscure the Venezuelan-Guiana boundary from instant consideration, and I therefore drew his Lordship's attention to the instruction above referred to, and stated its publication in the regular volume of the State Department's Correspondence for 1888 — of which, of course, a copy is in the Foreign Office.

In reading Mr. Phelps's acknowledgment of my No. 508 of February 17, 1888, you will perceive his uncertainty as to the wisdom or expediency of renewing our recommendations for a settlement by arbitration between the two powers.

I also asked the attention of his Lordship to the reply (his own) of Her Majesty's Government to Mr. Phelps, dated February 22, 1887, in which the declination of the offer of the United States (which had been made in December, 1886) was expressly placed "upon the attitude which General Guzman Blanco has now taken up in regard to the questions at issue, which precludes Her Majesty's Government from submitting these questions *at the present moment* to the arbitration of any third power" (the italics are mine), and the same note contains the statement that an offer to mediate in the questions at issue had been received from another quarter and declined "*on the same grounds.*"

As the grounds of declination in 1887, therefore, had been limited to objections personal to General Guzman Blanco, and "his attitude," and being confined to "the present

---

[1] In 1888 the editor of *Foreign Relations* confused his readers by printing two different serial numbers over the dispatches. Thus Bayard refers to the same document as "my No. 508" and "my No. 791."

moment," I suggested that with the absence of General Guzman Blanco and the lapse of time the grounds for the objections of Her Majesty's Government to consenting to arbitration might be considered as materially diminished or wholly removed.

I then proceeded to communicate the grave instruction with which I was charged, and having fully conveyed it, I placed as directed by you in his Lordship's hands a full and true copy thereof.

At the conclusion of my reading and statement, his Lordship made courteous expression of his thanks, and expressed regret and surprise that it had been considered necessary to present so far-reaching and important a principle and such wide and profound policies of international action in relation to a subject so comparatively small. That to make proper reply to so able and profound an argument, on a subject so important in its relations, would necessarily involve a great deal of labor, and possibly of time, both of which would be certainly bestowed. That he would at once submit the legal propositions thus propounded to the law officers of his Government and have the allegations of fact carefully examined.

He said it was his desire that Great Britain should be perfectly just in the matter, but that arbitration should only apply to cases where there was a real basis of justice and right, and was not demandable for *any* claim that could be set up, for otherwise a nation might be called upon to arbitrate its very existence.

That it was evident the questions raised by the instruction might give rise to a long and difficult discussion and much controversy, but that an answer would be made.

I enclose herewith a copy of a note addressed by me, on the day following this interview, to Lord Salisbury, in which reference is made to the question of official authority attachable to the two publications, the "Statesman's Year-Book" and the "Colonial Office List" which his Lordship stated were published only for the personal profit of individuals and not by Government authority.

I have thus stated the history of the communication of the instruction sent me.

Before closing the interview I dwelt upon the expression of the earnest desire of the President to receive a reply in time to enable him to lay the subject before Congress in his next annual message in December, and I commented upon the importance of keeping such questions in the atmosphere of serene and elevated effort, not merely "to tend to diminish the evils of war, but to extinguish war between nations," and to that end all irritating issues should if possible [be] avoided, and questions possibly containing them should not be thrown into the arena of party strife, and amid fury of excited and uninformed popular discussion — in all of which I understood his Lordship heartily to concur.

> I have the honor to be, Sir
> Your obedient servant
> T. F. BAYARD

Olney to Bayard [1]

November 20, 1895

MY DEAR MR. BAYARD:

...I telegraphed you this day suggesting that, if the answer of Great Britain to the Venezuelan dispatch cannot be given within the time asked in the dispatch, some reason should be expressly assigned by the British Foreign Office and another time fixed when the answer could be looked for. I sent the telegram in the interests of the good relations of the two countries. It certainly would not be regarded as courteous in this country if the British Government should neither answer the dispatch before the assembling of Congress nor give any reason for not answering....

> I am, with sincere regards
> Very truly yours
> RICHARD OLNEY

Olney to Bayard

December 2, 1895

MY DEAR MR. BAYARD:

I have yours of the 23d instant [ultimo] and am greatly obliged for your detailed account of the circumstances

Passages omitted have no bearing on the Venezuelan affair.

which have prevented Lord Salisbury from giving that uninterrupted attention to the Venezuelan question which would have enabled him to forward his views on the subject in time to be considered by the President before sending his annual message to Congress.

The result will be that the President will only briefly allude to the subject and will probably make it the theme of a subsequent special message when Lord Salisbury's letter has been received. Believe me

Sincerely yours

RICHARD OLNEY

Pauncefote to Olney

BRITISH EMBASSY, WASHINGTON
10 *December*, '95

DEAR MR. OLNEY:

Last night I received a telegram from Lord Salisbury to the effect that Her Majesty's Government propose to publish immediately your dispatch to Mr. Bayard of July 20th on the Venezuelan Boundary question and his own two dispatches to me of which I left copies with you on the 6th, and he directs me to ascertain whether there is any objection on the part of your Government to such publication. Would you kindly inform me at what hour I may call at the State Department to receive your answer to that inquiry?

I remain

Yours very truly

JULIAN PAUNCEFOTE

[Olney replied the same day that he was somewhat surprised, and that he would see the Ambassador at three o'clock. (Olney Coll.)]

Bayard to Olney, cipher cablegram, January 13, 1896

Lord Playfair, lately Liberal Cabinet Minister, came confidentially yesterday to my residence, at the request of Lord Salisbury and Secretary of State for Colonies, expressing earnest desire of both political parties here Venezuela dispute should not be allowed to drift, but be promptly settled by friendly coöperation. Suggests as solution, United States should propose Conference with United States of European countries now having colonies in American Hemisphere — Great Britain, France, Spain, Holland — to proclaim the Monroe Doctrine, that European powers having interests in America should not seek to extend their influence in that Hemisphere. If the United States would propose this, Great Britain would accept Monroe Doctrine, and it would become international law between countries named. Assuming from the President's message that any settlement of boundary satisfactory to Venezuela would be unobjectionable to United States, friendly arbitration is suggested. There being no Venezuelan settlements inside Schomburgk line, and no British settlements beyond that line, therefore, irrespective of that line, mutual condition be accepted, that all British and all Venezuelan settlements be excluded from arbitration, but all country between the settlements be settled by a court of arbitration drawing a boundary line, which should be accepted by both countries. Such court of arbitration to consist of two or three commissioners from England, two or three from Venezuela, and two or three from present United States Commission, to represent knowledge they have acquired. Under this principle, districts already settled by Venezuela or British Government or people would not be referred to arbitration, and there would be no difficulty in settling line by friendly arbitration. I will write you fully next Wednesday mail. But desire to express positive judgment that proclaimed recognition of Monroe Doctrine as international law between powers named would make it binding, not only on them, but practically on all other European powers, and would end all contemplated plans of future conquest, or intermeddling alliances, in the Western Hemisphere, by European powers, under any pretext.

BAYARD

Olney to Bayard, cipher cablegram received at the Embassy at
11.30 p.m., January 14, 1896

BAYARD, American Ambassador, London

Suggestions coming through Lord Playfair highly appreciated, and desire for speedy, as well as rightful, adjustment of Venezuelan boundary controversy fully reciprocated. But the United States is content with existing status of Monroe Doctrine, which, as well as its application to said controversy, it regards as completely and satisfactorily accepted by the people of the Western Continents. It does not favor, therefore, proposed conference of powers. Solution it suggests is this: let appropriate clause be added to Behring Sea Convention, or, if deemed wisest, let there be an independent convention, which shall provide for settlement by arbitration of all controversies between the two countries, including Venezuelan boundary, and which, as to that controversy, shall explicitly provide that long-continued occupation of territory by Venezuelans or by British subjects shall, with all the attending circumstances, be considered by tribunal of arbitration, and be given all the weight belonging to it in reason and justice, or by the principles of international law. Tribunal to consist of two members of present American Commission, of two persons chosen by Great Britain, and of a fifth agreed upon by the two Governments, or, in case of failure to agree, nominated by ....

OLNEY

Bayard to Olney

No. 572   EMBASSY OF THE UNITED STATES
Confidential   LONDON, *January* 15, 1896
SIR,

Your cipher telegram replying to mine of January 13th conveying the suggestions in the Venezuelan affair made to me through Lord Playfair, reached London last night at midnight, and now I have the honor to enclose herewith copies (deciphered) of both of the telegrams above referred to.

Having read your telegraphic instruction, I shall not proceed further in submitting my views, which I had commenced to embody in a dispatch to you upon the effect and value of a proclaimed concurrence by European powers having colonial dependencies in the Americas of the "Monroe Doctrine," advanced by the United States, as an accepted rule of international law, not restricted to the Western Hemisphere, but admitted and recognized as world-wide.

During my term of service in the State Department there were suggestions of the possibility of interference in regions proximate to the borders of the United States, which induced some apprehension followed by inquiry on my part, and proved not to be wholly groundless.

The attempted occupation of one of the Caroline Islands as a naval station by the German Government in 1886 led to a serious controversy between that Government and Spain, and the ominous rumor got afloat that, should hostilities ensue between Germany and Spain, a military occupation of the Island of Cuba by Germany would at once take place, and that the Island would then be held until a heavy indemnity should be paid by Spain, which in her financial condition would lead to an indefinite occupation by Germany.

The urgent desire for colonization and expansion of German commerce had led, and is leading, to large subventions by that Government of steamship lines to Paraguay, Brazil, and adjacent regions in South America.

An examination into the history of the Samoan Islands will disclose the movings of the same spirit of commercial greed, and it would not be a difficult task to trace most, if not all, the troubles that have befallen that unhappy distant group of semi-civilized islands to the maleficent disturbance of the natural laws of trade by the artificial forced creation of the beet sugar bounties of Germany, by which the native growth of sugar in Samoa was checked, and the unscrupulous occupation of their lands by a German trading company encouraged and sustained.

It was considerations of this nature that led me to believe it would save trouble to future Administrations of the United States if open public notice to all trespassers could be publicly posted on the *European* side of the Atlantic Ocean.

It is a consummation devoutly to be wished that the results of European diplomacy and wars — and systems of political control, such as we witness here to-day — should not be suffered to attach themselves to the soil of the Western Hemisphere.

I send to your personal address to-day a copy of the "Spectator," in which you will find a leading article on the German Emperor's policy.

I have just telegraphed you, in reply to your suggestion of yesterday's date, of a mode of settlement of all our differences with Great Britain, and inquiring whether Venezuela's consent is to be understood as being embodied in the decision which may be arrived at through the proposed action by the United States.

In the message of the President of December 17th, it is stated very pertinently that "any adjustment of the boundary which Venezuela may deem for her advantage, and may enter into of her own free will, cannot, of course, be objected to by the United States," but in your suggestion of the composition of the tribunal of arbitration of this boundary question (*inter alia*), two Commissioners are to be named by the United States, two by Great Britain, and one other to be chosen by them jointly, so that Venezuela does not appear to have any active participation, nor any voice, in the tribunal of settlement.

In the variance of time by latitude, I shall not receive your reply to my telegram of to-day until the mail of to-day shall have closed, and will therefore be obliged to await another post before I can make further comment.

I continue by this post to transmit to you full extracts from the leading newspapers bearing upon the present relations of the United States to Great Britain in respect of the various questions now under discussion between them.

There has been a welcome and unmistakable difference observable, in the manner in which the possibilities of conflict with the United States — and with Germany — were discussed and treated in this country.

In regard to a possible collision with the United States, amazement, disappointment, genuine distress, and manifest unwillingness to accept such a possibility were chiefly discernible, but as to the German Emperor's interference in the Transvaal, a prompt joinder of issue was tendered, and readiness for contest was almost universally expressed by the general public.

The many expressions to me personally have all been of sorrow that any misunderstanding should have arisen between the two peoples and of earnest desires for complete and friendly settlement of all causes of difference.

I have the honor to be, Sir

Your obedient servant

T. F. Bayard

The Honorable Richard Olney
Secretary of State

Bayard to Olney, cipher cablegram, January 20, 1896

Olney, Secretary, Washington.

Confidential. Had an interview with Lord Playfair this afternoon. Your declination of conference to declare international adhesion to Monroe Doctrine regretted chiefly because Her Majesty's Government anxious to remove finally from public mind in the United States all·belief that they desire to add one foot to their possessions on American soil. Her Majesty's Government is prepared to join United States in general arbitration of all disputed boundaries, including Venezuela, and state positively there are no British settlements or occupation whatever west of supposed Schomburgk line, and no Venezuelan occupation or settlements east of that line, and Venezuelan occupation much more close to that line than British. They submit, as a point of principle, that arbitration should mutually exclude all occupied settlements of either party. Definition of "settlements" to be arranged. They consider Venezuela must be represented in arbitration — but if United States stipulate for Venezuelan concurrence, I believe that would suffice. Precedents for delimitation between Great Britain and Russia and France cited, where exceptional cases were referred to respective Governments, and understanding reached without difficulty.

BAYARD

Bayard to Olney, Extract from No. 581

Confidential   LONDON, *January* 22, 1896

. . . If I comprehend aright the meaning of your instruction of July last, communicated by me to Lord Salisbury, and also of the President's special message of December 17th to the Congress, your insistence upon a submission to arbitration of the line of demarcation between the territories of British Guiana and of Venezuela was caused by your arrival at the opinion that the safety and interests of the United States were endangered by an apparently undefined, unexplained, and ever-progressive extension of British jurisdiction over the region lying eastwardly and northerly of the valley of the River Orinoco.

It may now be assumed that an absolute arrestation of any such expansion is expressly and positively avowed by Her Majesty's Government, coupled with an abandonment, *eo nomine*, of the "Schomburgk," or any other, "line," as a rigid condition precedent, and a willingness to submit the general question of rightful possession and boundary to the arbitrament of an impartial tribunal, coupled with the practical recognition, exclusive from the arbitration, of actual and undisturbed enjoyment and long usage of settled points of occupation, by citizens or subjects of either or both the parties claimant.

In such a state of facts, the difficulties of a practical and satisfactory solution would seem almost to disappear. . . .

Olney to Bayard, cipher cablegram, January 22, 1896

BAYARD, Ambassador, London.

With sincerest purpose to do so, am unable to comprehend the justice or pertinency of the proposition that mere occupation shall be decisive of title. The time, character, and all circumstances attending such occupation must necessarily be considered and must be interpreted and construed according to the principles of private and public law applicable thereto. Nor does the definition of settlements by agreement in advance seem to be feasible. Every one of the numerous elements involved in such definition would be subject of debate and of probable disagreement, while, as Venezuela must be consulted at every step, the inevitable delays would be interminable. As Great Britain desires the controversy should not drift, in which desire the United States heartily concurs, a resort to some form of arbitration which shall cover the real questions involved seems indispensable, since the moment it is agreed upon and the tribunal constituted, the controversy, so far as these two countries is concerned, is at an end.

OLNEY

Olney to Bayard, cipher cablegram

WASHINGTON, *January* 28, 1896

Suggestion to be communicated through Lord Playfair. Let there be new commission — two appointed by United States probably from present American Commission, two appointed by Great Britain, and if the four divide equally upon results, a fifth to be mutually agreed upon or nominated by . . . .

This Commission shall report, not a line, but the facts, to the two Governments which shall thereupon endeavor to fix a line satisfactory to all parties — Venezuela included. The endeavor failing, the facts reported shall be submitted to arbitral tribunal consisting of the Chief Justice of England, the Chief Justice of the United States, and a third arbitrator to be mutually agreed upon or nominated by . . . ., which tribunal shall ascertain and declare such a divisional line as the facts submitted warrant and which line so ascertained and declared shall be accepted by and binding upon all parties in interest — Venezuela included.

OLNEY

G. W. Smalley to Olney

THE ARLINGTON, *January* 31, [1896]

MY DEAR MR. SECRETARY,

Following dispatch just received (3.45 P.M.):

"Ultimate binding arbitration will be accepted provided

VENEZUELAN CORRESPONDENCE   235

that districts which have been *bona-fide* settled say for ten years by either English or Venezuelans were excluded. Note that we make two great concessions, first, practical admission of your right to intervene, second, abandonment of Schomburgk line. No official proposal been received here."

Signed as usual by Buckle. I wait to hear from you before answering, and would suggest it might be well if anything could be said about the sending of your official proposal. Of course if you like I will call.

Yours sincerely

G. W. SMALLEY

Olney to Bayard

Personal and confidential   *February 8,* 1896

DEAR MR. BAYARD:

I have your personal favor of the 29th ultimo and beg to express my thanks for the copy of the Armenian Blue Book which you were kind enough to send for my personal use.

I note your remarks upon the Venezuelan question, "that an amicable settlement on grounds consistent with the self-respect and honor alike of the United States and Great Britain" is unanimously desired in Great Britain. The same desire exists here, probably with the same unanimity. But it is coupled with the strongest conviction that self-respect and honor will not permit the United States to allow British occupation to be conclusive of British title unless it ought to be so in reason, justice, and by the principles of international law. The just effect to be given to such occupation — involving its duration, nature, and all its other characteristics — can be determined by only one of three parties — Great Britain, the United States (with Venezuela), or some impartial arbitral tribunal. As it is repugnant to all ideas of justice to let one party to a controversy lay down the rule for its decision, resort to the arbitral tribunal has always seemed to me, and still seems, inevitable. This suggestion has been met with no alternative that I am aware of except that "settlement" should be defined in advance and as one of the rules of the arbitration. It seemed, and still seems to me, that the attempt at definition would be most difficult, would involve great delays, and would probably prove abortive in the end — leaving the parties more irritated than they are now and the controversy in a more unmanageable shape. It appeared to me, and still appears to me, to be particularly inconsistent with the expressed purpose of the British Government — that the controversy should not "drift." I discern no chance of my being mistaken in this regard unless the British Government is prepared to offer a definition of "settlement" which could be more easily accepted and would be more easily justifiable in reason and on principle and by precedent than I have dared to suppose possible. Do you know what the idea of the Foreign Office on that point is? If so, or if you can find out what it is, I should be glad to be apprised. I should like the information for the information's sake — and, if I could make any use of it in the direction of a speedy adjustment of the Venezuelan question should of course be only too happy to avail myself of it.

With sincere regards, I am

Very truly yours

RICHARD OLNEY

Joseph Chamberlain to Lord Playfair [1]

40, PRINCES GARDENS, S.W.

February 25, 1896

MY DEAR PLAYFAIR, — I now return you, according to your request, the letter from Mr. Bayard of February 23d. I am sorry that I cannot but regard its contents as unsatisfactory.

I think it well at this stage to remind you of the course of our informal negotiations. When I first saw you, I pointed out that the message of the President appeared to place the two countries in direct antagonism, and that accordingly the object of all friends of peace should be to find some third

[1] Reprinted from Sir Wemyss Reid's *Memoirs and Correspondence of Lyon Lord Playfair* (London and New York, 1899), by permission of Messrs. Harper & Brothers.

course which both Governments could accept without going back on their previous declarations. I observed that while successive English Governments had uniformly refused an unlimited arbitration, it might be possible to arrange for an arbitration under conditions which might be acceptable to both parties; and I suggested *inter alia* that if settled districts on both sides of the Schomburgk line were excluded, there would probably be no difficulty in arriving at a boundary to be drawn by a competent tribunal, between the settlements in either country. This suggestion was submitted by you, and on the 17th January a telegram from Mr. Olney was received, which suggested that in the reference to arbitration specific provision should be made that long-continued occupation should be taken into account.

On January 19th I replied that the exclusion of the settled districts was a matter of principle, and that the words, "be taken into account," did not seem to me to be sufficient.

On the 20th January you gave me an account of your interview with Mr. Bayard, in which you reported that he was anxious that in the definition of settlement bogus claims should be excluded; but he stated that he quite understood that the principle of exclusion underlay our proposal.

On the 23d January I suggested five years' *bona-fide* occupation as the definition of a settled district.

On the 29th January you forwarded to me a definite proposal from Mr. Olney, in which, however, no reference was made to settled districts. You stated that you had pointed this out to Mr. Bayard, who said that he believed that the principle was understood and desired. On the same day I replied to you, pointing out that the exclusion of settled districts was stated to be the essence of the arbitration. Mr. Bayard explained that Mr. Olney insisted on *bona-fide* as contrasted with snatch settlements; and you suggested the words "effective occupation" as meeting the case.

This being substantially the history of the negotiation, I am surprised to find that in Mr. Bayard's last letter, of February 23d, he goes back to the original proposal for an open and unconditional arbitration, and ignores the continued insistence by both you and me on the principle of exclusion. To surrender this principle now would be to cut away the ground on which we have sought an amicable compromise, and would stultify the repeated declarations of the British Governments, from Lord Aberdeen to the present day.

As the abstract which I have given of our correspondence shows that this point has from the first been steadily kept before Mr. Olney, I must express my great disappointment that the United States Government should apparently desire to withdraw from the position which I think we both understood they originally accepted. In this case I can only hope that some other compromise may be found in the course of the negotiations, and as I understand that these are now officially in progress, I think no object will be served by continuing the informal discussion, which has unfortunately failed to bring about a complete understanding.

Sincerely appreciating the efforts which you have made, and trusting that although at present they have led to no practical result, they may have had the effect of clearing the ground for further negotiations, I am

Yours very truly

J. CHAMBERLAIN

Olney to Pauncefote

Private and confidential

DEPARTMENT OF STATE
WASHINGTON, D.C., *February* 28, 1896

THE RIGHT HONORABLE
SIR JULIAN PAUNCEFOTE
&c., &c., &c.

MY DEAR MR. AMBASSADOR:

Mr. Bayard wired me as follows yesterday:

"Interview with the Minister for Foreign Affairs who assents practically to commence negotiations Venezuelan boundary at Washington without delay. Will empower British Ambassador at Washington to treat with you. He suggests joint commission equal number American and English to ascertain all the facts and report to the two

Governments — which finding not obligatory, but may enable settlement or become basis for final negotiations."

If the suggestion above stated were to be regarded as final, I should not think it worth while to trouble you with negotiations which could have no result. But I have every reason to believe that the British Foreign Office are looking with favor upon a much more satisfactory solution.

January 28 — through a certain informal channel — I made the following suggestion:

"Let there be new commission — two appointed by the United States, probably from present American Commission, and two appointed by Great Britain, and if the four divide equally upon results a fifth to be mutually agreed upon or nominated by ...... This Commission shall report, not a line, but the facts, to the two Governments, which shall thereupon endeavor to fix a line satisfactory to all parties — Venezuela included. The endeavor failing, the facts reported shall be submitted to an arbitral tribunal consisting of the Chief Justice of England and the Chief Justice of the United States and a third arbitrator to be mutually agreed upon or nominated by ......, which tribunal shall ascertain and declare such a divisional line as the facts submitted warrant and which line so ascertained and declared shall be accepted and binding upon all parties in interest — Venezuela included."

It has been intimated to me informally that the principle of this proposition is acceptable and that there would be no difference about it except as to certain details which have not been specified. I communicate it to you now that you may know what, unless I have been deceived, is the present status of the negotiations from which, as a basis, we may proceed to perfect a positive agreement. It will be well for you to know, I think, all that has taken place formally or informally, and I shall ask you at an early day to give me a little of your time for that purpose.

I am, Mr. Ambassador,
With sincere regards
Your very obedient servant
RICHARD OLNEY

Honorable Henry White to Olney

Private and confidential   HARROGATE, YORKSHIRE

June 17, 1896

MY DEAR MR. OLNEY:

I was obliged, for want of time, to send you last Saturday a somewhat hurried letter stating that I had been informed that a further arbitration proposal has been made in reply to yours, and that this Government had recently assented to the inclusion therein, under certain conditions, of the Venezuelan boundary question. In view of which I thought it best not to urge upon as many people as I had intended, the importance of a prompt settlement of that matter — at all events, until I should hear from you again.

I expressed myself very fully on the subject, however, to Lord Salisbury and Mr. Balfour; also with considerable amplitude to Lord Rothschild. I explained that the inflammable materials which caused the explosion of warlike feeling at the time the President's Venezuelan message was sent to Congress, are quite ready — and will be sure — to break out again, the moment the public becomes aware of any serious hitch in the negotiations; particularly if our Commission should report adversely to the claims of this country and the President should be left with no alternative but to put into execution the threat contained in his message. I also explained that in view of the national feeling on the subject in the United States, no successor of Mr. Cleveland's will be able to modify in any respect the position taken by him, and I added some particulars as to the causes of these warlike tendencies among our people, which I need not repeat to you, who are aware of them.

They all seemed much interested in what I had to say, and neither Lord Salisbury nor Mr. Balfour manifested the slightest feeling of hostility or even irritation against the President or yourself; nor has any one with whom I have spoken done so.

I explained to Lord Salisbury that it would be absolutely impossible for you to give way on the subject of the "settled districts," and he admitted that there is considerable difficulty in defining them. I urged the impossibility of trusting to the accuracy of the statements, as to population, etc., of subordinate British colonial officials on the spot, any more than to those of the local Venezuelan officials, and that however favorable the United States might be to a settlement between Great Britain and Venezuela, it would be impossible to get the latter to assent thereto, as they believe that they will obtain better terms through us. I also touched on the importance of keeping the controversy out of the approaching presidential campaign.

Lord Salisbury replied that he would be glad to settle the question, but that he considers compulsory arbitration in matters affecting territory, without any power of appeal, a dangerous precedent to establish, and from the point of view of the British Empire, his reasons are forcible; viz., that claims to territory might — and probably would — constantly be made by countries having nothing to lose and hopeful of gaining some accession of territory through the submission of such claims to arbitration; that it would be very easy and inexpensive to make such claims, but not at all easy to find an impartial arbitrator, and the result might be that important powers might find themselves deprived, through arbitration, of portions of their territory; arbitrators being usually inclined to favor a weak power.

With a view to guarding against this danger, Lord Salisbury said he had suggested in his reply to your last proposal,[1] the form of appeal referred to in my letter of the 12th, which he hoped might strike you favorably and lead to a settlement of the Venezuela difficulty. I did not ask him particularly as to his views respecting the other points in your last proposal, but I infer that he does not object to your suggestion (to which I alluded) as to the refusal of Parliament or Congress to allow the submission of any particular question, as affecting the honor of either country, to arbitration. I think, had there been anything objectionable in the proposal he would have mentioned it. He also said, among other things, that he should like to avail himself of his conversation with

[1] This refers to the general arbitration negotiation, which was now in progress.

me to correct an impression which he understood had "got up the back" of our Government; viz., that he had insisted upon the immediate publication of his correspondence with you, notwithstanding your objection; of which he had no recollection and he had caused all the telegrams of that period to be carefully examined, but could find no trace of the incident. I told him I had never heard of it.

No reference was made in our conversation to the causes of the delay which has taken place in approaching the settlement of the Venezuela question. I have, however, ascertained from other sources (not within the Cabinet, but none the less trustworthy, I believe) some of those which have operated in that direction.

In the first place, I have good reason to believe that the Government has been advised through American channels, which I have as yet been unable to trace, that, being an eminent lawyer, and not a diplomatist, you are likely to take, in any international difficulty, the extreme view of an advocate anxious to win his case in court, and are more desirous consequently to make out a good legal case in the Venezuelan matter than to settle it; that you are animated, moreover, by feelings of hostility to this country, and if, as seemed probable from some of Smalley's telegrams to the "Times," you had recently appeared anxious to arrive at a settlement, it was merely in order to obtain for the Democratic Party, and for yourself in particular during the approaching presidential campaign, the credit of having compelled this country to give in. I was therefore careful, during my conversation with Lord Salisbury, without making any allusion to this rumor, to say that I had met you several times while in Washington and had never heard a word hostile to Great Britain or to himself fall from your lips; that you had spoken of the Venezuela question in a broad and statesmanlike manner; and that, while I had no authority to speak for you, my impression was that you thought it desirable, in the interest of both countries, that it should be kept out of the presidential campaign by being settled.

Another reason for delay is, I think, the alarm said to have been caused in Canada by the remark in your dispatch to Mr. Bayard as to the inexpediency of "any permanent political union between a European and an American state." Strong representations were made, I understand, to Mr. Chamberlain from that quarter to the effect that, if arbitration were assented to in the matter of Venezuela and territory should thereby be lost to British Guiana, there would be a loss of prestige throughout the Empire and particularly in Canada, where people would begin to feel that we might then turn our attention in that direction and endeavor to appropriate perhaps a portion of the Dominion.

I have no means of ascertaining to what extent these and other causes have operated in favor of delay; but our Ambassador has done nothing to counteract them, if indeed he has ever heard of them. It is not difficult to see, however, that, coupled with the assertion which so many of our countrymen of commercial eminence are constantly making here, to the effect that the Venezuela question is dead, and no one cares or thinks about it now in the United States, the aforesaid causes should have had the effect of not urging the Government to rapidity of action, but rather a contrary tendency.

I do not deem it necessary to add to the length of this letter by reporting my conversations with Mr. Balfour or Lord Rothschild, nor another which I had, at his own request, with Sir William Harcourt, the leader of the Opposition, *who is much interested in the subject, and anxious for a settlement.* The former, I think, quite sees that there are strong reasons for a settlement, but also feels that the question is not only between ourselves and Great Britain, and that the effect of such settlement upon other parts of the Empire must be considered. Both he and Lord Salisbury hope that the last proposal and the inclusion therein of the Venezuela question are an approach to a settlement. I enclose extracts from yesterday's newspapers containing an answer by the Foreign Under-Secretary to a question relative to the settlement of the Venezuela boundary, and that of Lord Salisbury to a

deputation from the Arbitration Society — both of them
hopeful in tone. . . .

Very sincerely yours

HENRY WHITE

P.S. I ought to add that before leaving Lord Salisbury I
turned the conversation to Cuba, and after ascertaining that
he is well aware of the deplorable condition of things in that
Island, I remarked that I had always assumed and stated in
the United States that it would be a matter of indifference to
Great Britain whether we were to annex the Island or not, to
which he at once replied, "It's no affair of ours [England's];
we are friendly to Spain and should be sorry to see her hu-
miliated, but we do not consider that we have anything to
say in the matter whatever may be the course the United
States may decide to pursue." He added that he thought an
independent Cuba would probably turn out to be another
Hayti on an enlarged scale, and that it would be difficult for
us to annex it under our system and difficult to deal with
afterwards.

All that I have herein written [is] *absolutely confidential.* I
should not wish it known — and least of all by the British
Ambassador — that I am in communication with you on
these confidential matters; nor would it be fair to those whom
I have quoted.

Olne) Honorable Henry White

Strictly personal   DEPARTMENT OF STATE
                                                   WASHINGTON, *June* 30, 1896
MY DEAR MR. WHITE:

I have your two favors of the 12th and 17th instant, and
am much indebted to you for them. . . .

The exact situation is this: The Venezuela boundary question and the general arbitration scheme are progressing quite
independently of each other, the Foreign Office having been
distinctly notified that, whatever this Government might be
willing to agree to in the way of a general arbitration plan,
no arbitral convention for the settlement of the Venezuela

boundary dispute could be entered into which did not make the award a finality as respects the entire controversy.

As regards the boundary dispute, the matter stands thus: Lord Salisbury has proposed a commission of four to fix the facts, to be followed by an arbitral tribunal of three to determine the conclusions from those facts — with the express proviso, however, that no territory *bona-fide* occupied by British subjects January 1, 1887, shall be affected. This Government has replied, objecting to the commission on the facts because it might stand two and two, and thus be not only abortive, but mischievous, and objecting to the arbitral tribunal because what are called settled districts are excluded from its jurisdiction.

The general arbitration plan, as proposed by Lord Salisbury, deals with two classes of subjects. No topic belonging to either class is arbitral if either nation concerned conceives and declares it to affect the national honor or integrity. Subject to that qualification, the first class of claims is apparently intended to include all except claims to territory, and, if not excluded from arbitration because the national honor or integrity is implicated, any award made respecting such a claim is to be final. The second class of claims, as above stated, comprises claims to territory. A power deeming itself aggrieved by the arbitral tribunal on such a claim may protest it even if the arbitrators are unanimous. Upon such a protest being made, Lord Salisbury suggested, first, an appellate tribunal consisting of six judges, three from the Supreme Court of each nation, who by a vote of five to one may sustain the award, which, however, failing such a vote in its favor, is to be null and void; second, a tribunal consisting of five judges of the Supreme Court of the protesting country who by a majority vote may set aside the award. This Government, while not assenting to either of the propositions just stated, and pointing out the objections to each of them, has not positively declined to accede to any of them, deeming it to be possible that it may ultimately conclude to acquiesce in some one of them as being better than nothing — as being a step in advance on the road to a satisfactory general arbitration scheme. The last suggestion made by it in this connection is that the award of the original arbitral tribunal shall stand unless the tribunal of review (composed of six judges, as above stated) shall set it aside by a majority vote.

You thus perceive that there is almost a deadlock as respects both the Venezuela boundary dispute and the. general arbitration scheme — it perhaps being more pronounced in the former case than in the latter.

I note that you will sail for this country some time between the 15th and 20th of next month. I regret it because there are soon to be developments which may make important changes in the situation. I should have been glad to hear from you whether they did or not, and what was their real significance. In the first place, the correspondence both as respects the boundary dispute and as respects the general arbitration scheme will soon be made public by being laid before Parliament. In the second place, an introduction to and summary of the Venezuela brief on the boundary question is ready to be published, and, if it is deemed expedient to do so, will be published within a few days. This brief, as I think I may have informed you, is being prepared by Mr. Storrow, of Boston, one of the most eminent lawyers in the country. It is very able, and I think will give the English people some idea of the strength of the case against the British claim. It is in the nature of a reply to the British Blue Book, which so far has had the field to itself, and I suppose has been considered by the British public generally as unanswerable. The inclination of my judgment is that the brief should be published, although I perceive that there are two sides to the question of what its effect may be. Instead of decreasing the chances of arbitration upon the boundary dispute, it may, by showing the defects in the British case, disincline the Government to resort to arbitration.

This letter is already too long, although there are many things in your interesting note upon which I should like to comment. I observe that you are to be at Newport this summer, and I count very much upon the opportunity of seeing you and having a full talk upon the situation in all its aspects. Of course everything that you have written me or choose to write me will be regarded as communicated in the strictest confidence. You will also, of course, regard what I now write you or may hereafter write you in the same light.

Trusting that Mrs. White will soon recover her usual condition of good health, and with the sincerest regards, I am,

Very truly yours

RICHARD OLNEY

To HONORABLE HENRY WHITE
9 Grosvenor Crescent
London, England

[To the foregoing letters the following from John Hay may well be added. It should be remarked, incidentally, that an article by A. Maurice Low in "McClure's" for July, 1900, erroneously pictures Hay as Olney's agent in London. Olney's letter-files show that neither he nor Hay was in any wise responsible for Mr. Low's erroneous representation.]

John Hay to Olney

R.M.S. TEUTONIC, *July* 31, 1896

DEAR MR. OLNEY:

The day before I left London I had a long and very interesting conversation with Sir William Harcourt on Venezuela, which followed, and was the result of, one I had had the day previous with James Bryce. In neither case did I seek the interview — and in neither case, I hope I need not say, did I assume any representative character, or any means of information not open to everybody. Sir William Harcourt spoke unreservedly, as the leader of the Opposition — and though nothing was said as to my repeating the conversation, I felt as if I ought confidentially to let you know one thing he said.

He expressed his gratification at the improved tone of the negotiations between the two countries, and said that you were perfectly right in your claim as to "settled districts"; that in an action for ejectment it was no defense that a wrongful occupier had built a house on his neighbor's land; that he had already let the Government know his views in the matter; that he had not wished to embarrass them by a public discussion while negotiations were in progress, but that he was using all proper means of pressure to induce them to come to an agreement with us at the earliest possible moment. He then asked my opinion as to the presidential canvass. I told him I thought McKinley would be elected. He asked what effect this would have on the negotiations, if they were not completed before next March. (It has been intimated that Lord Salisbury desired delay in the hope that the next Administration may be less exacting in its contention than the present.) I told him I thought any such calculation would be a great mistake; that the public sentiment of the United States was virtually unanimous in the support of the Administration's action in this question; that no steps backward would be taken by McKinley, and that only omniscience could guess what Bryan would do, if he got in.

He was anxious that I should let Mr. Chamberlain and Mr. Curzon know this view, and I accordingly conveyed to both of them, before I sailed, my impression that time was an element of considerable importance in the matter.

From what I have been able to gather in conversation I infer that most of the leading men are convinced that Lord Salisbury's tone a year ago was a mistake, and that our attitude is, on the whole, reasonable. Everybody wants the matter settled if it can be done without damage to the pride and prestige of England. Chamberlain seems afraid of making a precedent which may be injurious hereafter in Canada — and they all dread arbitration since Geneva.

I beg you will not think I have been meddling in what does not concern me. I said little or nothing myself, but the things that were said to me were so interesting that I thought I ought to communicate a word or two of them to you.

Please let me know this has reached you. My address is "Newbury, New Hampshire."

Yours faithfully

JOHN HAY

[At the time the following letter was written Cleveland was preparing the lecture on "The Venezuelan Boundary Controversy" which he subsequently included in "Presidential Problems." (The Century Company, 1904.)

Olney to Cleveland

BOSTON, 6 *March*, 1901

MY DEAR MR. CLEVELAND:

... I note your inquiry about the Venezuelan boundary arbitration affair. So much of the negotiation took place in the course of personal interviews between Sir Julian and myself that I cannot always easily recall the order of events. In general, the matter lies in my mind in this way: The term "settlements" was first used in Lord Salisbury's letter of November 26, 1895, toward the close of which he spoke of the gradual spread over the country of "British settlements," and intimated that under no circumstances would Great Britain submit to arbitration any claim which would affect them. After your special message to Congress, the first attempts at negotiation were between Mr. Chamberlain and Lord Playfair, on the one side, and Mr. Bayard on the other. One suggestion of Mr. Bayard's, you will remember, was that the United States should call a general conference of the great European powers over the Monroe Doctrine. It did not take us long to sit on that proposition. Pretty soon I found Mr. Chamberlain writing Mr. Bayard to the effect that he, Bayard — presumably acting for me — had committed the United States to the suggestion that there could be an arbitration of the boundary which should be exclusive of what was called "British settlements." That led to a note to Mr. Bayard stating quite emphatically that the United States would not consent to anything of the sort and instructing him to bring the communication to the notice of Mr. Chamberlain. Mr. Chamberlain thereupon withdrew from the whole affair, declaring, as I recollect with some positiveness, that it was idle to expect any results from negotiations through those channels. About the same time we concluded that negotiations had better be transferred to Washington —

to which suggestion Lord Salisbury acceded with cheerfulness — saying to Sir Julian, as Sir Julian confided to me confidentially, that now that the amateur diplomats had got through, perhaps serious negotiations could be set on foot. During the Playfair-Chamberlain-Bayard negotiations I had more than once, I think, asked Mr. Bayard to call for a definition of "British settlements," and, as you will see in one of Lord Salisbury's letters, he promises to furnish such a definition. It was in fact never given. After the transfer of negotiations to Washington, they went on continuously and almost daily between Sir Julian and myself, but almost always at personal interviews. The insuperable obstacle to progress, however, was the attitude of Great Britain as to "British settlements." Early in March, 1896, Lord Salisbury made a little diversion from the particular matter in dispute by entering upon the subject of a general arbitration treaty between Great Britain and the United States. I followed the lead and took up the subject. But after several letters had passed on this subject, I took occasion to say, as you will see by my letter of June 12th to Sir Julian, that the United States would not include the Venezuelan boundary dispute within the scope of such a general arbitration treaty as was then under discussion. I had been all along taking the same line with Sir Julian, intimating that the Venezuelan boundary question must be settled by an arbitration which would be final, and that the United States had taken its position on that particular subject, and would not depart from it. The result was that under date of May 22, 1896, Lord Salisbury wrote Sir Julian for *the first time* — perhaps this answers your special inquiry — *making* a definite suggestion as to the substance and form of a treaty for the adjustment of the Venezuelan boundary dispute. Sir Julian sent Lord Salisbury's letter to me in a note dated June 3, 1896. Some other correspondence followed — notably my letter of July 13th, in which I asked if Great Britain would submit to unrestricted arbitration the whole of the disputed territory, provided it were a rule of the arbitration that territory which had been in the exclusive, notorious, and actual use and occupation of either party for sixty years should be held to belong to such party. Later on that suggestion was accepted by Lord Salisbury as offering a solution of what had up to that time been an insuperable objection to the proposed arbitration. The summer vacation intervened and when Sir Julian and myself got back to Washington in the fall we went at the matter again in the most diligent and vigorous fashion — with the result announced, as you will recollect, by Lord Salisbury in his Guild-Hall speech early in November, in which he compared the American suggestion to Columbus's mode of showing how to make an egg stand on end.

The above is more of a dose than you have a right to expect from the simple inquiry contained in your note. I am going to let it stand, however, because it is possible it may recall or suggest something you would like to ask about or to which you would like to refer in your proposed addresses.

Further, the above is dictated from general recollection merely. If any special date or fact is called in question, I should want to verify any statement by reference to documents or papers before guarantying its exact accuracy....

I am

Very sincerely yours

RICHARD OLNEY

Heads of Proposed Treaty between Venezuela and Great Britain for Settlement of Venezuela Boundary Question, as agreed upon between Great Britain and the United States [1]

I

An arbitral tribunal shall be immediately appointed to determine the boundary line between the colony of British Guiana and the Republic of Venezuela.

II

The tribunal shall consist of two members nominated by the judges of the Supreme Court of the United States and

[1] From *Foreign Relations of the United States*, 1896, p. 254.

two members nominated by the judges of the British supreme court of justice, and of a fifth juror selected by the four persons so nominated, or, in the event of their failure to agree within three months from the time of their nomination, selected by His Majesty the King of Sweden and Norway.

The person so selected shall be president of the tribunal.

The persons nominated by the judges of the Supreme Court of the United States and of the British supreme court of justice, respectively, may be judges of either of said courts.

III

The tribunal shall investigate and ascertain the extent of the territories belonging to or that might lawfully be claimed by the United Netherlands or by the Kingdom of Spain, respectively, at the time of the acquisition by Great Britain of the colony of British Guiana, and shall determine the boundary line between the colony of British Guiana and the Republic of Venezuela.

IV

In deciding the matters submitted the arbitrators shall ascertain all the facts which they deem necessary to a decision of the controversy and shall be governed by the following rules, which are agreed upon by the high contracting parties as rules to be taken as applicable to the case, and by such principles of international law not inconsistent therewith as the arbitrators shall determine to be applicable to the case.

RULES

(a) Adverse holding or prescription during a period of fifty years shall make a good title. The arbitrators may deem exclusive political control of a district, as well as actual settlement thereof, sufficient to constitute adverse holding or to make title by prescription.

(b) The arbitrators may recognize and give effect to rights and claims resting on any other ground whatever, valid according to international law, and on any principles of international law which the arbitrators may deem to be applicable to the case and which are not in contravention of the foregoing rule.

(c) In determining the boundary line, if territory of one party be found by the tribunal to have been at the date of this treaty in the occupation of the subjects or citizens of the other party, such effect shall be given to such occupation as reason, justice, the principles of international law, and the equities of the case shall, in the opinion of the tribunal, require.

RICHARD OLNEY

JULIAN PAUNCEFOTE

November 12, 1896

[Note. A treaty for the settlement of the Venezuela-British Guiana boundary controversy was signed at Washington on February 2, 1897, by Sir Julian Pauncefote, on the part of Great Britain, and by Señor Don José Andrade, on the part of Venezuela.]

APPENDIX V

INTERNATIONAL ARBITRATION

[IN the text the diplomatic correspondence which led up to the Olney-Pauncefote treaty of general arbitration was necessarily summarized very briefly. Accordingly the principal documents are here given in full (from "Foreign Relations of the United States," 1896, pages 222–40), the main clauses of the treaty being included. The text will have reminded the reader that these official notes were accompanied by much informal discussion between the Secretary of State and the British Ambassador. See, also, several references to the general arbitration negotiations in the exchange of letters between Olney and Mr. Henry White and in Olney's letter of March 6, 1901, to Cleveland which have been placed in Appendix IV.

In this appendix is also included a paper which Olney wrote for the American Society of International Law entitled "General Arbitration Treaties." Few Americans have expressed themselves on this important subject with an authority comparable to Olney's.]

CORRESPONDENCE BETWEEN THE UNITED STATES AND
GREAT BRITAIN

Salisbury to Pauncefote

No. 65   FOREIGN OFFICE, *March 5,* 1896

SIR: In the spring of last year communications were exchanged between your Excellency and the late Mr. Gresham upon the establishment of a system of international arbitration for the adjustment of disputes between the two Governments. Circumstances, to which it is unnecessary to refer, prevented the further consideration of the question at that time.

But it has again been brought into prominence by the

controversy which has arisen upon the Venezuelan boundary. Without touching upon the matters raised by that dispute, it appears to me that the occasion is favorable for renewing the general discussion upon a subject in which both nations feel a strong interest, without having been able up to this time to arrive at a common ground of agreement. The obstacle which has separated them has been the difficulty of deciding how far the undertaking to refer all matters in dispute is to be carried. On both sides it is admitted that some exceptions must be made. Neither Government is willing to accept arbitration upon issues in which the national honor or integrity is involved. But in the wide region that lies within this boundary the United States desire to go further than Great Britain.

For the view entertained by Her Majesty's Government there is this consideration to be pleaded, that a system of arbitration is an entirely novel arrangement, and, therefore, the conditions under which it should be adopted are not likely to be ascertained antecedently. The limits ultimately adopted must be determined by experiment. In the interests of the idea, and of the pacific results which are expected from it, it would be wise to commence with a modest beginning, and not to hazard the success of the principle by adventuring it upon doubtful ground. The suggestion in the heads of treaty which I have enclosed to your Excellency will give an opportunity for observing more closely the working of the machinery, leaving it entirely open to the contracting parties, upon favorable experience, to extend its application further, and to bring under its action controversies to which for the present it can only be applied in a tentative manner and to a limited extent.

Cases that arise between states belong to one of two classes. They may be private disputes in respect to which the state is representing its own subjects as individuals, or they may be issues which concern the state itself considered as a whole. A claim for an indemnity or for damages belongs generally to the first class; a claim to territory or sovereign rights belongs to the second. For the first class of differences the suitability of international arbitration may be admitted without reserve. It is exactly analogous to private arbitration, and there is no objection to the one that would not apply equally to the other. There is nothing in cases of this class which would make it difficult to find capable and impartial arbitrators. But the other class of disputes stands on a different footing. They concern the state in its collective capacity, and all the members of each state and all other states who wish it well are interested in the issue of the litigation. If the matter in controversy is important, so that defeat is a serious blow to the credit or the power of the litigant who is worsted, that interest becomes a more or less keen partisanship. According to their sympathies, men wish for the victory of one side or another.

Such conflicting sympathies interfere most formidably with the choice of an impartial arbitrator. It would be too invidious to specify the various forms of bias by which, in any important controversy between two great powers, the other members of the commonwealth of nations are visibly affected. In the existing condition of international sentiment each great power could point to nations whose admission to any jury by whom its interests were to be tried it would be bound to challenge; and in a litigation between two great powers the rival challenges would pretty well exhaust the catalogue of the nations from whom competent and suitable arbiters could be drawn. It would be easy, but scarcely decorous, to illustrate this statement by examples. They will occur to any one's mind who attempts to construct a panel of nations capable of providing competent arbitrators, and will consider how many of them would command equal confidence from any two litigating powers.

This is the difficulty which stands in the way of unrestricted arbitration. By whatever plan the tribunal is selected, the end of it must be that issues in which the litigant states are most deeply interested will be decided by the vote of one man, and that man a foreigner. He has no jury to find his facts; he has no court of appeal to correct his law; and he is sure to be credited, justly or not, with a leaning to one litigant or the other. Nations cannot afford to run such a risk in deciding controversies by which their national position may be affected or a number of their fellow subjects transferred to a foreign rule.

The plan which is suggested in the appended draft treaty would give a court of appeal from the single voice of the foreign judge. It would not be competent for it to alter or reverse the umpire's decision, but, if his judgment were not confirmed by the stipulated majority, it would not stand. The court would possess the highest guaranty for impartiality which a court belonging to the two litigating nations could possess. Its operation in arresting a faulty or doubtful judgment would make it possible to refer great issues to arbitration without the risk of a disastrous miscarriage of justice.

I am aware that to the warmer advocates of arbitration this plan will seem unsatisfying and imperfect. But I believe that it offers an opportunity of making a substantial advance, which a more ambitious arrangement would be unable to secure; and if, under its operation, experience should teach us that our apprehensions as to the danger of reposing an unlimited confidence in this kind of tribunal are unfounded, it will be easy, by dropping precautions that will have become unnecessary, to accept and establish the idea of arbitration in its most developed form.

I beg that you will read this dispatch and the appended draft treaty to the Secretary of State and leave him a copy if he desires it.

[Enclosure]
Heads of a treaty for arbitration in certain cases

1. Her Britannic Majesty and the President of the United States shall each appoint two or more permanent judicial officers for the purposes of this treaty; and on the appearance of any difference between the two powers, which, in the judgment of either of them, cannot be settled by negotiation, each of them shall designate one of the said officers as arbitrator; and the two arbitrators shall hear and determine any matter referred to them in accordance with this treaty.

2. Before entering on such arbitration the arbitrators shall select an umpire, by whom any question upon which they disagree, whether inter-

locutory or final, shall be decided. The decision of such umpire upon any interlocutory question shall be binding upon the arbitrators. The determination of the arbitrators, or, if they disagree, the decision of the umpire, shall be the award upon the matters referred.

3. Complaints made by the nationals of one power against the officers of the other; all pecuniary claims or groups of claims, amounting to not more than £100,000, made on either power by the nationals of the other, whether based on an alleged right by treaty or agreement or otherwise; all claims for damages or indemnity under the said amount; all questions affecting diplomatic or consular privileges; all alleged rights of fishery, access, navigation, or commercial privilege, and all questions referred by special agreement between the two parties shall be referred to arbitration in accordance with this treaty, and the award thereon shall be final.

4. Any difference in respect to a question of fact, or of international law, involving the territory, territorial rights, sovereignty, or jurisdiction of either power, or any pecuniary claim or group of claims of any kind, involving a sum larger than £100,000, shall be referred to arbitration under this treaty. But if in any such case, within three months after the award has been reported, either power protests that such award is erroneous in respect to some issue of fact, or some issue of international law, the award shall be reviewed by a court composed of three of the judges of the Supreme Court of Great Britain and three of the judges of the Supreme Court of the United States; and if the said court shall determine, after hearing the case, by a majority of not less than five to one, that the said issue has been rightly determined, the award shall stand and be final; but in default of such determination it shall not be valid. If no protest is entered by either power against the award within the time limited, it shall be final.

5. Any difference which, in the judgment of either power, materially affects its honor or the integrity of its territory, shall not be referred to arbitration under this treaty except by special agreement.

6. Any difference whatever, by agreement between the two powers, may be referred for decision by arbitration, as herein provided, with the stipulation that, unless accepted by both powers, the decision shall not be valid.

The time and place of their meeting, and all arrangements for the hearing, and all questions of procedure, shall be decided by the arbitrators or by the umpire, if need be.

Olney to Pauncefote

No. 365

DEPARTMENT OF STATE
WASHINGTON, *April* 11, 1896

EXCELLENCY: I have the honor to acknowledge the receipt at your hands of the copy of Lord Salisbury's dispatch of March 5, 1896. His Lordship, after recurring to the negotiations of last year between himself and the late Secretary Gresham for the establishment of a general system of arbitration of disputes between the two Governments, and after in terms excluding from consideration the Venezuelan boundary dispute, expresses the opinion that the time is favorable for renewing discussion upon the subject. He thereupon proceeds to make a most interesting contribution to such discussion, which he concludes by submitting the draft of a proposed treaty, a copy of which, for convenience of reference, is annexed to this communication.

It is proper to state at the outset that these proposals of Her Majesty's Prime Minister are welcomed by the President with the keenest appreciation of their value and of the enlightened and progressive spirit which animates them. So far as they manifest a desire that the two great English-speaking peoples of the world shall remain in perpetual peace, he fully reciprocates that desire on behalf of the Government and people of the United States. To himself personally nothing could bring greater satisfaction than to be instrumental in the accomplishment of an end so beneficent.

If Lord Salisbury's draft had stopped with article 3, no criticism could have been made either of the arbitral machinery provided or of the arbitral subjects enumerated, except that the latter seem to be so cautiously restricted as hardly to cover other than controversies which, as between civilized states, could almost never endanger their peaceful relations. But article 3, as well as article 4, is apparently qualified by the provisions of article 5, since the national honor may sometimes be involved even in a claim for indemnity to an individual. Further, the arbitral machinery provided by article 4 is open to serious objection as not securing an end of the controversy unless an award is concurred in by at least five out of the six appellate arbiters. In calling attention to these features of the scheme as largely restricting its value, I am directed by the President to propose as a substitute for articles 4 and 5 the following:

IV. Arbitration under this treaty shall also be obligatory in respect of all questions now pending or hereafter arising involving territorial rights, boundaries, sovereignty, or jurisdiction, or any pecuniary claim or group of claims aggregating a sum larger than £100,000, and in respect of all controversies not in this treaty specially described: *Provided, however,* That either the Congress of the United States, on the one hand, or the Parliament of Great Britain, on the other, at any time before the arbitral tribunal shall have convened for the consideration of any particular subject-matter, may by act or resolution declaring such particular subject-matter to involve the national honor or integrity, withdraw the same from the operation of this treaty: *And provided further,* That if a controversy shall arise when either the Congress of the United States or the Parliament of Great Britain shall not be in session, and such controversy shall be deemed by Her Britannic Majesty's Government or by that of the United States, acting through the President, to be of such nature that the international honor or integrity may be involved, such difference or controversy shall not be submitted to arbitration under this treaty until the Congress and the Parliament shall have had opportunity to take action thereon.

In the case of controversies provided for by this article, the award shall be final if concurred in by all the arbitrators. If assented to by a majority only, the award shall be final unless one of the parties, within three months from its promulgation, shall protest in writing to the other that the award is erroneous in respect of some issue of fact or of law. In every such case, the award shall be reviewed by a court composed of three of the judges of the Supreme Court of Great Britain and three of the judges of the Supreme Court of the United States, who, before entering upon their duties, shall agree upon three learned and impartial jurists to be added to said court in case they shall be equally divided upon the award to be made. To said court there shall be submitted a record in full of all the proceedings of the original arbitral tribunal, which record, as part thereof, shall include the evidence adduced to such tribunal. Thereupon the said court shall proceed to consider said award upon said record, and may either affirm the same or make such other award as the principles of law applicable to the facts appearing by said record shall warrant and require; and the award so affirmed or so rendered by said court, whether unanimously or by a majority vote, shall be final. If, however, the court shall be equally divided upon the subject of the award to be made, the three jurists agreed upon as hereinbefore provided shall be added to the said court; and the award of the court so constituted, whether rendered unanimously or by a majority vote, shall be final.

The considerations which, in the opinion of the President, render the foregoing amendments of Lord Salisbury's scheme most desirable and perhaps indispensable may be briefly stated:

1. The scheme, as thus amended, makes all disputes *prima facie* arbitrable.

Each, as it may arise, will go before the arbitral tribunal unless affirmative action by the Congress or by the Parliament displaces the jurisdiction.

2. The scheme, as amended, puts where they belong the right and power to decide whether an international claim is of such nature and importance as not to be arbitrable, and as to demand assertion, if need be, by force of arms.

The Administration in authority when a serious international controversy arises must, in the nature of things, be often exposed to influences not wholly favorable to an impartial consideration of the nature of that controversy.

It may always be more or less controlled by personal predilections and prejudices inherent in the controversy or arising in its progress, while considerations connected with party success or failure are factors not likely to be wholly eliminated in determining upon a particular course of action.

It is liable to decide in haste — to view the honor of the country as not distinguishable from the good of its party — and to act without the advantage of a full discussion of the subject in all its aspects by party opponents as well as by party friends.

On the other hand, if the issue between war and arbitration be left to the supreme legislative tribunal of the country — to Congress on the one hand or Parliament on the other — there will be ample time for deliberation and for full investigation and debate of the subject in all its bearings, while it is in the face of such an issue and of all its responsibilities that mere party interests are most likely to be subordinated to those of the country at large.

A more conclusive consideration in this connection, however, remains to be stated. It is that, if war and not arbitration is to be evoked in settlement of an international controversy, the direct representatives of the people, at whose cost and suffering the war must be carried on, should properly be charged with the responsibility of making it.

3. The scheme, as amended, changes the arbitration

machinery provided by article 4 of Lord Salisbury's draft in important particulars.

In the first place, the award of the original tribunal of arbitration, if the arbiters are unanimous, is to be final, and the appellate tribunal is to give its decision in view of the record and proceedings (including any evidence adduced) of such original tribunal. It is hardly consistent with any reasonable theory of arbitration that an award concurred in by the arbiter of the defeated country should be appealable by that country. It is obvious, too, that the parties may properly be required to present all their facts and evidence to the original tribunal. Otherwise, and if the award is appealable in any event, the original tribunal might as well be dispensed with, since each party will be sure to make its real contest before the appellate tribunal alone.

In the second place, by the scheme as amended, an award is the result of each arbitration, so that the controversy is finally ended. Under the draft as proposed, on the other hand, there will be an award only in the rare cases in which the six appellate arbiters favor it, either unanimously or by a majority of five to one. Such an arrangement, it is believed, would be dangerous and rather mischievous than salutary in its operation. In all the cases in which the arbitrators were equally divided, or stood four to two, public feeling in each country would have been aroused by the protracted discussions and proceedings, and the chances of a peaceful outcome would be rather prejudiced than promoted. That would be the almost certain result in cases in which the arbiters stood four to two, and in which one judge of the highest court of his country had found himself compelled to give his vote in favor of the other country.

It is a possibility to be noted that the party defeated and disappointed by the award of the original tribunal, in a case where the stake is large and the public feeling intense, might find itself under irresistible temptation to make all subsequent proceedings purely farcical by making sure, before their selection, of the sentiments of two at least of the appellate arbiters.

It is submitted that precaution becomes excessive when the entire arbitration proceedings are made abortive unless the tribunal of six judges reaches an award by a majority of at least five to one. If they stand four to two — which means that at least one judge of the highest court of his country believes that country's claim to be ill founded — it is hardly reasonable to insist that the result should not be accepted and made effective.

It is believed, also, that there can be no arbitration, in the true sense, without a final award, and that it may be better to leave controversies to the usual modes of settlement than to enter upon proceedings which are arbitral only in name and which are likely to have no other result than to excite and exasperate public feeling in both countries.

It is objected by Lord Salisbury that to insist upon the finality of an award upon the controversies described in article 4 is to enable a single foreign jurist to decide matters of great international consequence.

But under article 4 as amended, the members added to the appellate tribunal need not be foreigners, and if foreigners and they control the result, it must be by the votes of at least two of them.

It may be pointed out, too, that if bias on the part of foreign jurists is feared, the United States, being without alliances with any of the countries of Europe, is certainly not the party to expect any advantage from that source. Great Britain could at least not fail to know in what quarters friendliness or unfriendliness might be looked for.

It is believed that the risks anticipated from the powers given to a foreign jurist as arbiter or umpire under article 4 as amended, if not purely imaginary, may be easily exaggerated. Before the foreign jurist could act, the questions in dispute would have been thoroughly canvassed and decided, once at least, and perhaps twice; so that the risks in question may fairly be regarded as reduced to a minimum.

Finally, to insist upon an arbitration scheme so constructed that miscarriages of justice can never occur is to insist upon the unattainable, and is equivalent to a relinquishment altogether of the effort in behalf of a general system of international arbitration. An approximation to truth — results which, on the average and in the long run, conform to right and justice — is all that the "lot of humanity" permits us to expect from any plan. Not to surround an arbitration plan with all reasonably practicable safeguards against failures of justice would undoubtedly be the height of unwisdom. But beyond that human skill and intelligence are without avail, while for actual results dependence must be placed upon the patient hearing and deliberate decision of a tribunal whose proceedings will attract the close attention and careful scrutiny of the civilized world. It may be conceded that a general arbitration scheme not perfected through repeated arbitration experiments entails the risks of erroneous awards. But in this, as in human affairs generally, there is but a choice between evils, and the non-existence of any arbitration scheme entails the far greater risks of controversies which should be arbitrated being settled by the sword. It would seem to be the part of wisdom, therefore, to establish the principle of general arbitration, even at the risk of the development of defects in the scheme originally adopted. The affirmation of the principle would of itself tend to greatly diminish the chances of a resort to war, while the imperfections of the scheme as disclosed by its actual working would be remediable at any time by the consent of the parties. That they would be so remedied, in fact, it is difficult not to believe, since a principle of such great value being once established, it is wholly unlikely that both parties would not desire to perpetuate its operation, and would not therefore be prepared to consent to reasonable changes in the necessary machinery. It would tend to insure such consent if the treaty were made terminable after a short term of years on notice by either party.

It only remains to observe that if article 4 as amended should prove acceptable, no reason is perceived why the pending Venezuelan boundary dispute should not be brought within the treaty by express words of inclusion. If, however, no treaty for general arbitration can be now expected, it cannot be improper to add that the Venezuelan boundary dispute seems to offer a good opportunity for one of those tentative experiments at arbitration which, as Lord Salisbury justly intimates, would be of decided advantage as tending to indicate the lines upon which a scheme for general arbitration can be judiciously drawn.

Begging that this communication — copy of which is enclosed for that purpose — may be brought to Lord Salisbury's attention at your earliest convenience, I avail myself of this opportunity to renew, etc.,

RICHARD OLNEY

Salisbury to Pauncefote

No. 128   FOREIGN OFFICE, *May* 18, 1896

SIR: I have to acknowledge your Excellency's dispatch on the 13th ultimo, enclosing a note from Mr. Olney in reply to the proposals made by Her Majesty's Government for a general treaty of arbitration.

Her Majesty's advisers have received Mr. Olney's dispatch with great satisfaction, in that it testifies clearly to the earnest desire which animates the Government of the United States to make effective provision for removing all differences of opinion which can arise between the two nations. They regret that in some essential particulars the opinions of the two Governments do not as yet seem to be sufficiently in accord to enable them to come to a definitive agreement upon the whole of this important subject. It appears to them, however, that there are some considerations bearing upon this matter to which the attention of the Government of the United States should be more particularly invited before the attempt to arrive at a general understanding ought to be laid aside.

I would say, in the first place, that Mr. Olney somewhat mistakes my meaning when he says that, in raising this question, I "in terms excluded the consideration of the Venezuelan boundary dispute." I wished to state our views upon the question of general arbitration without touching upon certain points in relation to which the two questions do not cover the same field. But I was well aware that any settlement to which we might arrive must, in its general principles, be applicable to disputes not only between Great Britain and the United States but between either of them and any other Government; and, therefore, with certain adaptations of detail, it would apply to a dispute between Great Britain and Venezuela. In this view I am glad to observe that I am at one with Mr. Olney, because I hold that, in discussing the safeguards by which a general system of arbitration should be sanctioned, it is important to bear in mind that any system adopted between our two nations ought to be such as can in principle be applied, if necessary, to their relations with other civilized countries.

Mr. Olney is satisfied with the provisions of Article III of my proposals and the plan of arbitration which it contains. The only fault he finds with them is that they are too limited in their application. He thinks that they "hardly cover other than controversies which as between civilized States could almost never endanger their peaceful relations." It is possible that the language of the article may be modified with advantage. It certainly was not intended to apply only to controversies of a practically unimportant character. The discussions which arise out of disputed claims to territory, which are dealt with in Article IV, are, or may be, much graver, as well as much more difficult to decide. But it would not, I think, be difficult to show by a consideration of the history of the present century that controversies which have issued in warlike action have not arisen exclusively or even mainly from disputed questions of territorial ownership.

To examine the individual instances would involve a somewhat lengthy investigation, which is not necessary now. It is more material on the present occasion to dwell upon the encouraging fact that Her Majesty's Government and the Government of the United States are entirely agreed in approving the language of article No. 3 and the policy it is designed to sanction. Under these circumstances it appears to me to be a matter for regret that the two Governments should now neglect the opportunity of embodying their common view, so far as it is ascertained, in a separate convention. To do so would not be to prejudice in the slightest degree the chance of coming to an agreement on the more difficult portion of the subject which concerns territorial claims. The first step would not prevent the ulterior steps being taken; it would rather lead to them.

With respect to the mode of dealing with territorial claims, the views of the two Governments are still apart. The United States Government wish that every claim to territory preferred by one neighbor against another shall go, as of right, before a tribunal, or tribunals, of arbitration, save in certain special cases of an exceptional character, which are to be solemnly declared by the legislature of either country to involve the "national honor or integrity"; and that any dispute once referred under the treaty to arbitration shall be decided finally and irrevocably without the reservation of any further powers to either party to interfere. Her Majesty's Government are not prepared for this complete surrender of their freedom of action until fuller experience has been acquired. In their view, obligatory arbitration on territorial claims is, in more than one respect, an untried plan, of which the working is consequently a matter of conjecture. In the first place, the number of claims which would be advanced under such a rule is entirely unknown. Arbitration in this matter has as yet never been obligatory. Claims by one neighbor to a portion of the land of the other have hitherto been limited by the difficulty of enforcing them. Hitherto, if pressed to the end, they have meant war. Under the proposed system self-defense by war will, in these cases, be renounced, unless the claim can be said to involve "the national honor and integrity." The protection, therefore, which at present exists against speculative claims will be withdrawn. Such claims may, of course, be rejected by the arbiter; if they are, no great harm is done to the claiming party.

In the field of private right, excessive litigation is prevented by the judgment for costs against the losing party; but to a national exchequer the cost of an arbitration will be too small to be an effective deterrent. Whenever the result is, from any cause, a fair matter of speculation, it may be worth the while of an enterprising Government to hazard the experiment. The first result, therefore, of compulsory arbitration on territorial claims will, not improbably, be an enormous multiplication of their number. Such litigation can hardly fail, from time to time, in a miscarriage of justice; but there will be a far more serious and certain evil resulting from it. Such litigation is generally protracted; and while it lasts the future prospects of every inhabitant of the disputed territory are darkened by the gravest uncertainty upon one of the most important conditions that can affect the life of a human being, namely, the character of the government under which he is to live. Whatever the benefits of arbitration may be in preventing war from arising out of territorial disputes, they may be well outweighed if the system should tend to generate a multiplicity of international litigation, blighting the prosperity of the border country exposed to it, and leaving its inhabitants to lie under the enduring threat either of a forcible change of allegiance or of exile.

The enforcement of arbitration in respect to territorial rights is also an untried project in regard to the provisions of the international law by which they are to be ascertained. This is in a most rudimentary condition, and its unformed and uncertain character will aggravate the other dangers on which I have dwelt in a previous dispatch — the danger arising from the doubts which may attach to the impartiality and the competence of the arbitrators.

There are essential differences between individual and national rights to land, which make it almost impossible to apply the well-known laws of real property to a territorial dispute.

Whatever the primary origin of his rights, the national owner, like the individual owner, relies usually on effective control by himself or through his predecessor in title for a sufficient length of time. But in the case of a nation, what is a sufficient length of time, and in what does effective control consist? In the case of a private individual, the interval adequate to make a valid title is defined by positive law.

There is no enactment or usage or accepted doctrine which lays down the length of time required for international prescription; and no full definition of the degree of control which will confer territorial property on a nation has been attempted. It certainly does not depend solely on occupation or the exercise of any clearly defined acts. All the great nations in both hemispheres claim, and are prepared to defend, their right to vast tracts of territory which they have in no sense occupied, and often have not fully explored. The modern doctrine of "Hinterland," with its inevitable contradictions, indicates the unformed and unstable condition of international law as applied to territorial claims resting on constructive occupation or control.

These considerations add to the uncertainty to any general plan of arbitration in territorial disputes. The projected procedure for this purpose will be full of surprises; the nature of the tribunal, its ability, and freedom from bias, may be open to much question; the law which it is to administer has yet to be constructed. Even if the number of such disputes is not much larger than those of which we have had experience in modern times, the application of so trenchant and uncertain an instrument to controversies in which the dearest interests and feelings of multitudes of men may be engaged cannot be contemplated without some misgiving. But if, as seems most probable, the facility of the procedure should generate a vastly augmented number of litigants desirous of rectifying their frontiers to their own advantage, the danger inherent in the proposed change may be formidable.

It appears to me that under these circumstances it will be wiser, until our experience of international arbitration is greater, for nations to retain in their own hands some control over the ultimate result of any claim that may be advanced against their territorial rights. I have suggested arrangements under which their interests might be indirectly protected, by conferring on the defeated litigants an appeal to a court in which the award would need confirmation by a majority of judges belonging to their nationality. I do not insist on this special form of protection. It would be equally satisfactory and more simple that no award on a question of territorial right should stand if, within three months of its delivery, either party should formally protest against its validity. The moral presumption against any nation deliver-ing such a protest would, in the opinion of the world, be so strong that no Government would resort to such a defense unless under a cogent apprehension that a miscarriage of justice was likely to take place.

Mr. Olney himself appears to admit the need of some security of the kind; only he would restrict the liberty of refusal to the period immediately preceding the arbitration. I do not in any degree underrate the value of his proposal, although if it were adopted it would require to be modified in its application to Great Britain in order to suit our special constitutional usages. But it would not meet the case of errors committed, from any cause, by the tribunal, which, in the case of a claim to inhabited territory, might have such serious results to large bodies of men.

I apprehend that if Mr. Olney's proposal were adopted as it stands, the fear of a possible miscarriage of justice would induce the Government whose territory was claimed to avoid all risk by refusing the arbitration altogether, under the plea, which he allows, that it involved their honor and integrity. The knowledge, on the other hand, that there still remained an escape from any decision that was manifestly unjust would make parties willing to go forward with the arbitration who would shrink from it behind this plea if they felt that, by entering on the proceeding they had surrendered all possi-bility of self-protection, whatever injustice might be threat-ened by the award.

I have no doubt that if the procedure adopted were found in experience to work with tolerable fairness, the rejection of the award would come gradually to be looked upon as a proceeding so dangerous and so unreasonable that the right of resorting to such a mode of self-protection in territorial cases would become practically obsolete, and might in due time be formally renounced. But I do not believe that a hearty adoption and practice of the system of arbitration in the case of territorial demands can be looked for, unless the safety and practicability of this mode of settlement are first ascertained by a cautious and tentative advance.

I have to request that your Excellency will read the substance of this dispatch to Mr. Olney, and will leave a copy with him if he should wish it.

Olney to Pauncefote

No. 419

DEPARTMENT OF STATE
WASHINGTON, *June* 12, 1896

EXCELLENCY: I have the honor to acknowledge the receipt from you of a copy of Lord Salisbury's dispatch to you of the 18th ultimo, relating to a proposed general treaty of arbitration between the United States and Great Britain. The contents have received the careful consideration of this Government, and I shall take the earliest practicable opportunity to submit some observations upon the propositions the dispatch sets forth and discusses.

Meanwhile, however, I deem it advisable to recall attention to the fact that, so far as the Venezuelan boundary dispute is concerned, the position of this Government has been plainly defined, not only by the Executive, but by the unanimous concurring action of both branches of Congress. A genuine arbitration issuing in an award and finally disposing of the controversy, whether under a special or a general treaty of arbitration, would be entirely consistent with that position and will be cordially welcomed by this Government. On the other hand, while a treaty of general arbitration providing for a tentative decision merely upon territorial claims, though not all that this Government deems desirable or feasible, might, nevertheless, be accepted by it as a step in the right direction, it would not, under the circumstances, feel at liberty to include the Venezuelan boundary dispute within the scope of such a treaty. It is deemed advisable to be thus explicit in the interest of both Governments that the pending negotiations for a general treaty of arbitration may proceed without any misapprehension.

I have to request that you will communicate the contents

of this dispatch to Lord Salisbury, furnishing him, should he so desire, with a copy, which is herewith enclosed for that purpose.

I have, etc.,

RICHARD OLNEY

Olney to Pauncefote

No. 425

DEPARTMENT OF STATE
WASHINGTON, *June* 22, 1896

EXCELLENCY: The dispatch to you from Lord Salisbury of the 18th ultimo, copy of which you have kindly placed in my hands, has been read with great interest. While this Government is unable to concur in all the reasoning or in all the conclusions of the dispatch, it is both impressed and gratified at the earnest and serious attention which the important subject under discussion is evidently receiving. It cannot refrain from indulging the hope that persistent effort in the line of the pending negotiations will have results which, if not all that the enthusiastic advocates of international arbitration anticipate, will be a decided advance upon anything heretofore achieved in that direction.

This last dispatch differs from the prior one of Lord Salisbury on the same subject in that, all general phraseology being discarded, an entirely clear distinction is drawn between controversies that are arbitrable as of course and controversies that are not so arbitrable. To the latter class are assigned territorial claims, while to the former belong, apparently, whether enumerated in Article III or not, claims of every other description. The intent to thus classify the possible subjects of arbitration seems unmistakable. In the first place, non-arbitrable subjects are expressly described as "territorial claims," instead of as matters involving "territory, territorial rights, sovereignty, or jurisdiction," the terms employed in Article IV. In the second place, all the arguments adduced against a treaty referring all differences to arbitration are arguments founded on the peculiar nature of territorial claims. The advantages of this sharp line of division between arbitrable and non-arbitrable topics are very great, and the fact that it is now drawn shows that the progress of the discussion is eliminating all but the vital points of difference.

Lord Salisbury criticizes an observation made in my dispatch of April 11th last to the effect that the subjects of arbitration enumerated in Article III are such as could almost never endanger the peaceful relations of civilized states. The remark, however, seems to me well founded when considered in its true connection — that is, when it is borne in mind that the subject of present discussion is a general arbitration plan, not for the world at large nor for any two countries whatever, but solely for and as between Great Britain and the United States. As between them, it still seems to me quite impossible that war should grow out of such matters as those described in Article III, whether a general arbitration treaty did or did not exist between the countries. Nor can I seriously doubt Lord Salisbury's concurrence in this view — his apparent opinion to the contrary being based, I think, on the supposed adoption and operation of Article III as the international law of civilized states in general.

Lord Salisbury's practical suggestion in this connection is that, as the two Governments "are entirely agreed in approving the language of Article No. III and the policy it is designed to sanction," those provisions may well be at once made effective by separate convention without waiting for an agreement upon other and more difficult points. Before a reply can be made to this suggestion, however, it becomes necessary to ascertain whether, in the view of his Lordship, Article V of the proposals is to form part of such convention. If it is, any present absolute accord of the two Governments as to Article III can hardly be predicated — the qualifying effect of Article V upon Article III having been distinctly pointed out and a substitute provision outlined in my note to you of April 11, 1896.

The remainder of Lord Salisbury dispatch is devoted to territorial claims. The suggestion on behalf of the United States being that such a claim shall be *prima facie* arbitrable, and shall be arbitrated unless Congress or Parliament declare it non-arbitrable, it is replied that this proposition involves a complete surrender of freedom of action for which Her Majesty's Government is not prepared. But each Government's freedom of action prior to entry upon an arbitration remains intact — the only change being that it is to be exercised through the legislature of each country. Hence, by the freedom of action that is surrendered must be meant the liberty to reject an award after entering upon an arbitration. But it will not be contended that a Government should be permitted to fly from an award after once undertaking to stand by it, so that, as respects a territorial claim, his Lordship's real position is that there shall be no genuine arbitration at all. There shall be the usual forms and ceremonies, a so-called arbitral tribunal, hearings, evidence, and arguments, but as the grand result, instead of a binding adjudication, only an opinion without legal force or sanction, unless accepted by the parties. Lord Salisbury does, indeed, propose that a protested award shall stand, either if approved by five out of six judges nominated three by one party from the judges of its Supreme Court and three by the other party from the judges of its Supreme Court, or, if not disapproved, by a tribunal of five judges of the Supreme Court of the protesting nation. But neither method makes any change in the essential idea, which is, that a decision upon a territorial claim shall not operate as a binding award unless the power aggrieved by it, acting through its political department, or through both its political and judicial departments, shall either affirm it or fail to disaffirm it. In Lord Salisbury's judgment, action by the political department alone is to be preferred as being "equally satisfactory and more simple." Now, it may not be wise to assert, though the obvious objections cannot be ignored, that the experiment of subjecting a territorial claim to all the processes it would be subjected to under a genuine arbitration may not have compensating advantages and may not be worth trying. But the experiment should be recognized and known for what it is — as an arbitration only in name, while in fact nothing but an uncommonly ceremonious and elaborate investigation.

It is suggested that the United States admits the principle of the British proposals, but gets security against a miscarriage of justice in respect of a territorial claim by reserving to itself a "liberty of refusal" prior to the arbitration. But the United States' proposals contemplate no rejection of an award when once arbitration has been resorted to — they reserve only the right not to go into an arbitration if the territorial claim in dispute involves the national honor and integrity. The British proposals also reserve the same right. The vital difference between the two sets of proposals is therefore manifest. Under the British proposal the parties enter into an arbitration and determine afterwards, when they know the result, whether they will be bound or not. Under the proposals of the United States the parties enter into an arbitration, having determined beforehand that they will be bound. The latter is a genuine arbitration; the former is a mere imitation, which may have its uses, but, like all other imitations, cannot compare in value with the real article. It is further suggested that under the proposals of the United States fear of a miscarriage of justice might induce the parties to make undue use of the plea that a claim is not arbitrable because involving the national honor and integrity. The possibility of such an abuse undoubtedly exists, and must continue to exist unless the principle of Article V of the proposals is to be altogether abandoned. The fact was fully recognized in my dispatch of April 11th last, where it was suggested that the risks of improper refusals to arbitrate questions on the ground of their affecting the national honor or integrity would be reduced, perhaps minimized, if the decision in each case were left to the legislature of each country. It cannot be necessary to now reiterate the considerations there advanced in support of that suggestion. It is sufficient to refer to them and to add that thus far no satisfactory answer to them has occurred to me or has been indicated in any quarter.

Lord Salisbury favors the practical exclusion of territorial claims from the category of proper arbitral subjects on two grounds. One is that the number of such claims is unknown and that, if arbitration respecting them became obligatory, there would be danger of an enormous multiplication of them. What grounds would exist for this apprehension were general arbitration treaties comprehending territorial claims universal and in force as between each civilized state and every other, it is difficult to judge and certainly need not now be considered. A treaty of that sort between Great Britain and the United States being the only thing now contemplated, it is not easy to imagine how its consummation can bring about the perils referred to. From what quarter may these numerous and speculative claims to territory be expected to come? Is the British Government likely to be preferring them against the United States or the United States Government likely to be preferring them against Great Britain? Certainly this objection to including territorial controversies within the scope of a general arbitration treaty between the United States and Great Britain may justly be regarded, if not as wholly groundless, as at least of a highly fanciful character.

It is said, in the next place, that the rules of international law applicable to territorial controversies are not ascertained; that it is uncertain both what sort of occupation or control of territory is legally necessary to give a good title and how long such occupation or control must continue; that the "projected procedure" will be full of "surprises"; and that the modern doctrine of "Hinterland" is illustrative of the unsatisfactory condition of international law upon the subject under discussion. But it cannot be irrelevant to remark that "spheres of influence" and the theory or practice of the "Hinterland" idea are things unknown to international law and do not as yet rest upon any recognized principles of either international or municipal law. They are new departures which certain great European powers have found necessary and convenient in the course of their division among themselves of great tracts of the continent of Africa, and which find their sanction solely in their reciprocal stipulations.

"Such agreements," declares a modern English writer on international law, "remove the causes of present disputes; but, if they are to stand the test of time, by what right will they stand? We hear much of a certain 'Hinterland' doctrine. The accepted rule as to the area of territory affected by an act of occupation in a land of large extent has been that the crest of the watershed is the presumptive interior limit, while the flank boundaries are the limits of the land watered by the rivers debouching at the point of coast occupied. The extent of territory claimed in respect of an occupation on the coast has hitherto borne some reasonable ratio to the character of the occupation. But where is the limit to the 'Hinterland' doctrine? Either these international arrangements can avail as between the parties only and constitute no bar against the action of any intruding stranger, or might indeed is right." Without adopting this criticism, and whether the "spheres of influence" and the "Hinterland" doctrines be or be not intrinsically sound and just, there can be no pretense that they apply to the American continents or to any boundary disputes that now exist there or may hereafter arise. Nor is it to be admitted that, so far as territorial disputes are likely to arise between Great Britain and the United States, the accepted principles of international law are not adequate to their intelligent and just consideration and decision. For example, unless the treaties looking to the harmonious partition of Africa have worked some change, the occupation which is sufficient to give a state title to territory cannot be considered as undetermined. It must be open, exclusive, adverse, continuous, and under claim of right. It need not be actual in the sense of involving the *possessio pedis* over the whole area claimed. The only possession required is such as is reasonable under all the circumstances — in view of the extent of territory claimed, its nature, and the uses to which it is adapted and is put — while mere constructive occupation is kept within bounds by the doctrine of contiguity.

It seems to be thought that the international law governing territorial acquisition by a state through occupation is fatally defective because there is no fixed time during which occupation must continue. But it is obvious that there can be no such arbitrary time limit except through the consensus, agreement, or uniform usage of civilized states. It is equally obvious and much more important to note that, even if it were feasible to establish such arbitrary period of prescription by international agreement, it would not be wise or expedient to do it. Each case should be left to depend upon its own facts. A state which in good faith colonizes as well as occupies, brings about large investments of capital, and founds populous settlements would justly be credited with a sufficient title in a much shorter space than a state whose possession was not marked by any such changes of status. Considerations of this nature induce the leading English authority on international law to declare that, on the one hand, it is "in the highest degree irrational to deny that prescription is a legitimate means of international acquisition"; and that, on the other hand, it will "be found both inexpedient and impracticable to attempt to define the exact period within which it can be said to have become established, or, in other words, to settle the precise limitation of time which gives validity to the title of national possessions." Again: "The proofs of prescriptive possession are simple and few. They are principally publicity, continued occupation, absence of interruption (*usurpatio*), aided, no doubt, generally, both morally and legally speaking, by the employment of labor and capital upon the possession by the new possessor during the period of silence, or the passiveness (*inertia*), or the absence of any attempt to exercise proprietary rights by the former possessor. The period of time, as has been repeatedly said, cannot be fixed by international law between nations as it may be by private law between individuals. It must depend upon variable and varying circumstances; but in all cases these proofs would be required."

The inherent justness of these observations, as well as Sir Robert Phillimore's great weight as authority, seems to show satisfactorily that the condition of international law fails to furnish any imperative reasons for excluding boundary controversies from the scope of general treaties of arbitration. If that be true of civilized states generally, *a fortiori* must it be true of the two great English-speaking nations. As they have not merely political institutions, but systems of jurisprudence, identical in their origin and in the fundamental ideas underlying them, as the law of real property in each is but a growth from the same parent stem, it is not easy to believe that a tribunal composed of judges of the Supreme Court of each, even if a foreign jurist were to act as umpire, could produce any flagrant miscarriage of justice. Lord Salisbury puts the supposed case of a territorial controversy involving multitudes of people whose prospects may be darkened and whose lives may be embittered by its pendency and its decision. The possibility of such a case arising may be conceded, but that possibility can hardly be deemed a valid objection to a scheme of general arbitration which is qualified by the proviso that either party may decline to arbitrate a dispute which in its judgment affects the national honor or integrity. The proviso is aimed at just such a possibility and enables it to be dealt with as circumstances may require. The plan of Lord Salisbury, in view of such a possibility, is that all the forms and ceremonies of arbitration should be gone through with, but with liberty to either party to reject the award if the award is not to its liking. It is respectfully submitted that a proceeding of that sort must have a tendency to bring all arbitration into contempt; that each party to a dispute should decide to abide by an award before entering into arbitration, or should decide not to enter into it at all, but, once entering into it, should be irrevocably bound.

The foregoing observations seem to cover such of the suggestions of Lord Salisbury's dispatch of May 18th last as have not already been touched upon in previous correspondence. By the original proposals of Lord Salisbury, contained in the dispatch of March 5th last, a protested award is to be void unless sustained by the appellate tribunal of six judges by a vote of five to one. He has since suggested that such protested award may be allowed to stand, unless a tribunal of five Supreme Court judges of the protesting country shall set it aside for some error of fact or some error in law. Without committing myself on the point, it occurs to me as worthy of consideration whether the original proposals might not be so varied that the protested award should stand, unless set aside by the appellate tribunal by the specified majority. Such a change would go far in the direction of removing that want of finality in the proceedings which, as has been urged in previous dispatches, is the great objection to the original proposals.

I have the honor to request that you will lay the foregoing before Lord Salisbury at your early convenience, furnishing him, should he so desire, with a copy, which is herewith enclosed for that purpose.

I have, etc.

RICHARD OLNEY

TEXT OF GENERAL ARBITRATION TREATY BETWEEN GREAT BRITAIN AND THE UNITED STATES

ARTICLE I

The high contracting parties agree to submit to arbitration in accordance with the provisions and subject to the limitations of this treaty all questions in difference between them which they may fail to adjust by diplomatic negotiation.

ARTICLE II

All pecunary claims or groups of pecuniary claims which do not in the aggregate exceed £100,000 in amount, and which do not involve the determination of territorial claims, shall be dealt with and decided by an arbitral tribunal constituted as provided in the next following article.

In this article and in Article IV the words "groups of pecuniary claims" mean pecuniary claims by one or more persons arising out of the same transactions or involving the same issues of law and of fact.

ARTICLE III

Each of the high contracting parties shall nominate one arbitrator who shall be a jurist of repute and the two arbitrators so nominated shall within two months of the date of their nomination select an umpire. In case they shall fail to do so within the limit of time above mentioned, the umpire shall be appointed by agreement between the members for the time being of the Supreme Court of the United States and the members for the time being of the Judicial Committee of the Privy Council in Great Britain each nominating body acting by a majority. In case they shall fail to agree upon an umpire within three months of the date of an application made to them in that behalf by the high contracting parties or either of them, the umpire shall be selected in the manner provided for in Article X.

The person so selected shall be the president of the tribunal and the award of the majority of the members thereof shall be final.

ARTICLE IV

All pecuniary claims or groups of pecuniary claims which shall exceed £100,000 in amount and all other matters in difference, in respect of which either of the high contracting parties shall have rights against the other under treaty or otherwise, provided that such matters in difference do not involve the determination of territorial claims, shall be dealt with and decided by an arbitral tribunal, constituted as provided in the next following article.

ARTICLE V

Any subject of arbitration described in Article IV shall be submitted to the tribunal provided for by Article III, the award of which tribunal, if unanimous, shall be final. If not unanimous either of the high contracting parties may within six months from the date of the award demand a review thereof. In such case the matter in controversy shall be submitted to an arbitral tribunal consisting of five jurists of repute, no one of whom shall have been a member of the tribunal whose award is to be reviewed and who shall be selected as follows, viz: two by each of the high contracting parties and, one to act as umpire, by the four thus nominated and to be chosen within three months after the date of their nomination. In case they shall fail to choose an umpire within the limit of time above-mentioned, the umpire shall be appointed by agreement between the nominating bodies designated in Article III acting in the manner therein provided. In case they shall fail to agree upon an umpire within three months of the date of an application made to them in that behalf by the high contracting parties or either of them, the umpire shall be selected in the manner provided for in Article X.

The person so selected shall be the president of the tribunal and the award of the majority of the members thereof shall be final.

ARTICLE VI

Any controversy which shall involve the determination of territorial claims shall be submitted to a tribunal composed of six members three of whom (subject to the provisions of Article VIII) shall be Judges of the Supreme Court of the United States or Justices of the Circuit Courts to be nominated by the President of the United States, and the other three of whom (subject to the provisions of Article VIII) shall be Judges of the British Supreme Court of Judicature or members of the Judicial Committee of the Privy Council to be nominated by Her Britannic Majesty, whose award by a majority of not less than five to one shall be final. In case of an award made by less than the prescribed majority, the award shall also be final unless either power shall, within three months after the award has been reported protest that the same is erroneous, in which case the award shall be of no validity.

In the event of an award made by less than the prescribed majority and protested as above provided, or if the members of the arbitral tribunal shall be equally divided, there shall be no recourse to hostile measures of any description until the mediation of one or more friendly powers has been invited by one or both of the high contracting parties.

ARTICLE VII

Objections to the jurisdiction of an arbitral tribunal constituted under this treaty shall not be taken except as provided in this article.

If before the close of the hearing upon a claim submitted to an arbitral tribunal constituted under Article III or Article V either of the high contracting parties shall move such tribunal to decide, and thereupon it shall decide that the determination of such claim necessarily involves the decision of a disputed question of principle of grave general importance affecting the national rights of such party as distinguished from the private rights whereof it is merely the international representative, the jurisdiction of such arbitral tribunal over such claim shall cease and the same shall be dealt with by arbitration under Article VI.

ARTICLE VIII

In cases where the question involved is one which concerns a particular State or Territory of the United States, it shall be open to the President of the United States to appoint a judicial officer of such State or Territory to be one of the arbitrators under Article III or Article V or Article VI.

In like manner in cases where the question involved is one which concerns a British colony or possession, it shall be open to Her Britannic Majesty to appoint a judicial officer of such colony or possession to be one of the arbitrators under Article III or Article V or Article VI.

ARTICLE IX

Territorial claims in this treaty shall include all claims to territory and all claims involving questions of servitudes, rights of navigation and of access, fisheries and all rights and interests necessary to the control and enjoyment of the territory claimed by either of the high contracting parties.

[Articles X to XV inclusive, which are not reprinted here, provide respectively, (Article X) for the appointment of the

King of Sweden and Norway, or a substitute, in case the nominating bodies designated in Articles III and V fail to agree upon an umpire; (Article XI) for the event of the death or incapacity of an arbitrator and umpire; (Article XII) for the expenses of arbitration; (Article XIII) for the time and place of meeting, for records and the manner of announcing decisions; (Article XIV) for a five-year term of duration for the treaty, "and further until the expiration of twelve months" after notice given by either party of its wish to terminate; (Article XV) for ratifications in the usual form.]

General Arbitration Treaties

Address read before the American Society of International Law at its Sixth Annual Meeting, Washington, D.C., April 26, 1912. Published in the "Proceedings" of the Sixth Annual Meeting of the American Society of International Law, Washington, D.C., April 26, 1912; also in "American Journal of International Law," July, 1912. (Reprinted by permission)

It is undoubtedly desirable, in the interest of the arbitration of international controversies, that at the next Hague Conference a form of treaty should be presented which, while covering all differences between states, shall steer clear of the difficulties which in the past have wrecked important treaties of that character. It is a matter in which the United States may be expected to lead, having by precept and example so often distinguished itself as a pioneer in movements tending to do away with war between nations. Facts must be looked in the face, however, and it is apparent that the present position of the United States with reference to this subject is not so advantageous as could be wished. No two countries of the world are so favorably situated for the purposes of an arbitration treaty between them inclusive of all differences as are Great Britain and the United States. Through racial, social, and commercial ties ever knitting them closely together, war between them has become almost unthinkable. Yet two trials for such a comprehensive treaty have failed, and the official position of the United States to-day seems to be that there is a class of questions which is necessarily to be excluded from any general arbitration treaty. The class covers controversies described as affecting "the vital interests, the independence, or the honor" of the parties. In the English-American treaty of 1897 such controversies were disposed of by sending them to arbitration, but so constituting the arbitral court that an award must have the assent of the representatives of the losing party or of a majority of them. In the treaty of 1911 it was sought to meet the difficulty by a joint commission of inquiry empowered to investigate and decide whether a question was or was not arbitrable and should or should not be arbitrated. But neither plan proved to be acceptable to the United States acting under the treaty-making power vested jointly in the President and Senate.

Notwithstanding past failures, it is not believed that the United States should be deemed to be irrevocably committed to the position that it will make no general arbitration treaty which does not exclude from its operation what are claimed to be non-arbitrable questions as above defined. Neither is there any controlling reason why its representatives at the next Hague Conference may not propose a draft of treaty between nations which shall be so framed as to minimize if not remove the objections to making all controversies at least *prima facie* arbitrable. Such a draft would, of course, be without the official endorsement of the United States Government. But it could be assumed to have the sympathetic endorsement of the American people, who are believed to have strongly favored the efforts of three Presidents to make an English-American treaty from which no subject of differ, ence should be excepted. A draft treaty of that character presented by our representatives at The Hague would be received not only with respect, but with great interest; would be discussed in all its aspects with earnestness and ability; and, if generally approved, could be urged upon the United States Government as something to be adopted and used in a renewed effort to substitute arbitration for war as the means of settling international disputes.

In considering the feasibility of such a draft treaty, it may not be wholly superfluous to note that matters of national policy, domestic or foreign, are universally conceded to be outside the category of arbitrable questions. Thus, the right of every independent state to determine for itself what persons and what property shall have access to its territory, or with what other state or states it will form amicable relations for mutual advantage, cannot be drawn in question by any other state. It is to be assumed also for present purposes that the discussion deals, not with weak states which cannot defend themselves against aggression either directly, or indirectly through alliances, but with states entirely competent to protect themselves from spoliation or outrage. No such state, it is claimed, should or will litigate its honor, its independence, or its vital interests. If that be admitted, two difficulties in connection with the making of a comprehensive arbitration treaty at once present themselves. One is that what differences will touch honor, independence, and vital interests cannot possibly be defined in advance, and that, even after a difference has actually arisen, its nature as being of the arbitrable or non-arbitrable class can hardly fail to be matter of real doubt and debate. The other difficulty is that, whether an actual difference touches its honor, independence, or vital interests every nation, it is urged, must decide for itself and cannot consent to have determined in any other way. The practical problem, therefore, is how to lessen the force of these obstacles and upon what lines an arbitration treaty between nations may be so constructed as, while recognizing the obstacles and not denying them any legitimate operation, shall yet be the nearest possible approach to a treaty covering all differences.

It will conduce to that result, it is believed, if such a treaty shall expressly declare that all differences between the contracting parties of whatever character, unless adjusted by diplomacy, shall be settled by arbitration, and that whenever a difference not so adjustable presents itself, the parties shall immediately proceed to set in motion the designated machinery by which the arbitration is to be made effective. The mere existence of such a treaty will have a desirable moral effect upon the Governments and peoples of both the parties.

It will accustom them to consider arbitration as the normal mode of settling their difficulties and to look upon any other mode as unusual and extraordinary and as justifiable only by some great and exceptional emergency.

It will also conduce to the same result, by removing the objections already stated, if such a treaty, after making all differences arbitrable, shall then reserve to the legislature of either of the contracting parties the right and the opportunity to withdraw a particular subject-matter from arbitration by a declaration that it concerns its honor, independence, or vital interests. In this connection, the modern organization of the Governments of the great states of the world is to be noted. On the one hand, the principle of democracy is so far accepted and so far controls that the legislative power is exercised by representatives chosen, theoretically even if imperfectly in practice, by the free suffrages of the people. On the one hand, the treaty-making power, together with the measures and proceedings incident to its execution, is practically vested in the executive branch of the Government. It is that branch which, under a treaty excluding the supposed non-arbitrable class of questions, would decide whether a difference was within that class, and, if deciding that it was, would block arbitration. Under the all-inclusive form of treaty now proposed, however, arbitration will go forward in the regular prescribed course unless arrested by the action of the legislative branch of one of the Governments concerned. It is that branch which will decide against arbitration if it is prevented, and which will assume the responsibility of such decision, as it properly should for obvious reasons.

The national legislature is the best representative of the people of a country and is the most closely in touch with the sentiments, views, and interests of its people.

The direct representatives of the people should take the responsibility of a decision which may lead to war because it is by the people that the losses and sufferings of war are to be borne.

The executive administration of a nation as the agent of

its dominant party may easily be influenced by motives of a secret and personal nature; may conceive party success to be identical with national honor, independence, or vital interests; and is only too likely to proceed without that thorough enlightenment which is only possible when the discussion of a measure is by party opponents as well as by party friends.

When the national legislature, on the other hand, is confronted with the alternative of risking or making war, or of permitting arbitration of a difference with another nation to take its appointed course, there will necessarily ensue such investigation, discussion, and deliberation as will bring out the merits of the dispute in all its aspects and will enable the dictates of genuine patriotism and sound policy to exert their legitimate influence.

In short, to refer the decision of such an issue to a national legislature insures bringing into play two forces of prime importance in the interest of peace — to wit, full publicity of all material facts and considerations, and sufficient time for reason to become the deciding factor in the result.

By reason of the solidarity of modern civilized states, public opinion, as manifested not only in those directly concerned, but in all, is sure to act with enormous force whenever war between any of them is seriously threatened.

When Earl Russell, speaking for the Government of the day, characterized the American proposition to arbitrate the so-called "Alabama claims" as inconsistent with the honor and dignity of the British throne and people, the door seemed to be finally closed upon any pacific settlement. It was reopened later by the pressure of public opinion, which had been given time to crystallize, which discovered that there was a real wrong to be redressed, and which led the British Government to seek and find a way to arbitrate the claims without prejudice to honor or substantial interests.

A similar case was presented and a similar result followed in respect of the boundary controversy between Venezuela and British Guiana, which was at first claimed to be impossible of arbitration by reason of the rights and equities of British settlers.

These instances are striking examples of time and publicity and an ensuing educated public opinion as potent preventives of war. It is a conspicuous merit of such an all-inclusive arbitration treaty as that under consideration that, while in and of itself a constant influence for peace, legislative interference with it cannot take place without giving such preventives their fullest operation.

It remains to note that it is possible for the legislative branch of a Government as well as the executive to go astray and to be misled into declaring an arbitrable difference to involve honor, independence, or vital interests. But such a declaration is not a finality and may be revoked by legislators of their own motion or through the influence of their constituencies. Further, if such a declaration brings war in sight, it also compels investigating the preparedness for war, comparing the warlike resources of the parties, and counting the cost generally — considerations of a most sobering as well as persuasive character. Here again the solidarity of modern states operates as a strong conservator of peace. The length of the purse rather than of the sword now determines the fortunes of war, and the most bellicose of great powers cannot but be staggered by the prospect of disrupting the closely interlocked relations, pecuniary and commercial, between its own country and the country to be assailed. In no quarter will the widespread ruin of such a disruption be more keenly appreciated than by the legislature of a country, intimately and practically acquainted as it must be with its industries and business interests — in no quarter is there likely to be more zealous effort to preserve "peace with honor." Nevertheless, when all is said, until the millennium arrives, the possibility of war is not to be wholly eliminated. Treaties of arbitration and all the other pacific instrumentalities the wit of man can devise can do no more than to make the possibility as remote as is humanly practicable.

RICHARD OLNEY

APPENDIX VI

CORRESPONDENCE REGARDING THE PACIFICATION OF CUBA

[THE following exchange of dispatches and two informal notes from the Spanish Minister to Olney are the documents referred to in the text at pages 158, 165, and Section XII *passim*. For the dispatches see "Foreign Relations of the United States," 1897, page 540.]

Olney to Dupuy de Lome

DEPARTMENT OF STATE
WASHINGTON, *April* 4, 1896

SIR: It might well be deemed a dereliction of duty to the Government of the United States, as well as a censurable want of candor to that of Spain, if I were longer to defer official expression as well of the anxiety with which the President regards the existing situation in Cuba as of his earnest desire for the prompt and permanent pacification of that Island. Any plan giving reasonable assurance of that result and not inconsistent with the just rights and reasonable demands of all concerned would be earnestly promoted by him by all means which the Constitution and laws of this country place at his disposal.

It is now some nine or ten months since the nature and prospects of the insurrection were first discussed between us. In explanation of its rapid and, up to that time, quite unopposed growth and progress, you called attention to the rainy season which from May or June until November renders regular military operations impracticable. Spain was pouring such numbers of troops into Cuba that your theory and opinion that, when they could be used in an active campaign, the insurrection would be almost instantly suppressed, seemed reasonable and probable. In this particular you believed, and sincerely believed, that the present insurrection would offer a most marked contrast to that which began in 1868, and which, being feebly encountered with comparatively small forces, prolonged its life for upward of ten years.

It is impossible to deny that the expectations thus entertained by you in the summer and fall of 1895, and shared, not merely by all Spaniards, but by most disinterested observers as well, have been completely disappointed. The insurgents seem to-day to command a larger part of the Island than ever before. Their men under arms, estimated a year ago at from ten to twenty thousand, are now conceded to be at least two or three times as many. Meanwhile, their discipline has been improved and their supply of modern weapons and equipment has been greatly enlarged, while the mere fact that they have held out to this time has given them confidence in their own eyes and prestige with the world at large. In short, it can hardly be questioned that the insurrection, instead of being quelled, is to-day more formidable than ever, and enters upon the second year of its existence with decidedly improved prospects of successful results.

Whether a condition of things entitling the insurgents to recognition as belligerents has yet been brought about may, for the purposes of the present communication, be regarded as immaterial. If it has not been, it is because they are still without an established and organized civil government, having an ascertained situs, presiding over a defined territory, controlling the armed forces in the field, and not only fulfilling the functions of a regular government within its own frontiers, but capable internationally of exercising those powers and discharging those obligations which necessarily devolve upon every member of the family of nations. It is immaterial for present purposes that such is the present political status of the insurgents, because their defiance of the authority of Spain remains none the less pronounced and successful, and their displacement of that authority throughout a very large portion of the Island is none the less obvious and real.

When, in 1877, the President of the so-called Cuban Republic was captured, its legislative chamber surprised in the mountains and dispersed, and its presiding officer and other principal functionaries killed, it was asserted in some quarters that the insurrection had received its deathblow and might well be deemed to be extinct. The leading organ of the insurrectionists, however, made this response:

> The organization of the liberating army is such that a brigade, a regiment, a battalion, a company, or a party of twenty-five men can operate independently against the enemy in any department without requiring any instructions save those of their immediate military officers, because their purpose is but one, and that is known by heart as well by the general as the soldier, by the negro as well as the white man or the Chinese, viz., to make war on the enemy at all times, in all places, and by all means, with the gun, the machete, and the firebrand. In order to do this, which is the duty of every Cuban soldier, the direction of a government or a legislative chamber is not needed; the order of a subaltern officer, serving under the general-in-chief, is sufficient. Thus it is that the government and chamber have in reality been a superfluous luxury for the revolution.

The situation thus vividly described in 1877 is reproduced to-day. Even if it be granted that a condition of insurgency prevails and nothing more, it is on so large a scale and diffused over so extensive a region, and is so favored by the physical features and the climate of the country, that the authority of Spain is subverted and the functions of its Government are in abeyance or practically suspended throughout a great part of the Island. Spain still holds the seaports and most, if not all, of the large towns in the interior. Nevertheless, a vast area of the territory of the Island is in effect under the control of roving bands of insurgents, which, if driven from one place to-day by an exhibition of superior force, abandon it only to return to-morrow when that force has moved on for their dislodgment in other quarters.

The consequences of this state of things cannot be disguised. Outside of the towns still under Spanish rule, anarchy, lawlessness, and terrorism are rampant. The insurgents realize that the wholesale destruction of crops, factories, and machinery advances their cause in two ways. It cripples the resources of Spain on the one hand. On the other, it drives into their ranks the laborers who are thus thrown out of employment. The result is a systematic war upon the industries of the Island and upon all the means by which they are carried on, and whereas the normal annual product of the Island is valued at something like eighty or a hundred millions, its value for the present year is estimated by competent authority as not exceeding twenty millions.

Bad as is this showing for the present year, it must be even worse for the next year and for every succeeding year during which the rebellion continues to live. Some planters have made their crops this year who will not be allowed to make them again. Some have worked their fields and operated their mills this year in the face of a certain loss who have neither the heart nor the means to do so again under the present even more depressing conditions. Not only is it certain that no fresh money is being invested on the Island, but it is no secret that capital is fast withdrawing from it, frightened away by the utter hopelessness of the outlook. Why should it not be? What can a prudent man foresee as the outcome of existing conditions except the complete devastation of the Island, the entire annihilation of its industries, and the absolute impoverishment of such of its inhabitants as are unwise or unfortunate enough not to seasonably escape from it?

The last preceding insurrection lasted for ten years and then was not subdued, but only succumbed to the influence of certain promised reforms. Where is found the promise that the present rebellion will have a shorter lease of life, unless the end is sooner reached through the exhaustion of Spain herself? Taught by experience, Spain wisely undertook to make its struggle with the present insurrection short, sharp, and decisive, to stamp it out in its very beginnings by concentrating upon it large and well-organized armies, armies infinitely superior in numbers, in discipline, and in equipment to any the insurgents could oppose to them.

Those armies were put under the command of its ablest general, as well as its most renowned statesman — of one whose very name was an assurance to the insurgents both of the skillful generalship with which they would be fought and of the reasonable and liberal temper in which just demands for redress of grievances would be received. Yet the efforts of Campos seem to have utterly failed, and his successor, a man who, rightfully or wrongfully, seems to have intensified all the acerbities of the struggle, is now being reinforced with additional troops. It may well be feared, therefore, that if the present is to be of shorter duration than the last insurrection, it will be because the end is to come sooner or later through the inability of Spain to prolong the conflict, and through her abandonment of the Island to the heterogeneous combination of elements and of races now in arms against her.

Such a conclusion of the struggle cannot be viewed even by the most devoted friend of Cuba and the most enthusiastic advocate of popular government except with the gravest apprehension. There are only too strong reasons to fear that, once Spain were withdrawn from the Island, the sole bond of union between the different factions of the insurgents would disappear; that a war of races would be precipitated, all the more sanguinary for the discipline and experience acquired during the insurrection, and that, even if there were to be temporary peace, it could only be through the establishment of a white and a black republic, which, even if agreeing at the outset upon a division of the Island between them, would be enemies from the start, and would never rest until the one had been completely vanquished and subdued by the other.

The situation thus described is of great interest to the people of the United States. They are interested in any struggle anywhere for freer political institutions, but necessarily and in special measure in a struggle that is raging almost in sight of our shores. They are interested, as a civilized and Christian nation, in the speedy termination of a civil strife characterized by exceptional bitterness and exceptional excesses on the part of both combatants. They are interested in the non-interruption of extensive trade relations which have been and should continue to be of great advantage to both countries. They are interested, in the prevention of that wholesale destruction of property on the Island which, making no discrimination between enemies and neutrals, is utterly destroying American investments that should be of immense value, and is utterly impoverishing great numbers of American citizens.

On all these grounds and in all these ways the interest of the United States in the existing situation in Cuba yields in extent only to that of Spain herself, and has led many good and honest persons to insist that intervention to terminate the conflict is the immediate and imperative duty of the United States. It is not proposed now to consider whether existing conditions would justify such intervention at the present time, or how much longer those conditions should be endured before such intervention would be justified. That the United States cannot contemplate with complacency another ten years of Cuban insurrection, with all its injurious and distressing incidents, may certainly be taken for granted.

The object of the present communication, however, is not to discuss intervention, nor to propose intervention, nor to pave the way for intervention. The purpose is exactly the reverse — to suggest whether a solution of present troubles cannot be found which will prevent all thought of intervention by rendering it unnecessary. What the United States desires to do, if the way can be pointed out, is to coöperate with Spain in the immediate pacification of the Island on such a plan as, leaving Spain her rights of sovereignty, shall yet secure to the people of the Island all such rights and powers of local self-government as they can reasonably ask. To that end the United States offers and will use her good offices at such time and in such manner as may be deemed most advisable. Its mediation, it is believed, should not be rejected in any quarter, since none could misconceive or mistrust its purpose.

Spain could not, because our respect for her sovereignty and our determination to do nothing to impair it have been maintained for many years at great cost and in spite of many temptations. The insurgents could not, because anything assented to by this Government which did not satisfy the reasonable demands and aspirations of Cuba would arouse the indignation of our whole people. It only remains to suggest that, if anything can be done in the direction indicated, it should be done at once and on the initiative of Spain.

The more the contest is prolonged, the more bitter and more irreconcilable is the antagonism created, while there is danger that concessions may be so delayed as to be chargeable to weakness and fear of the issue of the contest, and thus be infinitely less acceptable and persuasive than if made while the result still hangs in the balance, and they could be properly credited in some degree at least to a sense of right and justice. Thus far Spain has faced the insurrection sword in hand, and has made no sign to show that surrender and submission would be followed by anything but a return to the old order of things. Would it not be wise to modify that policy and to accompany the application of military force with an authentic declaration of the organic changes that are meditated in the administration of the Island with a view to remove all just grounds of complaint?

It is for Spain to consider and determine what those changes would be. But should they be such that the United States could urge their adoption, as substantially removing well-founded grievances, its influence would be exerted for their acceptance, and, it can hardly be doubted, would be most potential for the termination of hostilities and the restoration of peace and order to the Island. One result of the course of proceeding outlined, if no other, would be sure to follow, namely, that the rebellion would lose largely, if not altogether, the moral countenance and support it now enjoys from the people of the United States.

In closing this communication it is hardly necessary to repeat that it is prompted by the friendliest feelings toward Spain and the Spanish people. To attribute to the United States any hostile or hidden purposes would be a grave and most lamentable error. The United States has no designs upon Cuba and no designs against the sovereignty of Spain. Neither is it actuated by any spirit of meddlesomeness nor by any desire to force its will upon another nation. Its geographical proximity and all the considerations above detailed compel it to be interested in the solution of the Cuban problem whether it will or no. Its only anxiety is that that solution should be speedy, and, by being founded on truth and justice, should also be permanent.

To aid in that solution it offers the suggestions herein contained. They will be totally misapprehended unless the United States be credited with entertaining no other purpose toward Spain than that of lending its assistance to such termination of a fratricidal contest as will leave her honor and dignity unimpaired at the same time that it promotes and conserves the true interests of all parties concerned.

I avail, etc.

RICHARD OLNEY

Dupuy de Lome to Olney
[Translation]

LEGATION OF SPAIN, WASHINGTON, *June* 4, 1896

MR. SECRETARY: As I had the honor to inform your Excellency some time ago, I lost no time in communicating to the Minister of State of his Majesty the King of Spain the text of the note that your Excellency was pleased to address to me, under date of the 4th of April last, in regard to the events that are taking place in the Island of Cuba.

In his answer, dated May 22d last, the Duke Tetuan tells me that the importance of the communication here referred to has led the Government of His Majesty to examine it with the greatest care and to postpone an answer until such time as its own views on the complicated and delicate Cuban question should be officially made public.

The Minister of State adds that since the extensive and liberal purposes of Spain toward Cuba have been laid before the Cortes by the august lips of His Majesty in the Speech from the Throne, the previous voluntary decisions of the Spanish Government in the matter may serve, as they are now serving, as the basis of a reply to your Excellency's note.

The Government of His Majesty appreciates to its full value the noble frankness with which that of the United States has informed it of the very definite opinion it has formed in regard to the legal impossibility of granting the recognition of belligerency to the Cuban insurgents.

Indeed, those who are now fighting in Cuba against the integrity of the Spanish fatherland possess no qualifications entitling them to the respect, or even to the consideration, of the other countries. They do not, as your Excellency expresses it, possess any civil government, established and organized, with a known seat and administration of defined territory, and they have not succeeded in permanently occupying any town, much less any city, large or small.

Your Excellency declares, in the note to which I am now replying, with great legal acumen and spontaneously, that it is impossible for the Cuban insurgents to perform the functions of a regular government within its own frontiers, and much less to exercise the rights and fulfill the obligations that are incumbent on all the members of the family of nations. Moreover, their systematic campaign of destruction against all the industries on the Island, and the means by which they are worked, would, of itself, be sufficient to keep them without the pale of the universally recognized rules of international law.

His Majesty's Government has read with no less gratification the explicit and spontaneous declarations to the effect that the Government of the United States seeks no advantage in connection with the Cuban question, its only wish being that the ineluctable and lawful sovereignty of Spain be maintained and even strengthened, through the submission of the rebels, which, as your Excellency states in your note, is of paramount necessity to the Spanish Government for the maintenance of its authority and its honor.

While expressing the high gratification with which His Majesty's Government took note of the emphatic statements which your Excellency was pleased to make in your note of the 4th of April with regard to the sovereignty of Spain and the determination of the United States not to do anything derogatory to it, and acknowledging with pleasure all the weight they carry, the Duke of Tetuan says that nothing else was to be expected of the lofty sense of right cherished by the Government of the United States.

It is unnecessary, as your Excellency remarks, and in view

of so correct and so friendly an attitude, to discuss the hypothesis of intervention, as it would be utterly inconsistent with the above views.

The Government of His Majesty, the King of Spain, fully concurs in the opinion that your Excellency was pleased to express in regard to the future of the Island in the event, which cannot and shall not be, of the insurrection terminating in its triumph.

There can be no greater accuracy of judgment than that displayed by your Excellency, and, as you said with great reason, such a termination of the conflict would be looked upon with the most serious misgivings even by the most enthusiastic advocates of popular government; because, as remarked by your Excellency, with the heterogeneous combination of races that exist there the disappearance of Spain would be the disappearance of the only bond of union which can keep them in balance, and an unavoidable struggle among the men of different color, contrary to the spirit of Christian civilization, would supervene.

The accuracy of your Excellency's statement is all the more striking, as owing to the conditions of populations in the Island no part of the natives can be conceded superiority over the others if the assistance of the Spaniards from Europe is not taken into account.

The Island of Cuba has been exclusively Spanish since its discovery; the great normal development of its resources, whatever it is, whatever its value, and whatever it represents in the community of mankind, it owes in its entirety to the mother country; and even at this day, among the various groups of people that inhabit it, whatever be the standpoint from which the question be examined, the natives of the Peninsula are there absolutely necessary for the peace and advancement of the Island.

All these reasons fully and clearly demonstrate that it is not possible to think that the Island of Cuba can be benefited except through the agency of Spain, acting under her own impulse, and actuated, as she has long been, by the principles of liberty and justice.

The Spanish Government is aware of the fact that far from having justice done it on all sides on these points, there are many persons, obviously deceived by incessant slanders, who honestly believe that a ferocious despotism prevails in our Antilles, instead of one of the most liberal political systems in the world, being enjoyed there now as well as before the outbreak of the insurrection.

One need only run over the laws governing the Antilles, laws which ought to be sufficiently known in the United States at this day, to perceive how absolutely groundless such impressions are.

A collection of the Cuban newspapers published in recent years would suffice to show that few civilized countries then enjoyed to an equal degree freedom of thought and of the press — the foundation of all liberties.

The Government of His Majesty and the people of Spain wish and even long for the speedy pacification of Cuba. In order to secure it, they are ready to exert their best efforts and at the same time to adopt such reforms as may be useful or necessary and compatible, of course, with their inalienable sovereignty, as soon as the submission of the insurgents be an accomplished fact.

The Minister of State, while directing me to bring to the knowledge of your Excellency the foregoing views, instructs me to remark how pleased he was to observe that his opinion on this point also agrees with yours.

No one is more fully aware of the serious evils suffered by Spaniards and aliens in consequence of the insurrection than the Government of His Majesty. It realizes the immense injury inflicted on Spain by the putting forth, with the unanimous coöperation and approbation of her people, of such efforts as were never before made in America by any European country. It knows at the same time that the interests of foreign industry and trade suffer, as well as the Spanish interests, from the insurgent system of devastation; but if the insurrection should triumph, the interests of all would not merely suffer, but would entirely and forever disappear amid the madness of perpetual anarchy.

It has already been said that, in order to prevent evils of such magnitude, the Cabinet of Madrid does not and will not confine itself exclusively to the employment of armed force.

The Speech from the Throne, read before the national representatives, formally promised *motu proprio*, not only that all that was previously granted, voted by the Cortes, and sanctioned by His Majesty on the 15th of March, 1895, would be carried into effect as soon as the opportunity offered, but also, by fresh authorization of the Cortes, all the new extensions and amendments of the original reforms, to the end that both islands may in the administrative department possess a personnel of a local character, that the intervention of the mother country in their domestic concerns may be dispensed with, with the single reservation that nothing will be done to impair the rights of sovereignty of the powers of the Government to preserve the same.

This solemn promise, guaranteed by the august word of His Majesty, will be fulfilled by the Spanish Government with a true liberality of views.

The foregoing facts, being better known every day, will make it patent to the fair people of other nations that Spain, far from proposing that her subjects in the West Indies should return to a régime unfit for the times when she enjoys such liberal laws, would never have withheld these same laws from the islands, had it not been for the increasing separatist conspiracies which compelled her to look above all to self-defense.

The Government of His Majesty most heartily thanks that of the United States for the kind advice it bestows on Spain; but it wishes to state, and entertains the confidence that your Excellency will readily see, that it has been forestalling it for a long time past. It follows, therefore, as a matter of course, that it will comply with it in a practical manner as soon as circumstances make it possible.

Your Excellency will have seen, nevertheless, how the announcement of this concurrence of views has been received.

The insurgents, elated by the strength which they have acquired through the aid of a certain number of citizens of the United States, have contemptuously repelled, by the medium of the Cubans residing in this Republic, any idea that the Government of Washington can intervene in the contest, either with its advice or in any other manner, on the supposition that the declarations of disinterestedness on the part of the Government of the United States are false and that it wishes to get possession of the Island one of these days. Hence it is evident that no success would attend such possible mediation, which they repel, even admitting that the mother country would condescend to treat with its rebellious subject as one power with another, thus surely jeopardizing its future authority, detracting from its national dignity, and impairing its independence for which it has at all times shown such great earnestness, as history teaches. In brief, there is no effectual way to pacify Cuba unless it begins with the actual submission of the armed rebels to the mother country.

Notwithstanding this, the Government of the United States could, by the use of proper means, contribute greatly to the pacification of the Island of Cuba.

The Government of His Majesty is already very grateful to that of the United States for its intention to prosecute the unlawful expeditions to Cuba of some of its citizens with more vigor than in the past, after making a judicial investigation as to the adequacy of its laws when honestly enforced.

Still, the high moral sense of the Government of Washington will undoubtedly suggest to it other more effectual means of preventing henceforth what is now the case, a struggle which is going on so near its frontiers, and which is proving so injurious to its industry and commerce, a fact justly deplored by your Excellency, being prolonged so exclusively by the powerful assistance which the rebellion finds in the territory of this great Republic, against the wishes of all those who love order and law.

The constant violation of international law in its territory is especially manifest on the part of Cuban emigrants, who care nothing for the losses suffered in the mean while by the citizens of the United States and of Spain through the prolongation of the war.

The Spanish Government, on its part, has done much and

will do more every day in order to achieve such a desirable end, by endeavoring to correct the mistakes of public opinion in the United States and by exposing the plots and calumnies of its rebellious subjects.

It may well happen that the declarations recently made in the most solemn form by the Government of His Majesty concerning its intentions for the future will also contribute in a large measure to gratify the wish that your Excellency clearly expressed in your note — namely, that all the people of the United States, convinced that we are in the right, will completely cease to extend unlawful aid to the insurgents.

If, with that object in view, further particulars on the Cuban question should be desired, in addition to those it already has, by the Government of the United States, which shows itself so hopeful that the justice of Spain may be recognized by all, the Government of His Majesty will take the greatest pleasure in supplying that information with the utmost accuracy of detail.

When the Government of the United States shall once be convinced of our being in the right, and when that honest conviction shall in some manner be made public, but little more will be required in order that all those in Cuba who are not merely striving to accomplish the total ruin of the beautiful country in which they were born, being then hopeless of outside help and powerless by themselves, will lay down their arms.

Until that happy state of things has been attained, Spain will, in the just defense, not only of her rights, but also of her duty and honor, continue the efforts for an early victory which she is now exerting regardless of the greatest sacrifices.

While having the honor of bringing, by order of the Government of His Majesty, the foregoing declarations to the knowledge of your Excellency, I improve this opportunity, etc.

ENRIQUE DUPUY DE LOME

Dupuy de Lome to Olney

Personal and confidential LEGACION DE ESPAÑA, WASHINGTON

LENOX, *June* 17, 1896

MY DEAR MR. SECRETARY:

After our last interview I cabled to the Duke of Tetuan that I had understood from your words that you had been impressed by our note, answering yours of the 4th April ultimo, as [having] been a refusal of the proposition of the American Government.

The Minister of State cabled me, for my personal information, that after having been, as you were, so favorably impressed by the declarations of the Queen to the Cortes, in her address, he cannot understand the construction you have given to the official note.

The Spanish Government could not accept *officially* the intervention of a foreign power. Such a thing would have been a plain abdication of the sovereignty, and at the same time would have been a recognition, by Spain, of the belligerency, of the insurgents, two facts that would have been unanimously and bitterly opposed by the public opinion.

But both Governments have agreed in the principle, viz.: in the advisability of granting ample and liberal reforms to Cuba, and that has been promised, pledging the Queen's word.

There has been the solemn declaration you desired, in order to deprive the insurgents of moral and material aid and to be able henceforth to use your influence with the idea to impress the insurgents with the wisdom of laying down their arms, so hastening the new era in the government of the Island and the moment of the fulfillment by Spain of the pledge his Government has taken before the Cortes.

The Duke adds that, far from rejecting those friendly offices of the United States, the Spanish Government has plainly said that he accepts them with true gratitude.

The Spanish Government is, and will always be disposed to entertain, in a reserved, confidential, and unofficial (*oficioso*) way, a perfect understanding, to bring peace to Cuba, with the Government of the United States.

I have no doubt that you will receive this communication with the same friendly spirit that prompts it.

The Spanish Government desires to restore promptly the peace in Cuba and is disposed to do it in any way that can make it at the same time honorable, permanent, and possible.

It seems to me useless to repeat that if you want to see me you have only to send me a word by telegraph. I will be in Washington a few hours afterwards.

I am with my respectful regards

Truly yours

(Signed)   E. Dupuy de Lome

Dupuy de Lome to Olney

Personal and confidential   Legacion de España, Washington
The Waldorf, New York. *October* 24, 1896

My dear Mr. Secretary:

I have received a cablegram from the Duque of Tetuan saying that Mr. Canovas and himself have favorably considered your suggestion of embodying a declaration about the reforms in Cuba as a preamble of a convention of naturalization or in an exchange of notes in consequence thereto.

The Duque of Tetuan asks me to inform him, confidentially, of what you desire and how you do desire it to be done.

Tuesday or Wednesday I will be in Washington to remain, and I feel it is my duty to anticipate you this news, before seeing you.

You will have time to consider the matter and give me your views if you want me to cable to Spain.

Very respectfully yours

E. Dupuy de Lome

APPENDIX VII

PERSONAL LETTERS

THE five letters in this appendix were all written by Olney after he had retired from office. Three comment on political developments about which he was peculiarly fitted to express an interesting opinion. One characterizes the former President who has become a figure in American history and whom he knew so well. With the exception of the letter to John Fox and the quotation from the Nelson document, everything was written without expectation of publication, and therefore with more freedom, though not more candor, than marks Olney's public utterances. The reader will see that these letters deserve to be published for several reasons. The last note, to President Wilson, is printed on special grounds which are explained in the headnote.

To Grover Cleveland, written just after de Lome's resignation and the sinking of the Maine

[It will be recalled that a private letter of the Spanish Minister, de Lome, to a friend in Cuba fell into the hands of the insurgents and was published by them. Its comments on Cuban affairs and on President McKinley were such that there was nothing for de Lome to do but resign. The first paragraph of the following letter refers to this incident; the second to the sinking of the Maine.]

BOSTON, 19 *February*, 1898

DEAR MR. CLEVELAND:

I have your last note and have read the contents with the interest and satisfaction which anything from you always induces. I would give much for half an hour's chat with you over current events. Poor Dupuy must realize how much worse a blunder can be than a crime. Here is his country practically unrepresented at Washington at a time when its interests de-

mand a *persona grata* at our capital more imperatively than
ever before. I had much confidence in the man and thought
him able, sincere, and patriotic. I confess some expressions of
his letter stagger me, and, if they bear the interpretation the
President has put on them, and mean that Spain has been
tricking us as regards autonomy and other matters incidental
to it, I should have wanted the privilege of sending him his
passports before he had any chance to be recalled or resign.
His diplomatic career must, I think, be ended. What he can do
in domestic politics remains to be seen. But I would not give
much for his chances. The feminine portion of my family are
overflowing with sympathy for Madame Dupuy, who is certainly a charming woman.

What a horrible catastrophe in the harbor of Havana!
While it ought not — so far as I can now see — to bring us
any nearer to a rupture with Spain than we were before —
while the surface of things as yet shows little disturbance, I
cannot help feeling there is much suppressed and pent-up
wrath which may precipitate a crisis at any moment. As the
Maine was a comparatively well-tried and seasoned vessel
which had been in a good many foreign ports without misad-
venture of any sort, it is impossible to free the popular mind
of the conviction that she came to grief at Havana by foul
means — whether through any agency or fault of the Spanish
Government is for popular purposes quite immaterial. This
popular feeling is, I am sure, shared, if not created and intensified, by the officers of the navy, who will be likely to find
sympathy not to say a loud voice in the Assistant Secretary of
the Navy. His discretion is evidenced by his open communication to the New York police, made, of course, with the laud-
able intention of preventing any attempts upon the just arrived Spanish cruiser. But being publicly proclaimed, the
warning will operate almost like an invitation to cranks and
hot-heads to do the very thing it is desired to prevent. Then,
in our representative in Havana, we have a sort of firebrand
whose ruling idea, as we know, is that the Cuban troubles
offer an opportunity for the manufacture of a large stock of
political capital. Altogether, I do not like the look of it. The

Dupuy episode and the Havana explosion have furnished more material for the inflammation of popular passions against Spain than all that has happened during the last three years. Hitherto, while Congress has been fierce — rather in words than in real purposes — the people at large have been comparatively apathetic. The danger is now that the people themselves may become roused — in which case is it likely that this Administration will prove itself competent to prevent a collision with Spain?

This letter is becoming intolerable in length, and I feel certain, if I do not stop directly, your resentment will prevent you from ever writing me again.

Mrs. O. and Mrs. Minot send their best wishes to Mrs. Cleveland and all the children, as well as yourself — I do the same — and remain.

Sincerely yours

RICHARD OLNEY

HON. GROVER CLEVELAND
Princeton, N.J.

To Mr. S. B. Griffin — about Bryan and the Democratic prospects in 1900

[The struggle which went on from 1896 to 1912 between Mr. Bryan's wing of the Democratic Party and the conservative wing deserves a chapter of its own in the history of the times. With that the next letter and the one which follows are concerned. (Mr. Griffin has had no part in the publication of the letter to him, which follows an office-copy, and is printed by permission of Mr. Olney's family.)]

BOSTON, 23 COURT STREET
5 February, 1900

HON. S. B. GRIFFIN
[Editor of the "Springfield Republican"]
Springfield, Mass.
DEAR MR. GRIFFIN:
I am indebted to you for a recent copy of the "Springfield Republican" containing a most interesting editorial upon

Mr. Bryan and his candidacy — with an allusion to myself which I highly appreciate.

The article signifies a growing tolerance of Mr. Bryan's aspirations — which may culminate in support of them. The idea is not unfamiliar — I have asked myself many times of late, "Can I bring myself to vote for Mr. Bryan at the coming presidential election — are there reasons for so doing which are satisfactory to myself and which I should be willing to urge upon others as reasons which ought to be satisfactory to them?" I get over the "silver" issue which Mr. Bryan persists in bringing to the front without much difficulty. He is apparently wedded to an economic error. But his continued championship of the silver fetish may show that he is at least capable of convictions — convictions, too, which, however extraordinary and regrettable in themselves, are for present practical purposes of no real moment.

Indeed, had the 1896 Chicago platform embodied nothing worse than the silver heresy, I for one should never have thought of not supporting the Democratic nominee. As between the coinage of silver at the ratio of 16 to 1 and a Dingley tariff bill dictated by Hanna and his presidential syndicate, I should have thought the former the less evil of the two. The intolerable vice about the Chicago platform was and is its apparent attack upon law and order as existing and secured by our system of government. The leading and best speech on the Republican side during the campaign was made in New York by ex-President Harrison. He devoted but little time to silver, but put his whole force upon the "anarchical feature" of the Chicago platform. He was quite right in thinking it the most vulnerable point in the Democratic armor. Bryan, on the other hand, was so wanting in sense and sagacity as to permit Harrison's construction of the platform to stand as the true construction. He might well have interpreted it in his letter of acceptance or otherwise, not as a revolutionary defiance of the law, but as simply calling for a change of the law through the customary and accepted channels. In various parts of the country that view of the platform was put forward by Democratic candidates for Congress and other advocates of Bryan's election. That, so construed, the platform was not necessarily indefensible is shown by the fact that the Judiciary Committee of the Senate — Hoar, I think, chairman — actually decided and, as I recollect, reported in favor of certain changes of the law of contempt as now understood and administered by the courts. But Bryan, in 1896 as now, apparently stands for the Chicago platform as a whole and in every detail — as if it were a gospel of which any criticism or explanation would be a sort of blasphemy. While he maintains that attitude, he certainly makes it most difficult for any intelligent man to go with him — be Republican sins and shortcomings what they may.

He is now making a good deal of talk about "trusts." I don't know that his treatment is more superficial than that of most political orators, but it certainly does not give one exalted ideas of his practical statesmanship. For instance — and not to indulge in any extensive comments — he seems to think that a corporation is an essential feature of a trust, and so is hammering away at corporations, whose claws he proposes to cut by various devices which are neither original nor likely to prove effective. But the fact is (you are aware of it and I only wish you to notice it in this connection) that a trust of the intensest type may be and often is constituted without resort to the corporate form, so that Mr. Bryan's proposed remedies merely show that he is striking in the dark at a mischief he does not really comprehend.

Bryan's third issue is "imperialism," about which he seems to be floundering very much as in the case of trusts. He has already had to recall some of his early utterances and, if he must keep up an incessant stream of the talk he thinks adapted to the popular ear, will have to recall many more. He wants the people to trust him with the presidency. If he gets it, what is he going to do with it? What is he going to do about the Philippines, for instance? He will find them United States possessions which must either be got rid of or be controlled and administered in some way. If I understand Bryan, he considers the Declaration of Independence to be directly applicable to the case, and, construing it as literally as he does the Chicago platform, would, if he could have his way, get rid of the Philippines by immediately calling upon the natives to govern themselves. But as a practical proposition, could anything be more preposterous? As a solution of the Philippine problem the United States has to deal with, it is about what might be expected from the deliberations of some village debating society. The truth is that, while Bryan is to be credited with many of the attractive qualities which make a man the idol of the hustings, the moment he comes in contact with practical affairs, he makes an exhibition which seems to show that his development must have been arrested at the academic stage. He is undoubtedly a better-tempered man than Wendell Phillips, but is as inferior to him in sound practical sense (and Wendell had not too much of it) as in real oratorical genius.

Nevertheless, when everything is said, and lame and impotent as seems the conclusion, I may find myself compelled to join with the "Springfield Republican" in supporting Bryan.

The reason constraining me to that course, as I now view the matter, would be the vital importance of concentrating all the elements of opposition to the present Republican régime. Our government is a government by party, and the absence of a strong and coherent opposition to the party in power, if long continued, is sure to develop all the worst features of oligarchical or despotic misrule. Consider how the Republican Party has run riot during the last four years of its unchecked domination and what additional excesses are to be anticipated if its supremacy continues undisputed for another four years' term! To avert any such evil strikes me as the crying need of the present hour — is an absolutely necessary step in the direction of better and more rational government — and requires prejudices and predilections to be waived and even the claims of sound economic principles to be adjourned until the more serious and imminent danger confronting us is provided against.

This is a strictly confidential talk between us — for which I have found excuse, though not perhaps justification, in the instructive editorial to which I have already referred. If you have the time and patience to read so long a note and find that I am in error either as to facts or conclusions, I should be glad to be set right — and remain

Very truly yours

RICHARD OLNEY

[After Mr. Bryan had been nominated, Olney wrote a letter to Henry Loomis Nelson, with the expectation that it would be published, in which he reviewed the issues of the campaign and gave his reasons for supporting the Democratic ticket. It was published in the "World" of September 6th and became a campaign document. A few sentences from the beginning may be quoted as an addendum to the foregoing:]

"I need hardly say that Mr. Bryan is not the candidate I should choose could I have my way in the matter, and that I entirely dissent from parts of the Kansas City platform. But in laying his course upon the all-important subject of the presidency a citizen is bound to bear in mind that he is dealing with a practical matter, and must seek the best practical results through such legitimate practical methods as are available. Parties cannot be ignored, for example, because ours is a government of parties — the real issue is which of them shall control — and individual effort independent of party must at best be abortive, while it may further the success of the worst party in the field. So the choice between the parties, one of which must certainly prevail, calls for the exercise of the same sound common sense. Perfection in a candidate or platform is an idle dream, and infirmities in its creed and defects in its leadership will always characterize every party. . . . There is always a choice between the consequences of one party's ascendancy and those of its opponent, and therefore the true question before every citizen always is of the general attitude of a party upon the vital issues of the day, and whether, in view of that attitude, its success is not the best thing in sight. Such is the real issue now confronting every American citizen. Be it admitted that the Democratic Party, its platform and its candidate are open to much just criticism, yet, all things considered, would not its triumph be the best outcome of the present presidential contest?"

To his brother, Peter B. Olney — about the prospects of the Democratic Party, 1904, and current talk about his own nomination

[See the text at pages 177, 178 about the proposals to nominate Olney for the presidency in 1904.]

BOSTON, 15 *April*, 1904

MY DEAR PETER:

I am very much obliged for your note of yesterday. I have been feeling uncommonly cheap these last few weeks. The competition with Hearst, however successful, is inevitably demeaning of itself. I don't see, however, how I could decently keep out of it. It was insisted that it was not sufficient for the Democratic organization to be anti-Hearst — that it was essential to be *pro* somebody else — and that I was the only somebody else. The respectable wing of the Democratic Party here has worked as never before, while even Republicans have made substantial contributions to the sinews of war in the interest of decent politics.

I hope it is not true that I am so near a candidacy as you suggest. I have never taken the idea seriously and do not want to now. If I could have the presidency for the asking, I should refuse it unless considerations of duty made that course impossible, while the running for the office is something I actually loathe. I don't know any one less suited to such an ordeal. It is pertinent to add that, having been in public life for four years and got through without marked discredit, to try four years more is to tempt Providence and will probably ruin any little record I have already made.

The above are my honest sentiments which I expect you yourself to believe, though not to promulgate, as I am sure no one will believe in them.

As to Mr. Cleveland and his reported expressions to his friends — have I told you what his sister, Miss Rose Cleveland, said when Mrs. Olney called on her here the day after my speech at the McClellan dinner? She said she was reminded of the old conundrum, "Where is the best place to have a boil?" — answer, "On some other fellow's neck."

I am afraid my opinion on the Democracy's prospects of

carrying the next presidential election is worth very little. To tell the truth, I do not see where the votes are to come from that are to elect a Democratic candidate. The Democracy lacks, in the first place, a stirring and vital and moral issue, such as the Philippines might have made in 1900 and such as is necessary to secure the support of the Mugwumps and not over-zealous Republicans. In the second place, the Democracy has generally been strong with the wage-earning class. But in the coming campaign Roosevelt seems to me to have the ear of the leaders of that class as no other person has, either Republican or Democrat. In the next place, whatever chance the Democracy might have of capturing the labor vote or a large part of it, if the party were united, seems to me to be spoiled by the Bryan and Hearst faction, which, in the coming election, will, I anticipate, be infinitely more hostile to the Democratic candidates than it is to the Republican.

But in making political forecasts I am certainly getting beyond my depth. I apologize for so long a letter, and thanking you again for letting me hear from you, I am

Sincerely yours

RICHARD OLNEY

PETER B. OLNEY, Esq.
68 William St., New York

Richard Olney to John Fox — a characterization of Grover Cleveland

BOSTON, 16 *March*, 1910

JOHN FOX, Esq.
Prest. National Democratic Club
617 Fifth Ave., New York, N.Y.

MY DEAR SIR:

Circumstances beyond my control, as you are aware, prevent my attendance at the banquet of your club to be held on the 18th inst. in honor of the memory of the late Grover Cleveland. Though I cannot be with you in person, I gladly avail myself of the opportunity you give me to write you a brief estimate of Mr. Cleveland as formed from personal observation and intercourse. That observation and intercourse were practically limited to the four years of his second Administration and relate to him in his public capacity as President of the United States.

I regard Mr. Cleveland as the very model of an American constitutional President. There have been Presidents of the United States who were party leaders before entering upon the presidency and who remained party leaders afterwards. Mr. Cleveland belonged to a different class, and is one of the Presidents whose party leadership practically ended when the presidential office was assumed. From that moment Cleveland regarded himself as President of the whole people rather than the leader of one party. From that moment, in dealing with men or with measures, the paramount consideration with him was the good of the whole country. Was it identical with the good of his party, he stood for it for all he was worth; was it opposed to the good of his party, he was still for it, sorrowfully, perhaps, but with equal strenuousness. In his tariff message of 1887, for example, he threw to the winds his own as well as his party's political interests in the championship of a cause he believed of vital moment to the whole American people. It was but one of a series of memorable instances in which, on matters of principle and of great importance, Cleveland resolutely sacrificed party interests in favor of those of the country at large.

His conception of government under the National Constitution was clear and simple. Fully agreeing with Lincoln that it was government of the people, by the people, for the people, the rest of his creed was that what the people wanted and willed was expressed in the Constitution and the laws passed under it, and that Congress, the Judiciary, and the Executive were only agents of the people to carry out their mandates as set forth in the Constitution. The comparatively modern doctrine that the Constitution is an organic growth naturally and inevitably evolving not merely new applications of constitutional provisions, but vital changes in the provisions themselves, he would have been unable to understand because in plain and direct conflict with the one and only method of change and amendment provided by the Constitution itself. The proposition of sundry Republican statesmen that more power is needed for the National Government than the Constitution gives it, and that it should be got through congressional legislation, through judicial construction, and through Executive action, would have struck him as meaning treachery to the people and involving perjury by Government officials. It is not an uncommon assumption in these days, that if a thing seems desirable but is found not to be within the national jurisdiction, therefore the Constitution is defective and should be amended so as to confer the desired power. With Mr. Cleveland, in such a case, the strong, perhaps the conclusive, presumption would have been that the Constitution was right, and that either the object to be attained was not so desirable as it appeared, or that, however desirable, it should be accomplished by some other agency than that of the National Government. In short, Mr. Cleveland not only reverenced the Constitution as being all that Mr. Gladstone described it, viz: "the most wonderful work ever struck off at a given time from the brain and purpose of man," but regarded it as in the nature of a deed of trust, whose beneficiaries were the whole people of the United States, and could rightfully deem any disregard of the deed by the President or any other official as nothing less than a betrayal of trust.

Finally, Mr. Cleveland was in close touch, in intimate sympathy, with the great body of his fellow countrymen. Himself of the "plain people" as he loved to call them, he thoroughly understood their traits of character and realized to the full the feelings, wishes, prejudices, and aspirations by which they were animated. Popularity in the ordinary sense he can hardly be said to have obtained, nor did he possess or cultivate the arts of popularity. Yet the people appreciated him, felt him to be one of themselves, considered his character and achievements to reflect honor upon themselves, and retained their respect and regard for him even when they differed from him. During the four years between his two presidencies, he drew a greater share of public notice, perhaps even exercised a greater influence, than the actual President, and during the years that followed the close of his official life, he came to be the one man in the country whom men of all parties and all sections most delighted to honor. Mr. Cleveland's democracy was not limited to his views and theories as a public man. It accounts for much of the general esteem in which he was held that he was eminently democratic in the popular sense, in the simple and genuine and unaffected habits, tastes, and affections which distinguished his private life. He never failed to maintain the honor of the Government or the dignity of his own high office in all suitable ways. But he realized that all extravagant, ostentatious, wasteful, or foolish expenditure by Government was simply robbery of taxpayers, and he was unwilling to add an ounce to the weight of their necessary burdens. He believed the homely virtues by which individuals rise to better things to be not inapplicable to the government of communities and of nations, and that the affairs of the United States should be managed with the same industry, honesty, frugality, and thrift that private citizens use in the management of their own affairs. He consistently illustrated those virtues in his daily walk and conversation — in the White House as well as out of it, and in the whole tenor of a life that was fitly typified by the simple but impressive burial at Princeton.

Surely no more can be asked of the President of the United States than thorough and sympathetic understanding of its people, than patriotism which sinks the party leader in the Chief Magistrate of the Nation, and than a loyalty to the Constitution at once unflinching in the exercise of powers granted and equally unflinching in the refusal to exercise powers not granted.

Very truly yours

RICHARD OLNEY

To President Wilson

[As this letter shows, Olney was of the opinion that, as a matter of law, the United States might levy tolls on foreign vessels passing through the Panama Canal. It also shows how careful he tried to be not to embarrass the Government in its conduct of foreign affairs (compare the text at page 194). He was advised that President Wilson had no objection to the article referred to in the letter, and then published it in the "Proceedings of the American Society of International Law," 1913, page 81.]

Private and confidential   BOSTON, 21 *April,* 1913
HON. WOODROW WILSON
        President of the United States
                White House, Washington
MY DEAR MR. PRESIDENT:

As a member of the American Society of International Law I have been urged to read, or have read, at its annual meeting — April 24–26 — a paper upon some of the legal aspects of the questions raised by the Panama Canal tolls legislation.

I enclose copy of the paper I have prepared by way of precaution, and lest it may chance to add a feather's weight to the obstacles your Administration may encounter in enforcing its policy on the subject. What that policy may be I have no idea. But whatever it is, if there is a possibility of the document operating against it in any way or degree, I want to suppress it. Very likely your view of the possibility suggested may be that its existence is probably without warrant except in my own imagination — in which case please put the paper behind the back-log.

I should be much gratified if the Washington dispatches to Boston reported that you are a regular player of the royal game of golf. The first duty of an extra good President is to be both well and strong.

As the time is short, would you mind wiring your view — and oblige

                        Sincerely yours
                                RICHARD OLNEY

APPENDIX VIII

LIST OF PUBLISHED ARTICLES ABOUT OLNEY AND BY OLNEY

[THE list of references to what has been published about Olney takes no account of numerous and sometimes interesting notices and anecdotes in the daily press.

It will be obvious that the list of his own published utterances is only partial. His official reports and his dispatches in the volumes of "Foreign Relations" hardly call for enumeration. No attempt to collect a list of the interviews, letters to the press, and reports of remarks made on public or semi-public occasions has been made, although he frequently threw out very interesting observations in the course of such casual utterances. Similarly his legal arguments, able though they always were and permanently interesting as were some, like the income-tax arguments, have not been enumerated.]

A. ABOUT RICHARD OLNEY

Concerning Richard Olney the following may be consulted:

Richard Olney, by Charles P. Greenough; *Proceedings of the Massachusetts Historical Society*, Dec., 1917.

Memorial Exercises of the Boston Bar Association before the Supreme Judicial Court, In memory of Richard Olney, June 28, 1919 (including resolutions and addresses by Nathan Matthews, Esq., and Mr. Justice W. C. Loring); printed by Ellis & Co., Boston, 1919.

Attorney-General Olney (anonymous, but understood to have been based on statements supplied by Sigourney Butler). *The Green Bag* (Boston), v, 257.

Olney's association with his father-in-law, Judge Thomas, was so intimate that his memoir of Judge Thomas has documentary interest concerning himself. *See* Benjamin F. Thomas, LL.D., *Proceedings of the Massachusetts Historical Society*, Oct., 1900.

A Genealogy, of The Descendants of Thomas Olney, by James H. Olney, was published in Providence, R.I., in 1889. It has value, although it is incomplete with respect to Richard Olney's branch of the family.

320 RICHARD OLNEY

B. BY RICHARD OLNEY

International Isolation of the United States. *Atlantic Monthly*, May, 1898.
> This was an address delivered in Sanders Theater, Harvard University, in March, 1898. A vigorous argument against the popular interpretation of Washington's Farewell Address. Urges that the United States should take a more active and positive part in international affairs and should participate more cordially in solving problems of world adjustment. See the text at page 187.

Growth of our Foreign Policy. *Atlantic Monthly*, March, 1900.
> Discusses consequences of the Spanish War. Expresses the belief that the United States will be forced by circumstances to retain Cuba. Regrets the taking of the Philippines, but argues that, having taken them, the United States must realize that it is involved in foreign affairs both commercial and political as it never had been before.

Recent Phases of the Monroe Doctrine. *Boston Herald*, March 1, 1903.
> Concerning the enforcement by Germany and Great Britain of their claims against Venezuela, and the implications of American intercession. This was printed as an anonymous editorial.

The Nation's Parting of the Ways. *Harvard Graduates' Magazine*, Sept., 1904.
> This address, delivered at the dinner of the Harvard Law School Association on June 28, 1904, discusses the question of "imperialism" which was about to play an important part in the national election. It exhibits a strongly "anti-imperialistic" inclination.

The Development of International Law. *Proceedings of the American Society of International Law* (Washington, April 20, 1907), 1, 218; also *American Journal of International Law*, vol. 1, No. 2 (1907).
> In this paper Olney considers the growth of international law, particularly with reference to the Grotian presumption of the equality of all sovereign states as International Persons. He touches upon the problem of reconciling this presumption of legal equality with the fact of inequality in respect to political power and standing. He does not name and discriminate the two categories of equality, legal and political, as precisely as have others. (See F. Oppenheim, 1, §§115-17.) Nor does he lay down definite proposals. But he deplores the legal pretense of equality where it cannot be lived up to, and suggests that inasmuch as the law of nations is based ultimately, not on philosophy and logic, but on practice and custom, so limitations on the idea of equality should in time be carried over from the political to the legal field. "If the foregoing observations are of any value, it consists in noting and emphasizing the crucial fact that individualism as the essence of the relations between states must be regarded as largely modified by what may be termed internationalism. State independence as the basis of international law has become radically qualified by state interdependence" (p. 429).

Fortification of the Panama Canal. *American Journal of International Law*, April, 1911.

A brief legal opinion that the Hay-Pauncefote Treaty did not contemplate fortification.

The New Arbitration Treaty with Great Britain. *Independent*, Sept. 21, 1911.

Recognizes the force of objections advanced in the Senate against the Knox Arbitration Treaty as first submitted to the Senate.

General Arbitration Treaties. *Proceedings of the Sixth Annual Meeting of the American Society of International Law*, Washington, D.C., April 26, 1912; also *American Journal of International Law*, July, 1912.

Compares the conception on which the Olney-Pauncefote Treaty was based with the theory of later treaties. This is reprinted in Appendix V.

Panama Canal Tolls Legislation and the Hay-Pauncefote Treaty. *Proceedings of the American Society of International Law*, Washington, D.C., April 25, 1913.

A legal argument to the effect that the United States has the right to exempt its ships from toll, because it owns the canal and because its treaty stipulations provide only for equal treatment of its customers. (*See* letter to President Wilson at end of Appendix VII.)

A Tangible Goal. *Independent*, Oct. 26, 1914.

Extract from a letter to Hamilton Holt, Esq., expressing encouragement to the proposed League to Enforce Peace.

Our Latin-American Policy. *North American Review*, Feb., 1916.

This paper grew out of a letter to Dr. James Brown Scott in which Olney remarked, "It is time that our Monroe Doctrine should be overhauled and modernized to suit the changed conditions of the present time, especially those created by the Panama Canal and its ownership by the United States." Discusses with favor the possibility of a concert of American states. "The concert would put all American states behind the Monroe Doctrine so enlarged as to mean the protection of every American state, not only against European aggression, but against foreign aggression from whatever quarter," and should apply its discretion to determining when the independence of any particular state should be restricted and for the purpose of compelling it to perform its international duties.

CONCERNING CAPITAL AND LABOR AND ECONOMIC QUESTIONS

Legal Aspects of Railroad Rate-Making by Congress. *North American Review*, Oct., 1905.

A twenty-page article, almost a legal brief in form, which argues that the power to make rates cannot be separated from the ownership of the railroads, and consequently objects to rate-making by government.

Labor Unions and Politics. *Internation*, Dec., 1906.

Olney thought that the so-called "trusts" were a natural and to some extent beneficial economic development; but that they presented certain menacing features, particularly the power to oppress the wage-earner and extort unreasonable prices from consumers. To save the good and prevent the evil he believed not so much in attacking the trusts as in strengthening the hand of labor by encouraging it to organize and enter politics. Tariff reduction, revision of the patent laws, regulation of freight rates, and arbitration of disputes should be looked to for the protection of the consumer. These views were expounded in this article and in the two next enumerated. In the third of the series the incompatibility of the paternalism to which the socialist programme tends and the ideal of individual freedom by which western civilization has been guided is discussed.

Modern Industrialism. *Internation*, Feb., 1907. See above.

Paternalism and Personal Freedom. *Internation*, Jan., 1908. See above.

Discrimination Against Union Labor — Legal? *American Law Review*, March–April, 1908.

> A criticism of the United States Supreme Court's decision in Adair *v.* United States, 208 U.S. 161, which declared clause ten of the Erdman Compulsory Arbitration Act to be unconstitutional. (For Olney's connection with the drafting of this Act, see Section VI of the text above.)

The National Judiciary and Big Business. *Boston Sunday Herald*, Sept. 24, 1911.

Does the Court Exceed its Powers. The same, Oct. 29, 1911.

> Two popular articles deploring the application of the "rule of reason" to the interpretation of the Sherman Anti-Trust Law.

Address to the Merchants' Club of Boston, Jan. 21, 1913, printed as a pamphlet. See reference to this in the text at page 190.

Campaign Letters and Speeches

Reasons for supporting the Democratic ticket in 1900. (Letter to Henry Loomis Nelson, published in the New York "World," Sept. 6, 1900, and generally in the press the next day.

> Printed as a campaign document by the National Democratic Committee.

Address at the dinner of the Democratic Club of Massachusetts given in honor of William A. Gaston, candidate for Governor, Oct. 11, 1902.

> Reported in full in the *Boston Herald* the next day and published as a campaign document.

Speech delivered at a dinner arranged by Bourke Cockran and others in New York in honor of Mayor McClellan, Jan. 4, 1904.

> Printed in full in the *Boston Herald*, Jan. 5, 1904. The Democratic Party was trying to find a candidate who would represent the conservative wing of the party. The speech ended by proposing Cleveland.

Speech delivered at Cooper Union, New York City, Oct. 14, 1904.

> Reported in the press the next day. Speech in support of the presidential candidacy of Judge Alton B. Parker and of the Democratic Party.

Letter to the New York *World*, printed Sept. 17, 1908.
Supporting Bryan's candidacy and the Democratic Party.

Remarks of the Presiding Officer at a meeting in Tremont Temple, Boston, Sept. 27, 1912.
Printed in full in *Boston Herald*, Sept. 28. Mr. Wilson, then Democratic candidate for the presidency, was present at this meeting.

Letter to Colonel George Harvey. (Dated Oct. 17, 1914, given out at a rally in Springfield, Mass., and printed in full in the *Boston Herald*, Oct. 29. Also N.Y. *World* and *Times*.)
A letter urging voters to endorse the Democratic Administration at the approaching Congressional election.

Statement Advocating the Reëlection of President Wilson. New York "World," Sept. 27, 1916.

MEMORIAL ADDRESSES ON MEMBERS OF THE BENCH AND THE BAR

Remarks in the United States Supreme Court, April 24, 1893, presenting resolutions upon the death of Justice Lamar. (146 U.S. 708.)

Remarks in the United States Supreme Court, Nov. 13, 1893, presenting resolutions upon the death of Justice Blatchford. (150 U.S. 708.)

Remarks as Chairman of the Meetings of the Bar of the United States Supreme Court held to honor the memory of Justice Jackson, Nov. 18, 1895. (159 U.S. 701.)

Remarks in the Supreme Judicial Court of Massachusetts presenting resolutions upon the death of James J. Storrow, Sr., Oct. 30, 1897. Printed in full in *Boston Herald*, October 31, 1897.

Memoir of Benjamin F. Thomas, LL.D. *Proceedings of the Massachusetts Historical Society*, Oct., 1900.

Remarks in the Supreme Judicial Court of Massachusetts, Nov. 24, 1900, presenting resolutions in memory of Judge William C. Endicott. *Proceedings*. Printed as pamphlet by University Press, Cambridge, 1902.

Remarks in the Supreme Judicial Court of Massachusetts, Jan. 17, 1903, in presenting resolutions in memory of Justice Horace Gray. Printed in *Boston Herald*, Jan. 17, 1903.

Remarks in the Supreme Judicial Court of Massachusetts, Dec. 4, 1908, presenting resolutions upon the death of Lewis S. Dabney. *Proceedings*. Printed as pamphlet by University Press, Cambridge.

Remarks at a meeting of the Bar of the United States Supreme Court, Dec. 10, 1910, upon the occasion of the death of Chief Justice Melville W. Fuller. *Proceedings*. Printed as a pamphlet, Washington, 1911.

INDEX

Throughout the Index, *O.* stands for the subject of the biography.